From Tin Soldiers to Russian Dolls

Creating added value through services

To André, Emma and Meg with love

#28401352

From Tin Soldiers to Russian Dolls

Creating added value through services

Sandra Vandermerwe

D
658.8
VAN

BUTTERWORTH HEINEMANN

Butterworth-Heinemann Ltd
Linacre House, Jordan Hill, Oxford OX2 8DP

 PART OF REED INTERNATIONAL BOOKS

OXFORD LONDON BOSTON
MUNICH NEW DELHI SINGAPORE SYDNEY
TOKYO TORONTO WELLINGTON

First published 1993

© Sandra Vandermerwe 1993

All rights reserved. No part of this publication
may be reproduced in any material form (including
photocopying or storing in any medium by electronic
means and whether or not transiently or incidentally
to some other use of this publication) without the
written permission of the copyright holder except in
accordance with the provisions of the Copyright,
Designs and Patents Act 1988 or under the terms of a
licence issued by the Copyright Licensing Agency Ltd,
90 Tottenham Court Road, London, England W1P 9HE.
Applications for the copyright holder's written permission
to reproduce any part of this publication should be addressed
to the publishers

British Library Cataloguing in Publication Data
Vandermerwe, Sandra
    From Tin Soldiers to Russian Dolls:
    Creating Added Value Through Services
    I. Title
    658.8

ISBN 0 7506 0974 5

UNIVERSITY OF STRATHCLYDE
- 1 JUN 1993
UNIVERSITY LIBRARY

Composition by Genesis Typesetting, Laser Quay, Rochester, Kent
Printed on recycled paper in England by Clays Ltd, St Ives plc

Contents

Preface

Early in 1992, a new multidisciplinary services programme was launched by IMD (the International Institute for Management Development) in Lausanne, Switzerland. Why was this special? Because, like most management schools, we had tended to put services into its own niche. I, for one, had wanted to be an expert in services, and specialize in this field. But what did that really mean? I began to realize that the only experts were those who knew how to use services to create a competitive advantage.

Seven years ago, when I commenced my research in this area, I had assumed – like most others – that the issue was to uncover differences between service companies and manufacturers. But, what I found as the project unfolded were more similarities than differences. What I had been told was that there was a clear distinction between these two types of firms. What I learned was that, for a variety of reasons, the lines that had been drawn between classic goods manufacturers and their services counterparts had progressively become blurred. Irrespective of industry, geography, or whether they were manufacturing computers, credit lines, copiers or courier services, the really successful corporations would be those that created value for customers through services.

This was the common thread. And, more importantly, the common challenge.

For, almost anyone could produce high-volume, standardized products or services. It would be easy for firms to continue to add routines, standards, rules and regulations to already top-heavy organizations. But, could they bring the value down to where it really belonged – close to customers? Could they break with tradition and mechanistic mindsets in order to serve the unique needs of particular customers instead of mass markets, and so transform themselves from high-volume to high-value corporations? In sum, could they make the transition necessary to take advantage of new opportunities for adding wealth through services? What would it take to build organizations that would design, deliver and support these services, where customers and the people who serve them become the focal point?

That's what this book sets out to explore. In essence, my plan was to describe *why* there was a need for corporations to change and to focus specifically on services. I felt this could only be done by examining a broad range of subjects and industries. The next logical question was: *what* new concepts were most representative of the service ethos, a phraseology which seemed appropriate to me in a world where the immaterial had become the primordial source of value. Both in books and in boardrooms, many of the notions that I found were still in a state of flux. But one thing seemed certain: the artificial split that once had separated products and services was no longer as relevant as the need for solutions – of which the services component was clearly becoming the most dominant part. Next was to present my ideas and findings on *how* the shift from high volume to high value is being implemented. For this I went to executives, relying heavily on their insights and professional experiences. It also seemed appropriate to try to get some clarity on the kinds of metrics and measurements being put in place to assess performance. Not surprisingly, the intricacies of *how well* high-value corporations do – as perceived by customers – has had to be rethought as contemporary managers deal more and more with intangible offerings. The object was also to attempt to look beyond and suggest *how far* corporations may have to go as they adjust and adapt for the century ahead.

This is a book for practising managers. *Chapter 1* looks first at how the industrial precepts of the 1960s, 1970s and 1980s – so typical and successful in their time – programmed managers to think and behave in a particular way. Being immersed in technical innovations, manufacturing efficiencies and narrowly focused financial goals, however, they somehow forgot the customer. Such an attitude, as *Chapter 2* shows, began to prove less than desirable as the 1990s approached and these customers, more informed and demanding, asserted themselves in new and vigorous ways. But, by then, the pressures of increased competition and dramatic environmental changes had already caused high-value firms to begin shifting from bureaucratic concerns towards the marketplace. Orderly formats and predictable plans were being replaced by ideas that fit perfectly with concepts coming from other disciplines. Not least of which was that satisfying customers would become the responsibility of the distribution chain as a whole. And, they would have to learn to work together, to get the value down to the ultimate users. These users now wanted 'results' which, as described in *Chapter 3*, meant that the point of differentiation for corporations had switched: to services.

But, in and of themselves, these services meant nothing – unless they produced solutions for customers in their day-to-day activities. *Chapter 4* explains how, previously, managers had focused their attention on the minutiae of their own working processes, whereas now they would have to understand their customers' activities in more detail. It had all been very well to put efforts on the value adding within their own organizations. But this was no longer enough. Now, the acid test would be to provide the value added to customers and customers' customers. *Chapter 5* looks at new organizational forms, particularly the network, as it is more suited for the kind of service delivery that is necessary to modern customer satisfying processes. Unshackling hierarchies meant putting the power where it matters – on the front line – and the best people with customers. It also meant aligning structures to mirror customers' values and activities, capturing the interactions and interconnections among people. These feats, increasingly global, cannot be accomplished by one function or one firm any longer. Thus, complex barriers and clearly defined boundaries have had to be removed, replaced by activity-based bonds and bonding. Central to this whole philosophy is the service worker, endemic to high-value corporations. There are several ways to ensure that these employees transform their observations and expertise into the all-essential capabilities needed to sustain long-term customer relationships. But, as *Chapter 6* elucidates, the soft side is harder.

There can be no improvement if there are no standards. But, how does one define standards, measure them, and somehow continue to improve the quality of service delivery? This challenge is much more complex when trying to add value through services, especially over extended periods of time. It is this issue which *Chapter 7* addresses, before going on to tackle how firms can make services pay. Nowhere, as *Chapter 8* shows, does the move to services need more adjustments than in finding ways to cost and value these intangible assets. Contradictions and dilemmas in pricing, and in assessing profitability, have to do with both the nature of services and the nature of changing markets, for which resolutions have to be found. Partly it is through modern technology that corporations can offer their customers high-performing systems. And, partly it is through a new attitude to this technology. *Chapter 9* is concerned with how IT can be used to link, liaise and leverage services, eradicating once and for all the constraints of time, space and distance between firms and the marketplace. This theme is continued in *Chapter 10* where, based on several already discernible trends, I briefly suggest the way services may go in a future that has already begun. As well, this chapter looks at how growing ethical and environmental values may alter the ways that high-value corporations compete with services.

If this study differs from previous works of business strategy, it is because it makes services – or the 'immaterial' as I call these intangible offerings – the most important competitive lever for the 1990s and beyond. If it is untypical, as I think it is, from virtually all previous ones on services management it is because, rather than describing how a service company is run, it assumes that every high-value enterprise is in the business of providing services. For this I have drawn upon and distilled ideas from commentators, scholars, and writers in business, as well as other disciplines that may once have been considered too far afield. The concepts, frameworks and tools presented in the text reflect discussions with executives and academic colleagues worldwide, who have shared and explored ideas with me over the years. They are also the culmination of hundreds of interviews with executives, with just over 130 conducted specifically for this book, from thirty-five companies, mainly from Europe, North America, and Japan.

In a project such as this one, the choice of companies to be interviewed is crucial. I selected intentionally a sample that covered as wide a terrain as possible, rather than examine one industry or geographic region in particular, selecting a cross-spectrum of firms in manufacturing and traditional services engaged in diverse kinds of businesses. This I believed would give a greater opportunity to show the pervasive nature of contemporary service concepts, their applicability across the board and a richer base upon which to interpret how managers are thinking and behaving. Without such an input, this book would never have been possible. But, it is not a report. The text, examples and illustrations offer a combination of prescriptive and descriptive information, an analysis, synthesis and interpretation of current ideas and practices.

And now to an explanation of Russian dolls.

I had several reasons for choosing this metaphor. As the project progressed, it became obvious to me that, if this work were to make a contribution, it would somehow have to incorporate systems thinking. Linearity had become a relic of management's industrial past. No contemporary firm would be able to succeed unless it could see its people and processes, and the markets in which it operates, as a whole – made up of interconnected and interdependent parts. Yet, many of the existing frameworks and models were still rigid and one dimensional – built, it seemed, for tin soldiers.

Additionally, I discovered an interesting fact about the Russian doll – the matrushka. Strange as it may seem, it came to Russia from Japan at the end of the nineteenth century. A woodcarver in the town of Zagorsk near Moscow created the doll based on a Japanese character, Daruma who, it was said, lost the use of his legs because of constant meditation. The craftsman made the doll into a series, each one smaller than the previous one and each fitting smoothly into the next. These figures, he believed, would symbolize ongoing regeneration. . . .

Sandra Vandermerwe

Acknowledgements

From Tin Soldiers To Russian Dolls: creating added value through services would never have existed without the support of my colleagues at IMD. Here, in a climate which nurtures the expansion of international management horizons through research, I was encouraged to pursue this project and given the support this work required. Special tribute is due to the 'Managing Services' team, for their efforts to strengthen the body of knowledge in this area.

But in the academic world, there can be very little learning without the support of corporations. So to the executives who opened their doors and minds to me for this project, sharing so generously their time and insights, I am indebted more than I can say. I would like to be able to thank them by name but have decided instead to respect their personal privacy. I hope I have represented them well.

Several people at IMD deserve special mention for adding value to the manuscript: Josiane Cosendai, my secretary for her ongoing, conscientious efforts; Michelle Mayer who is responsible for the illustrations; and Faith Towle, whose masterful editing always makes a difference. Marika Taishoff, Research Fellow at IMD, worked with me from the inception of the book to its completion. She helped with the research and writing, assisting me in thinking through and clarifying many of my ideas. The credit for the literature review is hers. Thanks to her spirit and intellect – and her ability to understand mine – this book has become a reality. But the final word must go to my family whose never-failing devotion kept me going: my husband, André, who read through innumerable versions of the manuscript, and my daughters Emma and Meg. It is to them that I dedicate this work

1 *Products, tin soldiers and matter*

Th' consumers are full o'grievances, but ther'll be no strike.

Frank McKinsey Hubbard, *New Sayings by Abe Martin*, 1917

Among Frederick the Great's many talents and interests – ranging from warfare and empire building to composing music and playing the flute – was an unbridled fascination with the latest mechanical gizmo of the day: toy soldiers. These playthings were the origin of the modern battalion, a martial concept still used today by military strategists and commanders. Inspired by the idea of creating an army of reliable, unquestioning, and non-discerning automata, Frederick introduced among his conscripts clearly defined ranks, rules, and regulations, specialized tasks, and systematic training. His aim was to shape the army into an efficient war machine that worked well because each part followed a standard and routine set of directives which were pursued unquestioningly.[1]

Not surprisingly, then, when the corporation grew to overshadow the battalion, the same organizational precepts which Frederick had set for his rank and file were adopted by managers and taken a step further. Just as the principles had served armies well, so too they began to serve business. And as long as markets remained fairly predictable, resources controllable, competitive risks calculable, and customers reasonably pliable, they would continue to be appropriate to direct the tin soldiers who had learned to march to their corporate beat.

In its simple way, this mechanistic mentality personified what the economists, philosophers, and scientists had been struggling to demonstrate for centuries. As far back as 300 BC, the Greeks had said that the universe was orderly and that all form and change could be explained by the size, shape and movement of atoms. Both Aristotle in his study of animal movements and Archimedes in his mathematical equations demonstrated the relevance of mechanistic principles.[2] This idea was eagerly taken up by the neo-classical philosophers – like Descartes – for whom anything living was a machine: plants and animals were simply superior forms. The Cartesian philosophy mirrored Newton's physics, which was based on the same immutable and unchanging laws.[3]

So the stage was set for a Western mental model based on controllable causes and effects. Weren't the constant and crisply determined input and output flows of the Ford Model T cars that rolled off the production line at the famous Detroit plant in the 1920s, and the predictable manner in which markets performed, living proof that organizational life worked along these rigidly defined tenets? A clockwork pattern operating within a hermetically sealed box?

Of course, Ford's real contribution to our modern age was the assembly line. The principles upon which it hinged and the concomitant values which it spawned would persist into and throughout the twentieth century. An apogee for a method of making and moving 'things' and conducting profitable business operations, it altered the managerial world for a long time to come, affecting what firms made, the kinds of jobs people had, how they were paid, the structure of the organizations in which they worked, and the kinds of skills they needed in order to function. The ungainly little black car was more than just an innovative, horseless buggy. It became the metaphor for all that was valued, and it would continue to be so as long as the industrial mentality reigned.[4]

The 'hard' side of business

It was also Ford who, in an article written in the 1926 edition of the *Encyclopaedia Britannica*, coined the phrase 'mass production'. He knew that being better than all others at doing standard repeatable things would enrich society far more than anyone had imagined. And he was right.

Interestingly, although Ford may have been the first to make it happen, Adam Smith had already made the same point much earlier – that value would increasingly depend on machines. In *The Wealth of Nations*, written in 1776, he ousted the notion of agricultural productivity as *the* national source of wealth, replacing it with the industrial and manufacturing concepts which had only begun to appear in eighteenth century England. Smith made a strong case for the impact of machines and technology on work and productivity. It wasn't just that they could further subdivide manual tasks into more minute portions, thereby increasing efficiency and productivity, he said. The factory would also be able to produce standardized and affordable goods for an ever growing marketplace.

It didn't take long for manufacturing to become synonomous with mass production. But the Latin derivative of the word, *manufactus* – 'made by hand', had actually become a misnomer, no longer accurately describing the burgeoning number of manufacturing plants which were changing the commercial landscape. For most firms, mass production became *de rigueur*, whereas continuing to customize offerings was tantamount to commercial suicide. Take the French car maker, Panhard et Levassor (P&L), which had been making hundreds of cars a year two decades before anyone had heard of Ford or the Model T. It had built cars to customers' requests for years and made a fortune doing so. Like others, it would fold precipitously when the unique hand-built versions were bulldozed away by the standardized models.[5]

This trend swept all industries – those in goods making as well as the services sector. Industrial concepts resulted in unprecedented economic growth and led to the much vaunted 'conspicuous consumption' of the latter half of the twentieth century. Consumers were hungry for goods and services that, as never before, were so abundant, cheap and easily available. The system fuelled itself: as people bought more and more 'things', the productive machinery churned them out in increasing numbers and variety.

By the early 1970s, observers had began to talk about a shift in values. Sociologist Daniel Bell, in *The Coming of the Post-Industrial Society*, predicted the ebbing of an industrial society in the wake of the computer revolution and the resultant flood of information. Once basic needs had been met and capital growth requirements satisfied in the industrialized world, he warned, wealth and hence value would increasingly be due to the production and consumption of intangible items. A post industrial economy would be service-dominated. Instead of relying on material goods, the winning competitive strategy would become one based on the immaterial.[6]

The way things were

For the time being, though, business continued to concentrate on transforming factors of production into visible tangible output. Old-school economists looked at people as costs of production. Labour's worth, ever since Taylor's 'time and motion' studies, had been considered inferior to ever more powerful machinery. The role of people was essentially to serve the product and paper factories which made and moved 'things' – from loans and insurance policies, to computers and telephones, from animal feed and carpet fibre to cosmetics – all of which had a physical existence which could be quantified and measured. Concerned as they were with getting tangible output and determining the cost of material input, managers overlooked the less obvious capabilities of their employees. In his book *Postindustrial Possibilities – A Critique of Economic Discourse*, the American social economist Fred Block says:

> The concept of labour is both the most fundamental and the most inherently problematic of all economic categories. It is the category through which economists understand most of the human input into the production process. Yet in treating the major inputs into production – labor, capital, and raw materials – in a parallel fashion, economists tend to analyze labor in isolation from the social relations in which individuals are embedded. It is not actual human beings who are an input into the production process, but one of their characteristics – their capacity to do work.[7]

And, by the way industrial firms were structured, reporting lines arranged, and plans drawn up and executed, power was squarely in the hands of the corporate czar. Their attention was on strategies that were geared to bolster the firm's financial results. Information was kept in their central coffers and important decisions were made by them, distilled through middle management who were encased in boxes on carefully structured organization charts, ever ready to implement the carefully worked out plans of action.

As tasks and processes became increasingly subdivided, and jobs more rigid and specialized, so did the environment in which people operated. Managers attempted to increase efficiencies in their factories by curtailing worker discretion as much as possible. Archetypically, industrial leaders made certain that their staff remained dependent on the implicit knowledge, directives and sometimes whims of their bosses.[8]

All of these approaches were followed in the name of efficiency and productivity: car manufacturers worked to keep the assembly line going at full steam, airlines to fill space on routes, banks and insurance companies to sell as many loans and policies as possible in order to keep their paper factories fully occupied. The trick was to get large-volume orders to keep operations as standardized as possible. In this way, management could achieve the economies of scale they needed to be profitable or, put differently, to fill existing capacity and thereby have sufficient volumes of goods or services to be price competitive.

Those who held the corporate purse strings had the clout. The facts were analysed at monthly budget meetings: What had been sold? What were the costs? Would targets be reached in time for the quarterly reviews? Would annual profits be on target? This mentality jived perfectly with the assumptions made about how the market worked. But, unfortunately, as Canadian marketing academic George Day points out in his book, *Market Driven Strategy*, this attitude deflected attention away from customers, something which would, before long, prove to be a serious handicap for firms:

> Only retrospectively was it realized that these approaches to setting strategic directions were overweighted with top-down financial imperatives, and analyses of industry structures as guidelines to action. The main emphasis was on managing share, and allocating cash flows to conserve scarce financial resources. Even firms that had been market driven lost their focus on the customer, and marketing was relegated to short-run tactical concerns.[9]

By mid-nineteenth century, the marketplace had begun to resemble a competitive battlefield of giant industries and corporations. While most of the larger firms soaked up the mass markets, those which either would not, or could not, afford the huge investments stuck to smaller and more specialized niches. Either way, to dominate was a natural form of corporate life among suppliers and resellers. Having winners and losers was inevitable because the various pieces of the distribution channel operated sequentially, each invariably concerned only with achieving its own quotas.

Corporate success depended on minimizing unpleasant surprises. To create a 'fail-safe' world, certain conditions had to be met: tasks kept straightforward, different kinds of people and functions sharply separated, offerings standardized and exactitudes met. Absolute control was necessary if preconceived plans were to be successfully carried out. Under these circumstances, the human 'machine' parts – whether in the factories or on the front line – would have to behave as the corporate book of rules decreed. Variation was not appreciated anywhere, neither in input nor output.[10]

Yet, any and all of this paled against the gains achieved by firms which had successfully leapt into the industrial era. For some firms, this 'Ford–Taylorism' continued well into the 1980s and even the 1990s. Michael Porter's work, which brilliantly demonstrated that all the activities taking place in the firm form a chain and accumulate value along the way, had become a popular tool for managers. It underscored the importance of continuously applying pressure to keep their internal costs and efficiencies in check and so continue to protect their slice of the market.[11]

Customers out on a limb

Somehow, the theories of the time never included persuading managers to make customers the focal point for achieving competitive success. For better or worse, because business had become so very good at innovating and producing products and services en masse, the actual customers had been ignored, left to get on with the business of using the goods they had bought. It was as though managers had hit upon a lode source whose resources could be infinitely tapped. And the customers' needs did not particularly feature in this picture.

In truth, customers' appetites had not yet been sufficiently whetted for a better kind of treatment, especially in the regulated industries where services were more significant. It was safely assumed that they were all alike, basically after the same things, essentially captive, more concerned with their increasing desire to conspicuously consume more of everything money could buy. Above all, customers were distinct and separate from the main thrust of corporate life – the boardrooms – where the real action was.

Many firms kept their distance from end consumers, leaving them to the retailers, brokers and distributors further along the distribution channel. Typically, they believed their real and only customer was next in line in this distribution chain. Official buyers in companies had the power; they were the ones who set the ground rules, if not the product and price specifications as well. The old line that buyers 'never got fired for choosing an IBM' was easy enough to understand: many professional purchasers wanted what was known, reputable and 'safe'. Rational, cautious and technical by nature, their responsibility was to select the prime suppliers, and they based these decisions primarily, if not exclusively, on specifications and cost. Did the product or service conform to industry standards? Did it adhere to the technical or professional rigours demanded?

The bywords for any supplier were therefore 'productivity' and 'technical quality', and preoccupation centred on how to get volumes through the product and service pipelines. By creatively using advertising and promotion to entice customers, and make them aware of their wares, some of the more progressive consumer industries got market 'pull'. This was matched by equally aggressive distribution merchandising and selling techniques to 'push' their brands through the sequential trail to the end user.

The revenue and profit figures which oozed out of annual reports gave visible and quantifiable evidence that the formula was working. It was also self-generating, for it rewarded salespeople, and the managers to whom they reported, on the number of physical 'things' sold – be they units, seats, tonnage or 'black boxes'. The customers that firms valued most were those who gave them large predictable repeat orders. They provided the where-withal to design, make and sell the steady stream of rapidly improved offerings more efficiently and thus more profitably.

Services as an afterthought

Ford had made the point years earlier that no manufacturer was finished with a customer when the sale was over. What he meant, of course, was that any product that broke had to be repaired. Following this logic, corporations pretty much shunned any responsibility for products or services once they were delivered at the agreed upon price and place, unless they were faulty. As an afterthought or after-event, particularly in manufacturing, services were therefore there to fix what went wrong.

With few exceptions, these intangible activities were a deviation from the daily work routine – a necessary evil for the conventional corporation. They signalled trouble. A complaint, a claim, a problem. Worse still, extra costs. Encounters with customers were something managers clearly preferred not to have to face. It followed quite naturally, then, that the jobs on the front line and in services were badly paid and poorly esteemed. 'To serve, to be a slave' was a sentiment which carried such a stigma that it chased the good people away – into the jobs more valued by the firm and society.

These problems illustrated exactly what economists had long been saying. Value was tangible, something which visibly added to the stock of wealth. Services just didn't fit. In one of their rare points of agreement, both the capitalists and socialists had declared services to be worthless. For Adam

Smith, the situation was black or white: work was either productive or non-productive, and services fell squarely into the latter camp. Karl Marx considered services to be a waste of resources: since they didn't yield anything physical or material, they didn't yield anything useful.[12]

Managers, however, would soon have no choice. It didn't take long for new entrants to start streaming into ever more lucrative markets. By the late 1970s and early 1980s, the marketplace had become saturated with similar offerings, and substitutes were rife. Consumers became more jaded, more spoiled, more informed – and more powerful. Some manufacturers began to wonder whether building the proverbial better mousetrap was all it was made out to be. Especially now that the 'Made in Japan' label no longer provoked derogatory sniggers, as it had just a few years earlier.

The prospects of having real competition also began to shake up some of the service industries, a niche traditionally protected from the competitive inroads of foreign companies and industries. Although the pace differed from one industry to another, the 1990s would confront them all with the same challenges. And they did have one thing in common: customer values would have to point the way. As Peter Benton, the former chairman of British Telecom, states in his book, *Riding the Whirlwind*:

> Value as perceived by the customer; that principle seems to offer safe guidance in every sort of productive effort. Certainly in the competitive marketplace, failure to offer such value brings its own penalties swiftly. When markets are turbulent, success comes to those who can judge their customer's values well, and meet those criteria fast and efficiently. Where the market is not so perfect, and customers are constrained in their choice, the principle is no less valid; it just takes a little longer for the penalties of failure to hit home.[13]

2 Customers, Russian dolls and what matters

The functioning of the corporate system has not to date been adequately explained. . . .
The man of action may be content with a system that works. But one who reflects on
the properties or characteristics of this system cannot help asking why it works and
whether it will continue to work.

E. S. Mason, *The Corporation in Modern Society*, 1960

By the 1990s, trends which had begun, however loudly or even absurdly, with
the counter-culture and anti-establishment fringes of the 1960s began to
mellow into something much more profound. On the threshold of the third
millennium, despite earlier fears that standardization and globalization would
'massify' the human race still further, the individual had triumphed to become
more significant. Though technology and communications were now more
preponderant, rather than being dwarfed by them, individuals would be the
key driving force and agent for change in society.[1] This theme was quickly
swept up by management commentators around the world. In *Megatrends
2000*, social forecasters John Naisbitt and Patricia Aburdene say:

> Threatened by totalitarianism for much of this century, individuals are meeting
> this millennium more powerfully. The 1990s are characterized by a new respect
> for the individual as the foundation of society and the basic unit of change.
> "Mass" movements are a misnomer. The environmental movement, the
> women's movement, the anti-nuclear movement were built one consciousness at
> a time by an individual persuaded of the possibility of a new reality.[2]

What did this mean for business? Well, if it was the individual that counted
in society, then it was only a matter of time before this same sentiment would
be taken up by corporations. Indeed, there the notion began to take root on two
fronts. First, the pulse within firms started moving from machines and their
megapower to people and their mindpower – what they carried in their heads.
Second, individuals began to assert themselves more strongly as customers,
and particularly as users. They were no longer willing to be part of the vague,
so-called mass market somewhere down the distribution trail, accepting what
business could produce most efficiently. Nor were they prepared to hide in
their factories, plants and office blocks, satisfied with what had officially been
bought for them.

More informed and selective, with an accumulating power base unim-
aginable just a year earlier, this new breed of consumer was able and willing
to use both judgement and clout. They were hungry for information, aware of
their options and able to exercise them vigorously. The more information they
received, the more their decisions improved; their requests became increas-

ingly specific, weighed and fine-tuned to match what they were looking for and needed. Customers began operating at a new level, looking for concepts that could more closely fit with *their* values – at home, at play, and in their work environments. They were more discriminating about what they wanted and much more demanding if they didn't get it.

Kim Clark and Takahiro Fujimoto, Harvard production specialists, describe this new consumer behaviour as starkly different from the old days. In their worldwide studies on the car industry, they look at the implications for management – who had previously been able to get away with a lot less as far as their customers were concerned. In the book *Product Development Performance*, they expand:

> Accumulated experience has sensitized customers to subtle differences in product dimensions that go beyond technical performance and superficial design features to the degree to which a total product concept fulfills customers' needs at a deeper level. For customers, the deeper fit is with lifestyles and values: for industrial customers it is with other components that make up the system or a larger production process. The effect is to make customer expectations more holistic, complex, demanding and diversified and to increase opportunities for, and the necessity of subtle differentiation.[3]

But, many firms – in a flurry of product and process wizardry, designing, making and selling everything from bulk commodities to super sophisticated and powerful computers, from high-tech to high-touch products and services – had lost sight of the market. Weren't the people who *used* the goods and who actually had to *do* something with them, the critics now asked, the real customers? Undoubtedly, people still hankered for more advances in products and services; but paradoxically the more they did so, the more dissatisfied they had become. Additionally, the risk of poor use and misuse had grown as offerings became more complex.

The narrow-track managerial view of customers upon which the industrial age had been built had begun to flounder. Ford had said that those firms good–better–best at something specific and repeatable would win the day. Remarkably, some of his techniques would remain with us throughout the century. But, they would simply not be enough anymore to attract and keep customers. By the 1990s, business gurus had declared that a turning point had been reached: the context in which managers had to think and work would have to be radically altered.[4]

It becomes more difficult to compete with 'things'

Why did it become increasingly difficult for business to compete merely on a material basis, on their core goods – the computers, bearings, loans, seats, carpet fibre, paint, petrol? The answer to this question appears to be a confluence of a variety of social, technological, and economic forces. Each trend produced its own kind of change. Jointly, they metamorphosized the relationships between corporations and customers.

Globalization had opened corporate doors to new and aggressive trans-border competition. The previously self-contained national markets, once all-too-easy to control, were invaded by competitors who could offer products and services which were just as good and even less expensive. They came from across borders and seas, from both inside and outside industries, from goods producers and service providers. In many instances, this led to a supply glut because demand in any one area simply could not absorb the offerings which flowed ceaselessly into their boundaries.

Deregulation, primarily in monopolies and traditional service utilities, had changed the competitive vista for all time. In many more regions of the globe, the blurring between different industries – such as banking, department stores, credit cards, and insurance – had become common practice. Revelling in their newfound freedom, many different players were deciding where to put their emphasis to gain market acceptance, making it increasingly difficult to see who owned what market and who competed with whom.[5]

Design and added features, the classic product differentiation tools, were no longer as potent as they once were. As everyone discovered, technology could be bought off the shelf overnight by almost anyone. No longer did products have the built-in protection that had made them different from services. As technology cycles grew shorter, so did product life cycles, and manufacturers became ever more pushed to keep the treadmill churning to produce innovations they believed the market wanted and to recoup their investments.[6]

Convergences among different technologies began to whittle away at the once diligently erected boundaries between industries and markets. Distinct industries with little need or desire to compete on each other's turf previously – for instance computers, telecommunications and consumer electronics – suddenly found that the technologies used to base their differentiation in the past were now increasingly similar. No longer was there a regulatory, technological or managerial reason to prevent a telecommunications company from entering the household entertainment or information industry. Escalating costs and the similarities in their core technologies were persuading such firms to work together increasingly on joint projects. This meant that a single industry could never again take its market boundaries, or dominance, for granted.[7]

The impact of information technology (IT) had been felt for some time. Now it irrevocably altered the way goods makers and service providers competed.[8] Advances which compressed time and distance led to greater, easier and simultaneous communication and transparency of information. As space, no matter how great, was no longer an obstacle, companies had to grapple with a new set of challenges: mainly, learning how to really use IT to create a distinctly competitive advantage.

Japanese business philosophy and methods – used both at home and abroad – made Western companies sit up and rethink what else they could do to compete more effectively. The Japanese were not only cutting the prices of their high quality goods, as everyone knew, but also had unveiled the obvious: high quality was easier to sell, and also ultimately cost a firm less. Their language, which slowly began to creep into international business jargon, crystallized the differences in philosophical approach. '*Keiretsu*' in particular, loosely translated as 'commitment to a series of relationships', highlighted the Japanese ability to maintain a series of lifelong ties on different levels in a manner unmatched so far by traditional Western cultures.[9]

Customers at the centre of gravity

It was becoming apparent to all that a growing number of corporations were victims of their own success. In the midst of these converging trends, at an accelerating pace, core offerings resembled commodities. The proliferation of goods gushing out of product and paper factories – many of them *de novo* – began to confuse customers, who were increasingly wary of buying something for fear that a better or cheaper version would appear the following day. Products, as well as many services, were too complex. They were designed with buyers, not users, in mind. More and more technical features were being built in, which customers didn't necessarily want or understand. The insurance forms were too complex, the computer manuals impossible to understand. By the late 1980s, firms in products like office and home electronics and computers realized that only a handful of their customers were actually making use of specially designed features. It was time to look more intensely at users.

- Anyone could make a good bearing, as SKF discovered in the late 1980s. As a general rule, the Swedish global giant had overdesigned its products to ensure that the specifications of the machine manufacturers which bought SKF products were met. But, the lifelong features of the bearings were of only marginal benefit to users because they were being poorly installed and maintained in factories.[10]
- DuPont, renowned globally for differentiating by grafting powerful brand images onto constantly improved industrial products, found that sales were dropping in some of the division's stronger markets. Digging deeper as to why its carpet fibre sales had deteriorated in Europe, it discovered that, unlike PCs, holidays, videos, electrical appliances and curtains, homeowners simply did not like buying carpets. In fact, they delayed their decision as long as possible because they regarded the purchasing experience as an ordeal.

- British Petroleum (BP) had had no qualms about its product being perceived as a commodity – in fact, that concept had seemed only natural. Therefore, until the early 1990s, the company devoted attention and resources mostly to exploration and unit cost efficiencies. When the industry was jolted first by the price shocks and then by overcapacity, the needs of end-user customers began to enter into the company's thinking. Research revealed that a large chunk of the market was willing to pay extra per gallon to be served. Evidently, only in Texas do patrons actually enjoy pumping their own gas!
- American Express, creator of the credit card, did little to promote the use of its cards. Most of the advertising and promotion went into acquiring cardholders. Merchants were charged a service premium, which they regarded as an extra operating cost, for uppercrust customers who in any event carried at least one other card. Resulting resistance by retailers meant that cardholders found it increasingly difficult to use the card for their local shopping. American Express' unique position began to be eroded by low-cost competitors.
- Like most industrial suppliers, Rank Xerox had always dealt with the purchasing department at clients' corporations. Then, company representatives began to spend time with end users as well – the people who had to deal with the stresses and strains of printing on demand. These people could often provide an entirely different perspective. If told by official buyers, say, that their firm printed 400,000 sheets a month, Rank Xerox would base proposals for equipment on that data. But from discussions with users it might get other crucial information, like 350,000 of those copies were printed on the last three days of the month.
- Firms like Citibank were quick to realize that, in the years to come, providing more than a sophisticated electronic infrastructure would be needed to satisfy customers. If this kind of service were to be the company's differentiating feature, it would have to give more attention to the habits and needs of users making the several cash transactions daily. Time being of the essence, customers had to be able to use the service 24 hours a day, make their transfers quickly and accurately, and make better decisions.

Two things had become abundantly clear: one, that corporate success was inextricably bound up with a firm's ability to profoundly 'satisfy customers' – a phrase first enunciated by Peter Drucker,[11] and, two, that this proved to be a lot easier said than done. But for various reasons during the wonders of the industrial age, manufacturing firms had understood their customers less well than their internal operations. As for the traditional services – had they fared much better? In a legendary issue, *TIME* magazine's front page declared that customers were fed up with the service sector. Services, they claimed, had become maddeningly conspicuous by their absence.[12] By the late 1980s, a bevy of books and articles expressed fear that the service sector would be shaken, even shattered, by its inability to render effective customer satisfaction. Service specialists in the US, James Brian Quinn and Christopher Gagnon were among the many who were concerned. The title of one of their articles asks 'Will Services Follow Manufacturing Into Decline?' and they go on to say:

> Daily we encounter the same inattention to quality, emphasis on scale economies rather than customers' concerns and short-term financial orientation that earlier injured manufacturing. Too many service companies have . . . concentrated on cost-cutting efficiencies they can quantify, rather than adding to the product's value by listening carefully to customers and . . . providing the services their customers genuinely want. . . . if services are disdained or mismanaged, the same forces that led to the decline of US manufacturing stand ready to cut them to pieces . . . [13]

Irrespective of industry though, firms which either consciously or unconsciously avoided customers and their needs would be systematically weeded out of the market.[14] Which meant that some old die-hard attitudes would have to change even among the most stalwart and financially secure firms. Instead of customers being out on a limb, they would now have to become *the* focal point for corporate activities – the centre of gravity. In a sense, this would prove to be an important unifying theme for business as a whole, as well as single industries and firms, as they entered the 1990s.

Although this message wasn't exactly new, given changing conditions it was now imperative to corporate survival. Who could express this better than McKinsey's Japanese strategist Kenichi Ohmae? In *The Borderless World*, in which he examines the broader issues of competitive action and the managerial imperatives for winning global strategies, he makes this point rather profoundly:

> Of course it is important to take the competition into account, but that should not come first in making strategy. First comes painstaking attention to the needs of customers. First comes close analysis of a company's real degrees of freedom in responding to those needs. First comes the willingness to rethink, fundamentally, what products are and what they do, as well as how best to organize the business system that designs, builds and markets them.[15]

Robert Reich, the leading American political economist, also describes the situation in no uncertain terms in his book, *The Work of Nations*. By the 1990s, he states, no longer were businesses able to generate large earnings from high-volume production of standard products, no longer were they able to sustain profits by protection, no longer were they able to hold onto markets by cutting prices. The modern corporation could only succeed through the continuous discovery of how to serve the unique needs of its own particular customers.[16] But could firms make this turnabout to customers, particularly to the users of their goods and services? What were some of the fundamental differences between what they had already mastered and what they must now learn to do?

Foremost, instead of techniques aimed at making 'things' which they then persuaded buyers to purchase, they would need to have an intimate knowledge of the end users, where potential value-adding opportunities might lie and how they could best be achieved. Almost exclusive reliance on old orthodox research methods would have to be supplemented by spending more time with customers, understanding their attitudes and habits, knowing what mattered to them in their daily routines and how they used goods and services. These customers would have to be brought into the management process earlier on so that their needs could be firmly embedded into market concepts. Some firms would respond by sending employees out to 'become customers' – to live like them long enough so as to really know the way they felt and behaved.[17] The logic was simple: only when corporations see products and services from the outside in can they really understand what should be happening from the inside out.

The systemic progression of markets

Outside, markets were reconfigurating fast. Conspicuous consumption had progressed hand in hand with mass production – a successful formula for many firms, for which the 'average' consumer as an organizing principle had seemed quite valid. At the other extreme were some highly specialized markets for which certain firms opted, differentiating themselves accordingly.

But, quite a different picture had now begun to emerge, the effects of which would be far-reaching for corporations. It would challenge them to find a new, more systemic way to configure markets and satisfy the customers within them:

Then: markets were usually divided: either into the mass or into specialized pockets. Corporate profitability hinged on either reducing costs for the mass or adding differentiated features for the specialized.

Now: with the marketplace more complex, aiming successfully at these traditional extremes is not quite as simple. For to some extent, each market today contains a generic component, the 'mass within markets', and target groups – 'markets within markets' – each with its own distinctive characteristics and behaviour. Profitability hinges both on reducing costs and adding differentiated features.

Then: it was assumed that either within the mass markets or specialized pockets, customers were identical and therefore could receive the same treatment.

Now: it has become obvious that not only does the mass market consist of 'markets within markets', but within these are individuals – either single firms or people. These 'customers within customers', or units of one as they are sometimes called, must be catered to as well.

Take some examples:

- Digital, the international computer company, soon began to see that, although there were some shared generic characteristics among customers for networking technology, certain segments – like government, retailing, education, banks or manufacturing – were distinctly dissimilar. Over and above these differences within a sector – for example banking – one bank's needs are unlike another's, not to mention the various branches and even individual managers, depending on their client base, objectives and style of doing business.
- Despite similarities across all markets, it is not surprising that SKF found the 'before' and 'after' markets had their own peculiarities. Original equipment and automotive manufacturers, the 'before' market, regarded a bearing as a component, and wanted it reliable and cheap. Money was secondary to the 'after' market, where the bearing was a vital spare part that was needed in a hurry to keep a factory going or a customer on the road. The needs within each factory varied, however, depending on the physical environment, as did those of auto dealers according to their customer base.
- And, airline business corporations – like Scandinavian Airline Systems (SAS) and Singapore Airlines – had, by the early 1980s, already begun to divide the amorphous mass travel market into target groups. Business customers were recognized as distinct from leisure groups, short haulers from long haulers; frequent flyers were a breed of their own, and customers who wanted to sleep on longer hauls were very different from those who wanted to work. Even though passengers fly under one business class banner, Singapore Airlines acknowledges that, because these customers board from different time zones, some may want dinner while others want breakfast, some may be ready to eat immediately while others prefer to wait.[18]
- When it comes to telephony, British Telecom found that it's not good enough to simply split the market into homeowners, executives or the elderly. Customers, in their various roles – parents, employees, friends, or travellers – want different kinds of telephone services. The same people from the same division in the same company have distinctive telephone habits as well, depending on whether they are working, shopping or playing on the sports field at the time.
- Similarly, Citibank has shifted its emphasis from being an institution that gets things done for people and corporations in a locale to one that strives

to identify the needs of people as individuals, and organizations as units of one. Over and above what all people or firms expect from a bank and what certain groups may specifically require, customers – either personal or corporate – have their own special needs and habits, and they now demand to be treated on an individualized basis.

● Hoechst's European paint division says that every car factory is different, but so then is every production line. Nuances like the temperature of the ovens, the angle of the spray guns, and the movement of the machines can affect the colour of the paint and, consequently, the overall quality of their cars: so, it regards each line as an individual client.

● When it comes to insurance, there are some generic traits which cut across all markets. But, each sector – like manufacturing, retailing or transporta- tion – have certain critical application needs. Even within a sector like transportation, customers can't be handled in the same way. For a firm like Zurich Insurance it's a very different story when a fleet owner has an accident compared to, say, a bus company which relies on its vehicles to make a living.

● Apart from the size of the unit, most customer needs are uniform when it comes to laser printers. But, depending on whether it is an NCR, Unisys, or IBM system sending the data to the Rank Xerox machine, the end results could be very different for customers, even within the same business. And even within clusters of, say, IBM users, the individual combination of suppliers used makes each customer unique.

The new nature of markets goes beyond target marketing – splitting up the mass market into homogeneous segments – which is how managers began to get round the problem of undifferentiated mass offerings. It recognizes that individual differences are highly significant in buying decisions today. And for all practical purposes, if a firm can't come to terms with this there is no point in bothering to try to compete at all. Tom Peters, the well-known management consultant, makes this point clear in his essay, 'Time, information technology and the slicing of markets'. He puts it this way:

> Basically every market – from chemicals to steel, to automobiles, to semi- conductors, to financial and accounting services – is in the process of being fragmented, sliced, resliced and micronised. To put it at its simplest, at least in the high wage, high value added product nations, time is running out for the general purpose company and the general purpose product. In every business sector, tailoring and individualizing has become the name of the game.[19]

Actually, it's even more complicated. As the world has shrunk, thanks to the ease of travel and collapsing economic borders, and become universally bound by the media, most markets have also become more similar, though paradoxically individualization has made them more fragmented. In other

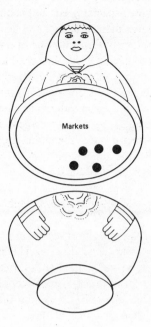

Figure 2.1   The systemic progression of markets: one market, some specialized pockets

words, people are more alike and less alike simultaneously today – both universal and unique in their buying demands. What all this boils down to is that very few markets nowadays, if any, fall into one huge mass with some specialized pockets. Nor does cutting the market up into ever finer bits provide an adequate description. Markets are systemic, to a lesser or greater extent, each with a generic, targeted, and individualized component. (Figures 2.1, 2.2, 2.3 show the progression.) Like Russian dolls, each of the components – the 'mass within markets', the 'markets within markets', and the 'customers within customers' – is separate and distinctive. Yet, they are also interconnected, linked, and inseparable, each an extension of the other.

Different ideas for changing times

Globally, by the late 1980s and early 1990s, ideas from other disciplines – hitherto unrelated to business – had seeped into managerial thinking. Perhaps it was because people in the arts and sciences – especially biology and physics

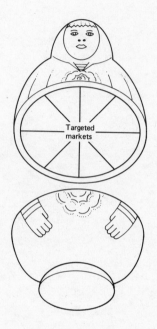

Figure 2.2   The systemic progression of markets: targeted markets

– argued more strongly and visibly that the fabric of life, indeed its very building blocks, in no way resembled the kind of world managers had long accepted. Or perhaps it was that management was listening more carefully. Either way, the fallacy fostered by business that organizations could be run in a rational, orderly and predictable way had become so remote as to hamper rather than help them cope with volatile and unfamiliar conditions. Here are some examples:

Back in the late 1950s and early 1960s, the theoretical biologist Ludwig von Bertalanffy had put forward his general systems theory. All living organisms, he said – including cells, individuals, groups and organizations – depend on a wider environment for their continued maintenance and survival. Unlike mechanical things, living things are organic and constantly evolving in response to their environment. These living things can't be isolated any more than organizations can, since they depend like them on their interaction with the environment for sustenance and growth.[20]

Building on his work, biologists – including such well-known names as James Lovelock who worked with cells, and James Watson and Francis Crick

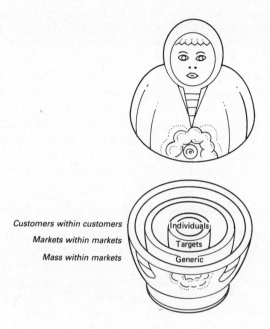

Customers within customers
Markets within markets
Mass within markets

Individuals
Targets
Generic

Figure 2.3   The systemic progression of markets: generic, targets, individuals

who together discovered DNA – demonstrated that living organic systems survive only by adapting to changing circumstances. They self-organize at the moment of need. New wholes are formed by parts which come together of their own accord in a perfectly natural way. This is in direct contrast to the mechanistic models managers had been working with where, if any part broke down, the whole system was jeopardized.[21]

In chemistry, Ilya Prigogine won a Nobel Prize for his work on 'open systems'. The whole is greater than the sum of its individual parts, he demonstrated. In contrast to the reductionist approach – in which systems are understood by breaking them down into their smallest constituent bits – his model looks at the whole picture, and in particular at the interaction of the parts to see how things work. Once managers began to look at the concepts around these open systems, they would begin to find that mechanistic principles no longer hold.[22]

Quantum physicists such as Werner Heisenberg, Max Planck and Niels Bohr had searched for the ultimate constituents of matter for some time. They wanted to know what an atom was actually made up of. What they found was that matter was both a particle and a wave simultaneously, but only one aspect could be perceived at a time. In other words, by observing one, the other was negated. That's why their work came to be known as 'the theory of uncertainty'. For ever more it would be impossible for anyone, including managers, to talk about what was being observed purely objectively, dissociated from the person doing the observing.[23]

For Newtonian science, there was total order in the universe. For so long as factors could be controlled, actions would lead to a reaction. Then, in the 1970s, an interdisciplinary group of scientists began to question why there was so much apparent disorder in the universe. Explain, they asked, the disorder in the atmosphere and in the turbulent sea. Why did the wildlife pattern fluctuate so dramatically, making predictions on numbers so difficult? What they revealed was that there were seemingly chaotic and unpredictable relationships at work within any system. In this chaos there were however patterns although they were impossible to forecast with accuracy. At best, prediction about the future based on the past could only be approximate and probabilistic.[24]

It was in the 1930s that Godel first showed the limitations of any logical system in mathematics. He proved that, no matter how thorough, in any mathematical equation one would always run into a contradiction. To resolve this another sort of logic was required. The fractal school carried this idea further in the 1970s and 1980s. One of its well-known advocates, Benoit Mandelbrot, looked at nature, from snowflakes to coastlines, showing that they did not follow strict geometric rules: bark was not smooth, lightning did not travel in straight lines, coastlines were jagged and snowflakes are all different. Nothing, it seemed, fit into neat equations as man had first supposed. What we have been measuring was all wrong, Mandelbrot said. Life was non-geometric. We should be looking at the exceptions rather than the rules to understand patterns better.[25]

Once mathematical equations were up for question, it was only natural for musicians to follow suit. A-tonal harmony, which had been toyed with but had never really taken off until the 1980s, was based on new non-sequential musical scales. Composers, from the American John Cage and the Frenchman Pierre Boulez – both modern classicists, to new-age Japanese composer Kitaro, threw out the old standards, pushing for greater individual expression rather than following strict rules. This, they argued, was more representative of contemporary life.[26]

As well, the sequential story lines with all-knowing narratives and a well-planned series of events faded off the literary scene. Instead, from all ends of the globe came novels presenting the reader with a kaleidoscope of interconnected but non-consecutive events, in which the dividing line between reality and fiction was difficult to determine. Authors from Thomas Pynchon in the United States to the Austrian Peter Handke began, in the 1980s, to describe a different world, where plots were not built block by block by the author's command but, rather, they evolved organically as the characters in the story demanded.[27]

And, finally, artists like Andy Warhol and Julian Schnabel began to ridicule conspicuous consumption, framing industrial artefacts – from soup cans to hub caps – on their canvases. Painters like Robert Motherwell, Ellsworth Kelly and Victor Vaserely stripped painting of any attempt to imitate physical objects, presenting life as a combination of light, colour, depth and perspective, rather than of objects. What they wanted was for the painting to be understood differently by each observer, without imposing one overriding view and to encourage a much more active relationship between the work and its audience.[28]

Industrial minds and contemporary mindsets

There were some important parallels between what these disciplines were saying and what managers had begun to experience. New minds and mindsets (such as those shown in Figure 2.4) had emerged within these managerial circles. Observers and practitioners pushed for more appropriate ways to operate companies. Tin soldiers worked in tightly controlled boundaries; they could not continue to do so. Tin soldiers were objective, logical, rational and competitive. But, it seemed that this orderly way of understanding the world no longer held up. Tin soldiers did not understand uncertainty; they had to learn to cope with it and to navigate their way through it. Tin soldiers were rigid and controlling; they had to be open and collegial. Tin soldiers managed 'things'; they had to manage flows. Tin soldiers weren't really atuned to customers; yet for them these customers were the bedrock upon which everything else depended. The old high-volume enterprise had its benefits of course. But to these had to be added new ideas and principles. For one thing, a more collaborative working relationship among members of the distribution chain was sorely needed, geared to the interest of end users. But from the underlying theorem of Darwinism had come the phrase 'the survival of the fittest'. There were winners and losers – the strong and the weak. Evolution would favour the strong. Or so we were told. Knowingly or not, Darwinism had permeated the corporate world, suggesting that the only way to survive was at the expense of anyone who got in the way. But as we now know, natural systems are not inherently competitive: they are collaborative.[29] The question was whether organizations could be made to work to this principle as well.

Some of the newer approaches had a familiar ring as, it seemed, the Japanese have been practising them for some time. If, for example, the whole distribution channel is ultimately more significant than the individual parts, then a spirit has to be fostered where firms collaborate rather than dominate. The Japanese have demonstrated successfully that this can lead to superior market performance. Firms have to look towards the market, beginning with the end user and working backwards. This practice has also already been attributed to the Japanese management style.[30]

But there is more. By the 1990s, it was obvious that the economies of scale which symbolized the industrial epoch served no purpose at all in isolation. A firm could produce all the oil, chemicals, feed or computers it wanted: it needed the services to get them to the market, and help customers use and maintain them properly. Optimizing the scale or scope of the whole distribution system would come to be as important for modern managers as achieving large production runs and building volume sales was to their predecessors.

'Either/or' choices about mass or specialized markets had to go, since all markets now consist of generic, targeted and individualized components. Mass production had achieved a startling economic victory for business. But, although it had provided economies of scale, and had therefore gained in productivity, it had lost in flexibility. The more that tasks became subdivided, the more regimented management became and the less able they were to offer the utility customers in key and select markets sought. Part of the problem was that with industrial logic managers inevitably traded off employees' capacity to serve customers more closely for machine efficiencies. Michael Piore and Charles Sabel, two economists who have studied the effects of industrial policies on American and European society, describe their findings in their book *The Second Industrial Divide*:

> The struggle to survive and prosper in a world where every satisfaction created new wants led to the constant improvement of productive efficiency; yet the constant improvement of efficiency subjected individuals to ever greater restrictions, according to the logic of divided labor and mechanization. The price of human liberation was thus subjugation. . . . whereas the worker had once defined the product, the product now defined the worker.[31]

So despite technological progress in the industrial era, as tasks were broken down, so customization disappeared, especially as it often did not coincide with corporate financial goals. Utility for customers would need a completely fresh approach. It would mean using the skills and talents of employees as a customer satisfying tool. It would require a capacity to collaborate in open interdependent systems rather than compete in closed and protected environments. And learning to focus concerns not on internal efficiencies for their own sake but rather as they relate externally to the needs of customers.

What had seemed so apt in bygone days had suddenly become clumsy and awkward. Hard core techniques were just too rigid to respond to unexpected customer demands, too inward bound to anticipate their needs and changes in their behaviour, too mechanistic to see the myriad of interactions inside the firm, as well as outside with the environment. As long as markets were prospering and competitors could be kept at bay, as long as customers' moves

Industrial	Contemporary
Get volumes for firm	Offer value to customers
Start with producer and work forwards	Start with end-users and work backwards
Compete in closed protective environments	Collaborate in open interdependent systems
Emphasize internal productivity	Focus on utility for customers
Pursue economies of scale for firm	Obtain optimization of scale/scope for total system
Choose mass or specialized markets	Markets consist of generic, targeted, individual components
Dominate mass markets	Cement key and selected markets
Machines add value	Man adds value

Figure 2.4   Industrial and contemporary mindsets

could be anticipated and everyone kept in his or her clearly defined place, the industrial model worked. And it worked well. But in the world we know today, a different managerial ethos would be needed.

3 *The market power is in the services because the value is in the results*

'Then you should say what you mean,' the March Hare went on. 'I do,' Alice hastily replied; 'at least – at least I mean what I say – that's the same thing, you know.'

'Not the same thing a bit!' said the Hatter. 'Why, you might just as well say that "I see what I eat" is the same thing as "I eat what I see"!'

Lewis Carroll, *Alice's Adventures in Wonderland*, 1866

When the anthropologists and linguists venture to the remote corners of the earth, what do they find? A new way of expressing things among the so-called primitives, that their words, sounds and syntax are totally unlike what we are used to. It isn't just that these people live in their own world: they interpret reality in a totally different way.

Primitive languages are in fact much richer than their modern counterparts, more complex in grammar and more baroque in expression. Whether Aborigine, Navajo, Hopi, or Amazonian, tribal people have one common feature: objects are described in terms of what they *do*, not in terms of what they *are*. Could it be that these people are more concerned than modern societies with how objects affect them, relate to their lives, and serve them?[1]

A tree, for instance, is described as a source of nourishment and protection. A room is where people live and work. A bowl is functional – it holds liquid, while the carved rim encircling the bowl is decorative: each part serves a distinct purpose and therefore is described differently. For these people, so far removed from industrial life, verbs seem to be more important than nouns. Descriptions of the environment are expressive and associative; they force people to think in terms of what the things are ultimately supposed to accomplish. Quite unlike our modern languages.

In business where, conscious of a need to constantly drive production and consumption up, many high volume managers were less concerned for the usefulness of their products and services than for their intrinsic technical qualities. How well they produced their offerings often took precedence over how well these goods could be applied, and they expressed this sentiment daily in their managerial discourse and language.

This couldn't have been more at odds with the kinds of needs increasingly being expressed by customers for whom utility had become paramount. No longer would a technical capability in and of itself produce corporations with better results, but rather better results for customers would produce more effective corporations. No longer would efficiency *per se* be the pivot around which a company's strength would depend. This would rest on its ability to provide utility for its customers and customers' customers.

But core offerings, whether products or services, were rapidly taking on the characteristics of commodities. Managers were beginning to realize that making heavy capital investments to distinguish their wares from those of the competition had finally reached a level of diminishing returns. Expressed in different ways, commentators and business practitioners were saying the same thing: services were growing at the expense of heavy manufacturing. Quite apart from what was happening economically in the macro sense of the word, this was glaringly apparent within corporations themselves. The point of differentiation had switched from the material to the immaterial – from making and moving 'things' to the value added services which could provide customers with the ability to 'do' things better.[2]

The value is in the results

The notion of value was based on the classic economic definition in industrial firms: something fixed in time, distance and space. It was determined by how much went into the product or service as opposed to what customers got out of it. Value was what customers were prepared to pay to increase their stock of wealth – a new computer, a line of credit, a ton of animal feed – at some fixed moment in time. It was a means to some desired end, an end which everyone – producers and consumers alike – simply accepted was the customer's responsibility. To put it more bluntly, the company's role ended when the ordered merchandise was delivered, in the right place, at the right time, at the agreed on price.

Was this a true reflection of economic value? According to some experts, a more realistic way of describing economic value would have been the proper utilization of goods and services, and their useful functioning. Viewed in this way, the word productivity takes on a new meaning: it becomes a measurement of the improved and increased use of goods in any economy or society, rather than an increase in the production figures. Two French economists, André Barcet and Joel Bonamy, who have been particularly involved in research to determine the impact of post-industrial trends on enterprises, express this concept in their article, 'Services et Transformations des Modes de la Production':

> There has been a total reshuffling in economic thinking: new ways must be found to integrate the customers and their use of products and services. During Ford's days, consumers were only slightly interested in utility: their primary concern was in the accumulation of goods and hence more production. The challenge in the present age is to move from the principles of accumulation to those of

utilization. And the new frontier in economics is one of functionality, where value is associated with productivity not in terms of production but in terms of what the customer gets.[3]

This matched perfectly with the more micro, managerial world, where new needs were being exhibited by consumers. To be more explicit, these needs had become increasingly concerned with the kinds of activities which made work in particular and life in general more productive. What customers now wanted was not just products or services for all the conventional reasons, but 'results' or, put differently, 'applied performance'. And this determined their more carefully thought out choices about with whom to do business, and what to buy.

To the uninitiated, the phrase 'applied performance' may seem no more than a slight nuance. In fact it represented a profound shift touching at the heart of the problem and also at what was to become the opportunity: the difference between what customers buy and what firms actually sell. The drive towards accumulation, with all the imaginable consequences, was what industrial values, or 'order winning criteria' as some prefer to call buying needs, were all about, while contemporary motives would be based on a whole new set of additional criteria (as the list in Figure 3.1 shows).

Industrial	Contemporary
Goods or services which conform to industry standards	Applied performance of goods and services
Compatibility of products, parts and components bought	Interconnectivity of working system
Buyers dealing with technical sales people	Multi-level links with various specialists
Curative features after the event	Preventative maintenance throughout use
Being on time according to schedule	Respond instantly and just in time (JIT)
People there if and when needed	People present and accessible all, and any time
Updated offerings and new features	Ongoing support and potential for improvement
Variety in range and depth of offering	Multichoice and flexible menus
Firms conscientious in their business	Firms easy to do business with

Figure 3.1   Industrial and contemporary customer values

The gadgets, bells and whistles so loved in the 1960s and 1970s had lost their lustre by the mid-1980s. Customers wanted functionality – not instead of, but in addition to everything else. Rather than buying just the product or the service, they wanted the solutions these goods could provide. In business-to-business markets, relationships could no longer solely centre around official buyers and sellers, as links had become much more multi-faceted, operating on different levels between buying and consuming organizations. In fact the roles of the buyer and the salesperson had changed to become brokers between producers and users, rather than just negotiators. Customer decisions were being based increasingly on applied performance rather than industry specification, with customers keener on the application potential and the interconnectivity of systems than in buying an assortment of bits and pieces from various suppliers, hoping to fit and operate them together.

In contemporary terms, competitive prowess means responding instantly and just-in-time as opposed to simply being on-time, according to some schedule. It means having people present and accessible to the customer at all and any time, not just if and when they make a request. It entails support that has ongoing and potential improvement for customers, not just updating models and features which entice them to replace what they've already got. Making customers happy may have more to do with flexibility in a range than depth, with preventing things from going wrong than fixing them when they do, and the ease with which customers are able to deal with the firm rather than just its level of conscientiousness.

In any case, the real value for customers today comes not from the core good but from how well it serves their purpose. By and large, anyone can produce and distribute the material 'things' well enough. Competitive strength for a corporation – be it large or small, in the traditional manufacturing or service sector – comes from the capability of making things work for customers. Here are some cases in point:

● From having been a traditional manufacturer, successful for its bearings design, production, distribution and sales acumen, SKF had to aim at providing customers with ongoing productivity. What's necessary for the industrial aftermarket – such as steel, textile and paper mills – is not just bearings: they need 'trouble-free operations', a working system which either prevents downtime or, when inevitable, predicts or plans for it in advance. Round-the-clock performance of the machinery into which the bearings are placed became the new mission for SKF's factory clients. Helping the automobile dealers and the body shop customers get rid of their biggest headache – finding the right bearing and getting it installed quickly – an integral part of the company's new value-adding strategy.

● When things go wrong with a computer, it often has nothing to do with the product itself – less than 1 in 100 network failures are hardware defects. The remaining 99 per cent are due to the customer's business processes and the computer's inability to function well *in situ* for some reason. After the shock of losing key accounts, management at Digital decided to change gears and concentrate on the ongoing functioning of its clients' systems rather than continue to only bring out sophisticated 'black boxes'. These sentiments struck just the right chord. While Digital's salesforce had been dealing with technical buyers, the users and their day-to-day problems had been overlooked. By then, customers were pretty much taking the high-tech hardware for granted. And users began to ask: how can the machines enhance their personal and corporate objectives? Where were the specialists they could talk to about their personal needs and applications? Where was the support to ensure non-stop functioning of their system? Could Digital have people on the spot to help when systems went down?

- Though it's in a very different industry, Citibank also is just as concerned today about making the bank work for customers as it is with making the bank work. Which means moving away from selling cheap credit – which anyone can do – to providing customers with the financial support they need to have the results and lifestyles they want. On the corporate front, for instance, it involves the movement and management of the funds that customers need, including better returns and reporting. Electronic transfer is one small aspect of this kind of service, where the object is now to make sure that customers can use the system effectively, at any time, in any place.

- 'I've moved, please link me up' was a typical request from British Telecom customers who were moving house. Until recently, they would have been put on a waiting list to get a new line and a phone. Today, the object is to be sure that the phone lines are in homes and offices before the customer arrives, making the service instantaneous at the lift of the receiver. Now, jointly with architects and builders, British Telecom works on projects and renovations upfront, pre-wiring buildings in anticipation of an eventual corporate or homemover's request.

- A hotel chain, restaurant or hospital can buy the best coffee in the world. But, unless their employees know how to prepare it properly, the beverage will be undrinkable after 30 minutes. Not only does this amount to excess costs for Nestlé customers also but it creates a lot of unhappy patrons. The firm's objective is to help give these clients a better overall result. The same principle is being applied to retailers. Increasingly, professional organizations and their buyers want improved results from shelf space or 'category of shop', as the trade calls it. So the international Swiss-based manufacturer has responded by developing category management and forecasting systems for key retailers to help them optimize their purchasing and organization of brands.

- The dyestuffs division of Hoechst found that it had two options in the United States: to become an outright commodity or to take the initiative and update its market offering to include more of the value-added guarantees that customers wanted. India was already offering an almost identical dye at only 30 per cent of the price. Since the dye contributed only 2 per cent of the overall added value to dyehouses – which in turn supplied the textile industry with coloured cloth – the situation remained problematic. Although dyehouses simply added the dye to water and immersed the product in the mixture, if the dye is not up to scratch, it can cause enormous damage and expense. Thus, Hoechst has moved from selling dye to offering 'risk-free dyeing production'.

● Mandelli, the Italian manufacturer supplying automotive engine machinery to firms around the world, made a leap from being what it called an 'iron supplier' – in other words, a pure commodity firm – to creating fully-automated, flexible manufacturing systems for clients. Before, the company would typically be given a machine specification or a prototype by customers who would ask Mandelli and others to place a bid for the machinery to manufacture the new engine. Now, the company goes into a customer's factory – say, Caterpillar or Ferrari – at the developmental stages of a new model. Jointly, they design the engine, then the machine needed to make the engine and, finally, the factory itself, thus optimizing the entire operation. [4]

● Why were so many customers dissatisfied with the insurance industry? Like all the others, Sprinks in France, Kansa, a Finnish insurer, and some Zurich Insurance companies like those in Canada, Australia and the United States (Universal Underwriters and The Maryland) used to sell policies to their customers that were essentially curative: any benefits were received after the event. Too late, customers complained. While the companies were focused on selling and processing claims, customers were also looking for help to prevent disaster and for support when it invariably happened. Now, these firms put their efforts into also forestalling accidents and hazards, thereby getting at the root of what many customers need.

What are the implications of all this? Customers want results to be sure. But, in truth, while most firms have been very good at producing results for themselves, they have never seriously had to deal with results for their customers. Herein lies a very different challenge. More than a semantic argument, more than a gentle nudge, it's a reversal in managerial logic, language and creed.

Companies, instead of achieving productivity for themselves, then selling the fruits of it outside in the marketplace, first have to achieve benefits for their customers which are then translated back into their own operational efficiencies. Instead of producing goods in high volume in order to benefit from larger markets, companies must become high-value organizations capable of providing utility for customers and thereby obtaining larger chunks of the revenues the market is prepared to spend. In a manner of speaking, firms must learn to package and sell results, that is, get a return – financial or otherwise – for customers.[5] This approach fundamentally changes what corporations do, what managers do well and how they make money. As Peter Drucker reminds us in the book, *The New Realities*:

> The single most important thing to remember about any enterprise is that results exist only on the outside. The result of a business is a satisfied customer. The result of a hospital is a healed patient. The result of a school is a student who has learnt something and puts it to work ten years later. Inside an enterprise there are only costs.[6]

Companies move to a total solutions approach

When SAS first explored a new travel package for business class passengers, the company wanted to minimize the amount of time wasted by customers doing unproductive and unnecessary things. The idea was to identify all the problems that travellers faced from the moment they thought about a trip to the moment they returned to their homes or offices. In the rush to reduce costs-per-seat-mile, airlines worldwide had up until then acquired large, wide-bodied aircraft, placing the focus squarely on capacity. The planes had to be filled, otherwise the costs-per-passenger-mile were too high. Classically, aircraft stopped several times en route to load on more passengers, a move which aggravated customer problems, adding time and inconvenience to their already pressed schedules. In a then legendary move, SAS eliminated its big planes and kept only the short-haul passenger aircraft to transport business class passengers to destinations quickly and comfortably.

The fact that customers ultimately bought things to solve problems was not a new thought, though few firms were explicitly gearing their strategies to achieve this. The famous marketing expert Ted Levitt, for instance, had already made this point 10 years earlier in several different pieces of work – that customers attach value to offerings in direct proportion to their perceived ability to solve problems. An extract from his article, 'Differentiation of Anything' is worth repeating here:

> Products (whether purely tangible, intangible or hybrids of the two) . . . are problem-solving tools. If the buyer won't buy for lack of help in design and application, it's not a product because it does not fulfill a problem solving need. Certainly it is incomplete. . . . A product is, to the potential buyer, a complex cluster of value satisfactions. The generic 'thing' or 'essence' is not itself the product. It is merely, as in poker, the table stake, the minimum necessary at the outset to allow its producer into the game. But it's only a 'chance', only a right to enter play. Once entry is actually attained, the outcome depends on a great many other things. Mostly it depends on how the entrant plays the game, rather than on the table stake (the generic product) that entitles one to play.[7]

What was different now?

Then: companies concentrated on solving internal problems, limited to their own working domain. Any solutions they sought were invariably isolated from the marketplace.

Now: the customers' problems had become the company's own problems. Solutions had to be found first. Then and only then could the problems that have to be resolved within the firm be determined.

Then: the main challenge for managers was how to modify, revamp and update existing corporate offerings, and solve problems related to producing and selling items better and more cheaply.

Now: selling results involves customer problem-solving concepts. Traditional products and services are mere components in a much wider system.

Then: the challenge was how to limit scope, confining resources to the immediate problems to be solved.

Now: it's how far to go beyond an existing range of activities and capabilities and what should be included in offerings to resolve customer problems.

Then: expertise was acquired specifically to solve corporate problems which were definable and imminent.

Now: pockets of expertise are tapped inside and out, to ensure that customers get ongoing results.

But the customer satisfying process involves more than eradicating obstacles to solve customers' problems. It implies that firms can actively seek opportunities for clients as well, to get them optimum results. Identifying and transforming potential or unmet customer needs into these opportunities often means being at least one step ahead of customers, building organizations that can anticipate their needs; take existing concepts, stretch and even overturn them if necessary. Quick to make this point, many business academics and commentators are adamant that a firm's capability to fulfill these goals is crucial in any competitive strategy today.[8]

This example illustrates the point. Looking at the human gains to be had from electronics as opposed to simply perfecting the technology, Matsushita has changed its concept of 'home electronics' to 'humanizing electronics'. What does this mean? While increasingly sophisticated and powerful, its machines no longer suffice to attract customers. Matsushita must gain value, its management believes, from adding to the physical, mental and spiritual well-being of its customers, all of whom have their own aspirations, lifestyle needs and worries about what goes on in their homes. Japanese youth want to watch American television, to learn languages and be expanded culturally. The elderly want all controls for entertainment in one place, so they don't have to keep getting up. Business people want to know when they have received a fax while they are travelling. And all customers want to keep track of their electronic equipment when they are away from home – whether or not the refrigerator is leaking, etc!

Moving from traditional concepts to value for customers through solutions is rather like going from the Indo-European languages back to primitive ones: from nouns, the material, to verbs, the immaterial. The language metaphor shifts products and services from 'being' to 'doing', and managerial priorities from making and supplying 'things' to seeking and providing value added. (More examples from firms which have made this transition are shown in Figure 3.2.)

Industrial (Noun)	Contemporary (Verb)
Bearings	Trouble free operations
Animal feed	Productive pig farming
Insurance	Risk protection (industrial) Lifetime investment (personal)
Dyestuffs	Risk free dyeing
Air trip	Total travel management
Cable machine components	Productive cable capacity
Carpet fibre	Floor covering expertise (industrial) Floor covering enhancement (personal and contract)
Computers	Network capability
Calls	Interpersonal communication
Trucks	Cost-per-mile
Retail brands	Category management
Carrier service	Logistics management
Printers and copiers	Document management
Home electronics	Humanized electronics

Figure 3.2 Traditional and contemporary solution concepts

Expanding on this:

● Customers can and do buy vehicles from several suppliers. Volvo Trucks, after discovering that the average capacity utilization of a truck in Europe is only 50 per cent, developed a system to cut down on the end user's empty mileage time when the vehicle is not fully loaded. Thereby, the company provides fleet owners with a reduced 'cost-per-mile' solution, of which the vehicle is only part. As little as a 1 per cent saving – produced by various means – can translate into tens of millions of Kroner of added revenues to Volvo's customers' bottom line.

- Nokia-Maillefer Cable Machinery was known as a world leader in cable machinery by virtue of its high-quality equipment. The global corporation, based in Europe, decided to move from selling machinery and components to providing its clients using cable machinery with solutions or, in company terminology, with 'productive capacity'. The kinds of problems customers needed to have solved typically were: which components and machines to use, where to find them, and how to combine and configurate them to gain the maximum possible meterage of cable wire. Once the appropriate machinery had been selected by customers, the lines have to be set up and kept running at peak performance. And, to keep these lines and factories updated in a cost effective manner, technologies have to be chosen and implemented on an ongoing basis.[9]

- As the largest supplier of animal feed to pig and chicken farmers in Holland, Hendrix Voeders continually improved its feeds, providing specialty mixes to suit its customers' individual circumstances. But, of course, competitors did the same, leading to an increase in the costs of serving customers without any commensurate expansion in the market. Hendrix then took the lead in developing an entirely new approach. Working on the philosophy that 'if the farmer is doing well, we'll do well', the company switched from being a feed supplier to being a provider of 'productive animal farming'. The results? Twenty years ago it took 2.8 kg of Hendrix feed to add 1 kg to the live weight of a chicken. Today, the same breed of chicken gains 1 kg when fed 1.8 kg.[10]

- During a routine sales call to a large hotel chain, one Nestlé representative was told, 'It's not more coffee we want; we have a breakfast problem. We serve 3,000 cups of coffee between 7am and 9am every morning. Our taste is not up to par, our customers are fed up, our staff can't cope and we've got a massive amount of waste. If you can't help us solve this problem, we'll have to find someone who can.' After analysing the client's entire coffee-making process, a solution was found that increased productivity, decreased congestion, improved taste and minimized waste. Doctors at a Marseilles hospital decided that the time had come to stop serving 'sad food' to patients. Good, interesting and nutritious meals were essential to their morale and recovery. Nestlé, as the hospital's culinary supplier, began asking patients what kinds of food they liked. Based on this feedback and medical recommendations, the company created first new menus and recipes, and then redesigned the kitchen equipment and layout to achieve better productivity for the hospital and improved service for patients.

- InterForward, a carrier service operating primarily in Europe, was rather good at handling its customers' physical distribution and paperwork. But, by the late 1980s, the company went way beyond merely getting things on and off lorries, planes and trains, and began to handle all activities related to moving things for clients, both inside and outside their premises. Such a physical transportation and materials handling concept was closer to logistics management than to traditional carrier service practice.

● Several companies within the Zurich Insurance group now provide customers with risk management systems. The object of the exercise is to minimize the risk of accidents, liabilities and losses. For instance, each aspect of a customer's factory process is analysed to ascertain where potential danger may lie. Then preventative methods, ranging from changing the lifting method on a factory floor in order to reduce employees' back injuries to implementing a procedure for storing keys to reduce car thefts, is put into place.

● From selling single 'box' copiers, Rank Xerox has extended its offering to 'document management'. Now, the company provides all the products and services needed for customers to print and publish their documentation. A total solution enables corporations to produce forms for use in-house, and publish and distribute such material as magazines, annual reports, newsletters and mailings electronically or in hard format, both creatively and productively. Instead of working with ivory tower solutions in the company's own laboratories, offices, and factories or trying to change its clients' cultures, Rank Xerox now carefully abides by users' workstyles and existing operating parameters.

The evolution of adding value through services

After taking a look at the approach to services during the second half of this century, we can see that slowly but surely they have moved from being mere afterthoughts to become *the* value creators in any firm's offering to the market. Though, today, the effects of this process are quite dramatic, it has been a gradual build-up, which for interest's sake can be traced over various stages, culminating in the total solution approach now found in high-value corporations (as shown in Figure 3.3).

What began as a relatively imperceptible move during the 1950s, 1960s and 1970s, then gathered some steam in the 1980s has, in the 1990s, become a necessity for any firm that wishes to maintain its competitive grip. Regardless of the products and services sold, value-added services are now a *sine qua non*: it's just a question of degree.

As services have become more powerful in market offerings, so the role of the 'core' item in the value bundle has changed. Whereas in the past this 'core' was the sole determinant of market success, today the computer, bearing, telephone, copier or unit of animal feed can no longer be relied upon to get or keep an edge. In fact, as some people suggest, with the passing of the

Stage	Contents	Object	Market
1 Stick to core	Core products *or* services	Volume	Generic
2 Augment core	Core products or services *and* value added services	Volume Value	Generic Targeted
3 Extend core	Solution modules products *and* services	Volume Value Results	Generic Targeted Individualized

Figure 3.3 Evolution of value adding services

high-volume industrial economy, over-preoccupation with the 'core' is restrictive, making firms rigid and unable to stretch beyond current business boundaries into activities more in line with customers' needs.[11]

Stage 1: Stick to the core (1950s, 1960s and 1970s)

During this phase, the core product and service was the firm's chief priority. Everything that was done and everyone who was hired was determined by how much could be added to the company's technical and commercial success. 'Concentrate on doing better what you do best' was the underlying principle which echoed the fundamental sentiment of the times and which undoubtedly managers had, over and over again, proved worked.

From this core, everything else emanated: research and development (R&D), budgets, recruiting, production, sales and, of course, services – such as they were. As a rule of thumb, corporations stayed within their own domain. 'Stick to the knitting' was a phrase made popular by Tom Peters and Robert Waterman who, in *In Search of Excellence*, retrospectively tried to find the common denominator for successful companies.[12] This notion synchronized perfectly with perceptions about customers and the then vigourous pursuit of mass production and consumption targets.

Stage 2: Augment the core (1980s and early 1990s)

Managers knew that if they didn't get the core right, everything else was bound to go haywire. But, with fiercer competition and goods becoming commodities much more quickly, they realized that this could only be a starting point for future strategies – the 'poker stakes' in Levitt's words. It was certainly no guarantee of success anymore or of winning a customer, and, perhaps more importantly, no guarantee of keeping one.

Adding services to the core was marketing's way of trying to differentiate offerings from those of competitors. It served two purposes: firstly, the marketing gurus had been pushing hard for a targeted approach to markets, aiming at chosen groups of customers – homogeneous in their desires and reactions – and this seemed to be an ideal way to tailor products or services more specifically to these groups. Secondly, by augmenting the core, firms could begin to combine the advantages generated by volume sales with value specific to the needs of these customer segments.[13]

Gradually, corporations began to add extra bits to their offerings – such as financing, transportation, insurance, guarantees and JIT delivery. But, what had probably begun as a promotional tool soon took on a more profound character. The value-added services were becoming *the* primary differentiating vehicle. Customers could, in theory, get the 'core' items anywhere. Of course, specifications and price would always be a major competitive factor to them. But they had begun to attach a different kind of meaning to the intangibles which added the real gains. The balance of power between the almighty 'core' and the augmented parts of the offering had begun to change.[14]

Stage 3: Extend the core into solutions (1990s and beyond)

A firm's ability to identify, package and deliver value-added service capabilities will determine its success in contemporary markets. From every industry – even those in traditional bulk industrial products or regulated service utilities – have come the same overriding remarks. One interesting example emanates from John Harvey-Jones's memoirs as ICI chairman, *Making It Happen: Reflections on Leadership*:

> Increasingly as the world becomes more and more competitive and as the skills of manufacture become more easily replicated, the selling of a defined product against a formula becomes, from a competitive point of view, a matter of cost and the ability to command a market position. . . . It could be and indeed it is my belief that the chemical industry of twenty years hence will be more of a service industry and less of a manufacturing industry. One can already see the trends in this direction as the successful companies are those which have developed an ability to provide a chemical service to customers rather than selling a product in a bag.[15]

This doesn't suggest that firms are about to dispense with their core products or services. On the contrary, that move could cause yet another sort of vacuum which would thwart the new aim – to provide solutions. But, by the late 1980s, early 1990s, two things had become clear. One, the mythical choice between products and services was at an end and, two, the value added had less to do with the 'core' – be it a product or a service – and more to do with the environment where it would be used. Managers had begun to expand their notion of the core as they transformed their basic offerings into solutions for customers. One executive from SKF describes this change:

> Our 'core' now encompasses the whole life of the bearing. The objective is to increase the productive time that people can get from the component. This means taking care of the number of things that have to be done with the bearings and the surrounding environment. Customers may ultimately even buy fewer bearings, but at least this way they will buy from us.

With this move, firms have had to become as proficient at the new value-added services which create the solution as they previously were at making and moving their core. The net result has been that services have begun to dominate operations of classic goods producers to such an extent that it's no longer clear what the word 'manufacturer' really means. Traditional goods producers must recognize, say James Brian Quinn, Thomas Doorley and Penny Pacquette, working in the area of services and technology, that not achieving a strong enough competitive performance in these services will result in an inevitable loss of strategic advantage, lower profitability and a high risk of takeover. The major portion of incremental value and gain, they say in their article, 'Technology in Services: Rethinking Strategic Focus', will continue to come from the chain of services integrated into a form most useful to customers, and much of the remaining enterprise will exist to let these activities take place. [16]

The anatomy of solutions

Ironically, when translated from the Latin, the word solution literally means 'to unravel and dissolve'. Originally, the term referred to its use in chemistry. A solution is made up of several elements, and in order to really understand its effects, a chemist had to first break it down into its various parts and smallest constituents.

Solutions, as it applies to providing results for customers, are comprised of several modular components (as illustrated in Figure 3.4). Although they are sometimes difficult to separate, and indeed some companies would prefer not to do so, each one is vital for delivering satisfying solutions to customers. Since a solution can only be as good as its weakest link, the modules need to be integrated into one cohesive whole. Take one piece out and the effect will be felt – its absence diminishing the overall result for the customer.

Goods

Goods are the basics, the material 'things' – the credit, chemicals, computers and copiers. It is these that are invariably fast becoming commodities. From them the solutions first emanate. But, because they don't necessarily create

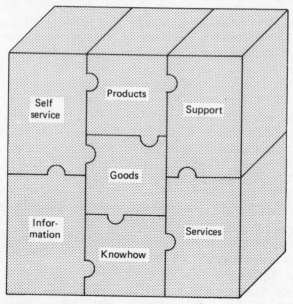

Figure 3.4   Anatomy of solution system modules

the added value any longer, many managers are increasingly less preoccupied with them. Here is some of the thinking on this subject, although it is neither conclusive nor consistent from one firm to another:

> *The R&D in basic technologies should be shared with other firms.* This is happening especially in high-tech industries such as computers and consumer electronics. The approach saves money and the needed time to reach the market, particularly on goods that are very easy to copy. The disadvantage is that larger portions of these goods have become identical, and this is accelerating the pressure to create value added in other ways.
>
> *The production and the R&D of goods can be outsourced.* Who cares, some managers say, who designs and makes the core so long as its quality is acceptable? Their argument is that such items, even the most sophisticated, can be made or bought out. They reason this way on two counts. First and most obvious, it's cheaper; second and more subtle, customers can't perceive the difference and, if they could, they wouldn't care or be prepared to pay. Some firms go so far as to 'give away' these goods as the price of market entry. The real potential, they argue, comes from elsewhere.
>
> *The R&D and production of goods providing an applications platform must be retained.* This rationale comes from firms which believe that only by holding onto basic goods can they maintain their edge – not only for these goods themselves, but for the applications technologies surrounding them,

including the value added services. They nonetheless acknowledge that, unlike the past when this core had to be sold first to get the service deals, today it's often the other way round.

Products

Moving into solutions means there will be a need to have new products outside the firm's traditional portfolio. These products may be sold to customers or just leased. Or simply used by the firm in the delivery of its solutions. Either way, they are products fundamental to providing an overall solution. These examples help demonstrate the point:

● In order to provide its customers with 'trouble-free operations', SKF had to invest in new diagnostic equipment, installation tools and an array of other devices needed to predict downtime, circumvent it, and get bearings into machines more accurately and quickly.
● For years, SAS tried to promote a 'Passenger Pleasing Plane' for short-haul passengers. The idea was to sacrifice space in the freight and pilot compartments to give passengers more seating space and room for their baggage, thus improving comfort in the air and decreasing time delays on the ground.
● With a credit card, American Express customers can now withdraw cash from almost any international airport or hotel. Similarly, British Telecom and other phone companies give customers a credit card to trigger their services from almost any city in the world.
● Using specially designed products, solutions can be better implemented. That's why Nestlé's Food Services division has worked closely with kitchen supply manufacturers to make a range of hospital culinary equipment available to their clients.
● When Kansa discovered that 95 per cent of the child deaths in car accidents could be avoided by using seats with specific features, the firm commissioned a Finnish manufacturer to produce such car seats for young children. When the youngsters outgrow the product, it is returned to Kansa, restored and rented to other customers. In a similar vein, the insurance company, The Maryland, gives its customers a catalogue of safety products for all common accidents which may occur in the home. The more important ones – such as swimming pool alarms and door hinge protectors – are supplied by the company.
● To provide risk-free dyeing, Hoechst builds containers on the customer's site. This ensures hitch-free JIT delivery to each individual consumer's production line. Hoechst has also redesigned the packaging in which the dye is transported so that customers can simply throw the product into the machine and switch it on, thereby avoiding spillage and inexact measuring, which endangers the outcome.

Services

The kinds of services that facilitate the use of goods can range from training, installation, repairs and logistics to financing, stock control or facilities management. Referred to sometimes as 'service products', they are definable, packagable, confinable and relatively repeatable. They are traditional activities which exist by virtue of someone selling a basic good in the first place. To illustrate:

- In keeping with Volvo Truck's response to its fleet owner market to provide cost-per-mile rather than vehicles only, the company has embarked on a programme to design, deliver and support several services. The difference between this approach and making, delivering and repairing trucks is huge. Trucks have to be maintained, petrol and credit supplied, breakdown services put in place throughout Europe, and various technologies built in to enhance and monitor utilization of the trucks within the fleet.
- Petrol is a grudge purchase, as no one likes to spend time at a petrol station. Can extra services provide a better solution for customers? BP has tried other innovative services in addition to the usual ones – such as upgrading the facilities, restrooms and restaurants; its customers are able to get cash, to use fax machines and other work facilities. The company's 400 convenience stores carry a wide assortment of products so that customers can really shop, not just make some impulse purchases.
- The firm InterForward collects some 500 different components required to build IBM's printers in Sweden. These parts are then taken to Inter-Forward's warehouse to be unpacked, inspected, repaired if necessary, housed and, eventually, delivered JIT. Once they have been assembled by the computer manufacturer, InterForward packs and delivers the finished product to the customers.
- In addition to regular financing, Rank Xerox also gives financial advice to its customers. This service is most critical because the financial arrangement can affect the economics of the documentation management system. By using this professional advice, costs and depreciation can be correctly matched to the revenue generation of the machines, often as important a consideration in the solution as the quality of the document itself.
- For Citibank to make the movement and management of cash work for customers, the company has to go beyond PCs and banking. A slow printer in the customer's office may, for instance, wreck the chances of getting the whole transaction – including hard copy – done fast. So, in providing solutions for customers, Citibank will also make available other services such as an analysis of the customer's office equipment relevant to creating a fully functioning system.

Self-service

What a firm can do for customers is important in any solution offering, but just as important, is helping them serve themselves. The industrial mentality encouraged customers to self-serve so as to cut costs, usually for the firm: the contemporary mindset includes self-serve modules within offerings which add to the customer's purchase. It increases value rather than subtracts from it, facilitates rather than causes inconvenience, with time and money saved for both the buyer and seller. As examples:

● Sprink's Insurance uses an extensive database, which is made available to its customers in France through the electronic Minitel network. If clients who are about to take a vacation want to find out, for example, which vaccinations are needed, what diseases are rife and how to protect against them, the necessary kinds of visas, the amounts of currency allowed in and out of various countries, or legal rights in the event of an accident or damage, they can access this information instantly themselves.

● AT&T and British Telecom both offer phone systems which can now be modified by customers when the occasion arises. Screens can be attached to the basic product to link them into a modem and give them networking capability. Or clients can plan the uninterrupted use of telephone lines to their key country markets at critical times by self-programming their needed slots beforehand.

● Taking the idea from office equipment and implementing it in homes, Matsushita has built a self-inspection and self-fix component into its electronics. If a TV, video or refrigerator begins to malfunction, a display panel alerts the user as to the cause and what to do. The owners are given instructions for handling routine repairs but, if the problem is more serious, they can phone for help. And repair people can come properly equipped since they already have all the relevant data, thus taking less time to fix the machine.

● Federal Express now has a 'powership management system' for 30 per cent of its customers whereby they can handle all their own ordering, tracking, and even billing of a parcel. Once customers' computers are hooked into the system at Federal Express, all they have to do is key the information in and the parcel is picked up automatically. Clients can then weigh the parcel on special scales, track its progress, prepare the bill themselves and, finally, pay Federal Express directly every 6 weeks.

● Most airlines now use some form of automatic boarding system. SAS, for instance, has five different methods to help customers find a convenient way to avoid standing in a queue – by phoning in beforehand and by using machines in taxis, hotels and office blocks, as well as at the airport.

Support

These 'behind the scene' activities enable the functioning of the entire system to be effective. Like a safety net, they are important; they help to ensure that problems are staunched before they arise, and handled rapidly and quickly when they do. Less routine by nature, support activities deal with problems that cannot be anticipated and help the solution provider to be ultimately sure that results will be ongoing. This kind of support includes activities such as scheduled maintenance, contingency planning, remote diagnostics and damage control. Some typical trends in support services include:

● *Supporting wares of other firms*. This requires that companies know their competitors' products and services as well as their own. Digital and IBM both support and maintain machines of other manufacturers, taking on these functions as part of their overall commitment to customers.
● *Ongoing services to minimize if not eradicate interruption*. Digital has put 'self-help' desks in its major clients' premises. In this way, potential problems can be fixed before any disaster occurs, and people are on the spot when the unforeseen has to be dealt with. SKF has set up maintenance support centres in forty-five countries, which are responsible for the planned maintenance of the company's worldwide customer base.
● *Support systems that warn of potential breakdowns*. These services can switch into a backup mode simultaneously or give a firm the opportunity of fixing a problem before it affects the customer. For American Express, having less than 100 per cent uptime is unacceptable. The company managed to achieve 99.8 per cent, but when the system was down, even for only 30 minutes, twenty-four times a year, huge numbers of transactions were still lost, and innumerable merchants and cardholders aggravated. With its new system it has backup which immediately comes into play, doing away with even the slightest interruption.
● *Remote electronic linkups when face-to-face support is impractical*. To diagnose, advise, instruct and send help to truck drivers in need, Volvo Trucks has set up a remote Euro-wide mechanism which fleet drivers can tune into 24 hours a day wherever they happen to be. Local dealers trained for this purpose by the Swedish manufacturer go to the scene to assist drivers with their problems.

Information

Information services can entail anything from the simple collection, processing, interpreting and tranferring of data to sophisticated, intelligent systems applications. Over and above this, every part of a solution in some way uses information which is handled by firms differently depending on the circumstances. Some embed it into other modules, like support; others package the information portion separately. However it is fashioned, its significance is becoming ever more profound:

● Federal Express has found that information about a package is as important as getting it delivered on time. Just telling customers whether or not their parcel has arrived on time is not enough. The courier company knows that they now want to be able to find out how their package is doing at any moment. As soon as a phone call starts the process to the time the delivery is signed off, a whole tracking mechanism is set in motion which can relay information to the customer and anyone else who happens to be involved with the parcel's fate.

● Largely by virtue of its information system, Hendrix Voeders is able to optimize overall farm productivity for Dutch pig farmers. Data is fed into the system from two sources: the farmers who give details on feed, treatment and the general status of the pigs, and consultants who monitor various aspects of the livestock. What transpires is a real-time information flow encased in a technical advisory service.

● Ciba-Geigy has created a separate information service unit in its restructuring which serves internal users with a more competitive spirit than previously – when divisions took what they got and were arbitrarily allocated costs. Information is now a part of a total solution designed for colleagues in agro-chemicals or pharmaceuticals to help them respond to the thousands of problems they need to solve – ranging from a corn disease in Africa to the potential side effects of a new drug.[17]

Know-how

To do all of this well requires know-how. For the same reasons – like information – this expertise is difficult to separate from other modules, as the portfolio of experience and capabilities within a firm is contained in everything it does. So important are these vast pools of knowledge becoming – and potentially very lucrative too – that those firms that are excelling in this service are undoubtedly taking the lead:

● Corporations like Digital and IBM sell their know-how to customers independently of the hardware. To call this merely 'information technology' is a gross understatement. Their know-how extends over computer expertise touching on all aspects related to helping customers achieve their strategic global goals through networking systems.

● Nokia-Maillefer's skill today is in knowing which machines to put together and how. The company packages this know-how in the form of productive capacity which is sold to its cable making clients. Knowing what, where and how to put the relevant components, lines and systems together, and getting the lines, systems and factories up and going more quickly than the customers could do it on their own has, in essence, become Nokia-Maillefer's competitive edge.

- InterForward's considerable accumulated experience with regulations in Europe related to vehicles and transportation, including motorcycles, is being applied in many diverse ways. For example, it does all the legal work for Harley-Davidson associated with the distribution of its motorcycles, as well as determining the physical modifications of the bikes so that they conform to national and European requirements.
- Why buy know-how from Nestlé on category management or design know-how from Mandelli? One reason is that their exposure to other customers has given them know-how which spans a wide spectrum of corporations. Combine this with the in-depth knowledge that individual customers have about themselves and the end result for everyone is better than any single firm can hope to achieve on its own.

Mass custom-alization of solution systems

Limitations of technology and the way customers and markets were viewed gave prudent managers one of two options during the 1960s, 1970s and even into the 1980s: either produce en masse for the generic end of the market, or customize offerings for smaller selective niches. Two incompatible ideas – the twain simply could never meet. Then, as targeting became a more common approach during the 1980s, managers began to tailor their offerings to segments, intentionally catering to differences in the 'markets within markets'. By the 1990s, thanks to technology, they were able to both capitalize on the substantial economies of scale to be gained from producing for the 'mass within markets', and provide special features for these 'markets within markets' – their chosen segments.

Mass customization was an idea whose time had finally come. In theory, both product and service sectors could industrialize and specialize their offerings simultaneously, allowing the two techniques that had once seemed so contradictory to coexist. Served markets were better off because the same large numbers of customers would receive the benefits of mass-produced items while, by customizing added features, these items could be more suited to the more specialized needs of identified customer groups.[18] With a little creativity, corporations could both reap the economies from mass producing products and services, and at the same time give target segments what suited their tastes and circumstances.

Not only had the combination of standardization and flexibility become possible but also it had become a necessity. But, in reality, did mass customization go far enough? Probably not. With individual needs now so important to the competitive position of firms, it had become essential that solutions cater to the generic, targeted and individualized components of the market. If firms did not truly create benefits for individual users – the only people who could really assign value to an offering and make results happen

Stage	Contents	Object	Market	Offering
1 Stick to core	Core products *or* services	Volume	Generic	Mass or customized
2 Augment core	Core products or services *and* value added services	Volume Value	Generic Targeted	Mass customized
3 Extend core	Solution modules products *and* services	Volume Value Results	Generic Targeted Individualized	Mass custom- alized

Figure 3.5   Evolution of value adding services

– then they could not compete. Extended core concepts only made sense if they included this personalized dimension. Which meant that mass customized offerings had now to become 'mass custom-alized' (as shown in Figure 3.5).

Included in mass custom-alized solutions would have to be the 'mass within offerings' for the generic 'mass within markets', to keep costs down; the 'customized within offerings' for 'markets within markets', so that modules can be applicable for targeted groups; and the 'personalized within offerings' for 'customers within customers' – individuals or markets of one, to ultimately ensure utility. (Figure 3.6 illustrates this mass custom-alization graphically.)

Markets are reconfigurating quickly and on a wide scale today. In high-volume economies, mass markets had time to mature before they fragmented. Now customers demand relevance immediately. Mass custom-alization represents a true opportunity for firms to get down to the crux of what users really need. It also addresses some of the challenges of how to match customization and personalization with the untold potential for producing solutions on a global scale economically.

Goods and services: body and soul

It was inevitable that the classic distinctions between services and manufacturing companies would become blurred. Neither goods nor services could sensibly be confined to one fixed domain anymore. For all practical purposes then, firms today can no longer opt to be either in products or in services if they are to remain competitive.[19]

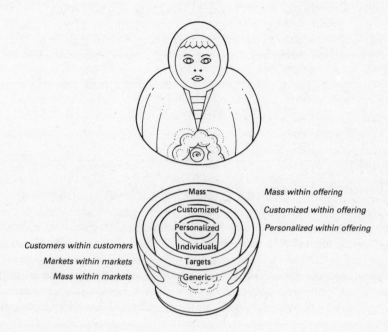

Figure 3.6   The mass custom-alization of market offerings

Manufacturers need services to make their offerings relevant to targets, markets and individuals. Already products have a large proportion of services built into them. But we now know that a profusion of newer and better products does not reduce the need for services. In fact, the opposite is true. It's really a vicious circle, because the more advanced products become, the greater it seems is the customer's appetite for intangibles.[20] One way of putting it is that manufacturing and services have converged, with far reaching implications. Several academics have come to the same conclusion, including Jean Gadrey, whose work at University of Lille in France confirms this. As he says in his article, 'Le Service N'est Pas Un Produit: Quelques Implications Pour l'Analyse Economique et Pour la Gestion':

> It will no longer be enough to offer product or service alone. Rather, more and
> more complex services will have to be integrated to create increasingly complex
> solutions. Convergences between manufacturing and services will occur on a
> more frequent basis for two reasons: services will become a more common
> feature in product companies, and, in particular, more corporations will not be
> selling products as they did in the past but processes and capabilities.[21]

In the same way that manufacturers moved into services, the services sector began to develop, make and use more products to deliver their intangibles. Also, hoping that they could discover what manufacturers had already learned, many service firms began to industrialize their activities. The benefits were clear enough, so long as the objectives were kept within limits. Unfortunately, though, some firms went overboard and therefore experienced all of the drawbacks of the tin soldier mentality: lack of flexibility, internal and upward focus, and loss of the human touch.[22]

But by the 1990s, for one reason or another, most manufacturing and service firms had concluded that products without services, or services without products, was an untenable situation. Both were patently necessary in order to compete. Besides, were products and services so different from each other?[23]

Certainly, for decades economists had maintained that the two were different. They had insisted on distinguishing services from products, relegating them first to the 'tertiary' sector, and later classifying them as 'residual' activities – in other words, what remained after agricultural and industrial production.[24] But, when statistics in the mid-1970s revealed that services made the greatest contribution to wealth in the developed countries, there were some questions posed that had no ready answers.[25] Where was the real value coming from? With know-how so integral to offerings, could services be distinguished from the product any longer? What was software – a product, a service, or both?

Could a manufacturer really be considered part of the industrial sector anymore if such a large portion of its revenue depended on services? Most contemporary firms were involved in a compendium of activities – with some of them ending up as products, others adding value to these products, while still others did not relate directly to the material at all. Were artificial demarcations between products and services justifiable in a world concerned more about utility and the immaterial than with the 'things' themselves? The differences between service and manufacturing companies had clearly faded. While the debate on the finer points of what was, and wasn't, a service would rage on, managers had to learn how to run corporations where, like body and soul, products and services had become so interdependent that they could hardly be distinguished. And, they had to figure out a way to manage the immaterial that permeated their offerings – now *the* generator of market power.

4 *Jumping into the customer's activity cycle*

'To every Form of being is assigned,'
thus calmly spoke the venerable Sage,
'An active Principle.'

William Wordsworth, *The Excursion*, 1814

Picture a busy street, pavement, restaurant or park in New York, Paris, London or Tokyo. In addition to the normal pedestrians going to and fro, there could also be some people staging, on their own small platforms, what has come to be known as 'performance art'. At the beginning, it may seem unfamiliar and even awkward to those observers who have never before experienced this kind of activity. Most people expect to see drama in a theatre, music and dancing in a concert hall, painting in a studio or gallery, poetry recited in a literary salon or book store.

They may think at first that the players are improvising, but soon it's clear that this is not the case at all. Early on, the various acts may appear to be just a series of disjointed sketches. In fact, they are usually very well rehearsed and connected. This avant-garde performance may not fall into any traditional framework, but it is a solid new art form. No longer the fringe activity it once was, it's a mainstream discipline today. A far cry from the song and dance acts which used to liven city streets and carnivals. Sophisticated multimedia techniques are being used to explore new ways of combining disparate art forms and create another unique brand of customer experience. The classical 'high' arts proclaim from atop, 'this is it': performance art, or 'low' art as it is sometimes called, says 'let's figure this out together.'

Sometimes performance art is known as living art because it is never quite the same each time around. Each performance unfolds as it goes along, including the spectators' daily routines in the act. The theme is woven around the observers' experiences, in this way breaking down the traditional distance and formality between those doing and those observing. Both the doers and the observers contribute to the end result because the artists deliberately draw the audience into the act. There is constant exchange going on throughout the spectacle so the rapport between the two groups and the individuals within them grows and, jointly, they determine the nature of the ultimate outcome.

Time, in these events, is not fixed to the typical 2-hour slot. Instead, the reaction of the audience and the intent of the actors as the drama unfolds determine how long they will be together. Since the barriers between them are less pronounced or formal, exchanges are more spontaneous, occurring on the spot in real time, often changing the course of the performance. Rather than being lodged into a conventional format, the performance is held in the customers' space. How else could the artists adapt what they do so well to the activities going on in the audience's own unique setting?

Services are acts that must be performed by someone and experienced by someone else if they are to exist at all. They cannot be possessed or accumulated: they must be rendered and experienced, often simultaneously. Whereas material objects can be fixed in time and space, the immaterial cannot. Since they are social by nature, they demand a constant interplay of give and take. And, as in the performing arts, those who are serving and those who serve cannot be kept apart.[1]

Because of the nature of relationships today, a firm frequently must literally be in its customers' space, sharing activities with them. The distance between buyers and sellers so characteristic of previous working styles has practically disappeared. So has the narrowly focused ideology that firms can continue to do better what they already do well in the hope that this will be sufficient. Moreover, the steadfast time horizons they have been used to have had to be stretched, since results can seldom be accomplished in the short term. Paradoxically, though, while the experiences of high-value corporations reveal that satisfying customers requires longer time frames, activities still must be achieved in ever speedier ways.

A renaissance in customer relationships

In the craftsman-like days of the pre-industrial era, firms were close to their customers by definition. They had to be. People with the means and wherewithal to buy something – whether at the corner store or from an auto manufacturer – had a set of individual problems and requests they expected to have resolved. Between buyers and sellers an open channel existed, and relationships were close and personal. From their knowledge of customers' lifestyles and work patterns, sellers gradually built generic features into their wares. Such was the nature of the commercial relationship during those times. Until Ford and the assembly line entered the commercial picture and the inevitable tradeoff occurred: customer relationships suffered as the more pressing concerns of producing voluminously and affordably for the masses took hold.[2]

Strange as it may now seem, managers assumed that customer relationships simply happened. It was seldom explicitly suggested that these relationships might have to be earned or that customers were investments which had to be developed over time.[3] Because of the compelling need to produce and sell, managers concentrated on finding new clients rather than taking more time with those already in the fold. This was aggravated by the fact that the prime management task was to obtain financial results quickly – managers could not realistically think more broadly than the prevailing rules of the industrial game allowed.

But, there was also something deeper at work. Most managers just weren't programmed to think systemically. Consequently they didn't venture beyond well-defined parameters of time and space. Deliberately they distanced themselves from the market, often content with short-term answers to longer-term problems. Frequently, it was the symptoms that were dealt with rather than the real issues therefore. Managers had been taught to compete, not collaborate, shifting the burden to others whenever possible so as to optimize the position of their organization.[4]

With the benefit of hindsight, we now see that this attitude can and does damage relationships between members of the distribution chain and ultimately endanger, even destroy, an industry's or firm's ability to satisfy end users. By the 1990s, a more systemic approach had begun to take hold in management. What really hit home was the realization that no individual firm in a distribution channel could single-handedly accomplish total customer satisfaction. Nor could any supplier of products or services delegate totally its relationship with end users to intermediaries. Put differently, if businesses could learn to collaborate, they would be able to achieve more jointly than any one firm or industry could on its own. Had the damage already been done? The question was posed by several commentators, including the organizational consultant, Ronald Ashkenas. He, like others, feared that for a variety of reasons shifting the burden had become a habit, *the* prevailing Western archetype. This point he makes in his article, 'A New Paradigm for Customer and Supplier Relationships', and he says:

> Rather than collaborate with other members of the value chain on systemic solutions . . . many companies are putting their faith in 'go-it-alone' programs, competitive awards, and other symptomatic fixes, or they are forcing other members of the value chain to 'conform' to their view of what's needed. . . . When some firms in the chain cannot handle the extra cost or the reduced margins, they collapse and weaken the overall chain.[5]

How had this situation become manifest in well-known industries?

- Some manufacturers in consumer goods were so intent on getting volume throughput that retailers became choked with products. Manufacturers stoked consumer demand creatively, and retailers were expected to push their stock through to the final users. This process was happening worldwide. Like others in the cosmetics industry, Kao – the renowned Japanese manufacturer – maintained a continuous policy of filling up the retailers' shelves, many of whom by the late 1980s were slowly going bankrupt.
- Adversarial overtones and conflict – described by some writers as 'warlike' – characterized relationships between buyers and sellers in many other sectors.[6] Food is one good example. Nestlé was one of many firms using

the classic formula to gain its chunk of the market: products were so good, branding so strong, promoted so well and vigorously through wide distribution, that a derived demand was created among end-user customers. As retailers grew, they became more powerful in the scheme of things. What fresh approach could replace the relationship between manufacturers and the trade – which had become increasingly based on margins – so that they could watch their markets grow jointly?

● As pushing volume through the pipeline was the only way to get rid of the gigantic quantities of products coming out of industrial factories, manufacturers lost contact with end users. In linear fashion, component manufacturers followed the same principles as consumer manufacturers. They moved products through the system with one difference: because they were dealing with industrial buyers, they couldn't do much 'pull' promotion. Salespeople were given incentives to make volume sales down the line – something they did and did well. SKF is one case in point. Prior to moving to 'trouble-free' operations, the company sold to, not through, their 35,000 distributors, regarding them as the prime aftermarket target.

● Whoever did the selling to end users was also expected to be their link and information channel in both product and service sectors. This was tantamount to leaving end user relationships to intermediaries. This contributed to an already growing rift between those who produced the goods and those who consumed them. DuPont had an interesting experience relevant to this point. The quality of service in the retail stores was so bad that customers would actively postpone making a carpet purchase. Consequently, the sale of DuPont's carpet fibres deteriorated, despite their technical excellence.

Was it an underlying feeling of security and infallibility that programmed some manufacturers to keep users at bay? Or was it just the way that they conducted their business at that time? Perhaps the kind of reputation and clout held by many well-known firms simply enabled them to set the conditions. This attitude was certainly not confined to the manufacturing sector. In services as well, especially where size or regulatory protection tended to give corporations a false sense of infallibility, this was common practice.

Closing the gap between producers and consumers

If one traces the relationship between producers and consumers in some historic kind of framework (as in Figure 4.1), it's clear that over the last few decades the gap between them has gradually narrowed. By and large, relationships were mostly 'transactional' in the 1960s, assigned to professional sales people who were expected to sell as much and as many 'things' as possible.[7] A more 'relational' approach began to catch on in the 1970s,

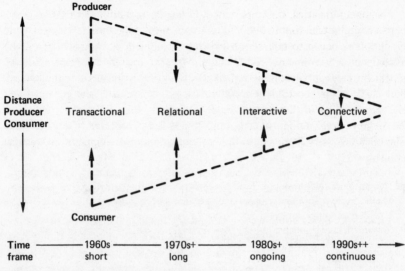

Figure 4.1   Stages in customer relationships

when marketing began seeking a better understanding of markets and strategies to satisfy customers more fully. Again, the idea wasn't entirely new but, for a variety of reasons, it had not been implemented. What the experts were now proposing was that corporations analyse their customers more rigorously and thereby get a better reading on their needs. Pursuing this course assumed, obviously, that customers would be able to express their needs. It was, most people acknowledged, a step forward. But only a step.

Some writers suggest that during this period the 'marketing mix', or rather management's interpretation of it, had been responsible for some of the general dissatisfaction in the marketplace. It had, they claimed, chased after new customers but had not been concerned about long-term relationships. It had relied too much on mass, instead of person-to-person communication. It had enticed instead of delighted customers. It had spent its energy getting instant gratification, not real satisfaction. Its forecasts were backwards. Its tools made it an expert in the past, often unable to assess future consumer behaviour in the face of new attitudes and values.[8]

Had it all seemed too easy then? Management had left the delicate job of customers to a single function, which happened to be marketing. Yet, it was impossible for any one function to handle alone because, as it became increasingly clear, a focus on customers is an attitude rather than a task, a state of mind as opposed to a functional responsibility.[9] Marketing was also placed in the double bind of having to care for customers on the one hand, but also sell as much to them as possible on the other. In practice, this led to complex and divergent relationships with the other functions, as well as ambivalent goals.

For most industries, the importance of customers as long-term assets only began to really take root in late 1980s. By the turn of the decade, management practitioners began to talk seriously about customers as *the* most important investment any company could make. Writers stressed the importance of repeat business in sustaining a firm's future competitiveness. In any event, they said, happy customers were the richest source of new business. In Europe, working in the area of trade in services, John Richardson and Leif Edvinsson were among that group. Their essay entitled 'Services and Thoughtware: New Dimensions in Service Business Development' makes the point strongly:

> The customer relationship itself is the asset . . . Confronted with a new product, whether it be a new financial service, a computerized hotel reservation service, a mail order opportunity, a new form of consultancy or a software system, consumers may be unable to judge its usefulness or value. Hence a company that has established a relationship based on trust with its customers possesses a priceless asset and can build on this asset by offering new packaging to the same customers.[10]

Observers were now advocating so-called 'interactive' relationships, specifically demanding stronger, ongoing bonds between a company and its customers, longer-term outlooks, more intuitive assessments of needs, and more apt responses in tune with contemporary values. By then, the services school had made management more acutely aware that, certainly when it came to the intangible aspects of business, customers and firms could not be separate because they were part of the same process. The 'moment of truth' idea, made popular in Scandinavia, seemed to crystallize what many firms had known instinctively for a long time but few had, in reality, been able to practise. Relationships were made up of a series of encounters with customers at many levels in the organization. If any of these interactions were badly handled, no marketing – however professional, no product or service – however good – could save a firm from ultimate oblivion.[11]

But how, writers in both manufacturing and services had been asking, were managers going to eradicate the seeming gap between producers and consumers? A new orthodoxy began to surface late in the 1980s which had a different kind of nuance, based on relationships more 'connective'. Connective because it meant doing things not only *for*, but also *with* customers. Partnering between a firm and its customers – a concept borrowed from classic professional service firms – entered the general management vocabulary. What it intended to convey was an end to the distancing between corporations and their customers. It implied collaboration.[12]

It was different from the arm's-length relationships of the industrial years, in which the pivot was the relationship between professional buyers and professional sales people. In partnering, power and with it responsibility, are spread more evenly between producer and consumer, between firms and end users, which jointly endeavour to reach a desired common goal. Take banking as one example. Many often had to base their offerings solely on margins.In the long run neither the customers nor the bank got what they wanted. Today, a firm like Citibank will of course provide credit at the cheapest possible price but in addition will supply to its customers the higher margin, value added services. This way, the bank can develop the best possible solutions for customers while they in turn get cheap finance plus the fuller benefits of funds, cash and currency management.

In connective relationships, partnering takes place at various levels. People who have to deal with customers, and who were previously blocked or locked into the formal buyer-seller type situation, are able to work with more freedom because they have access to the correct people and information. Rosabeth Moss Kanter, whose research and writing is on mastering some of the challenges in modern organizations, discusses the impact of these new relationships on the people who are involved in their execution. In the book, *When Giants Learn to Dance*, she says:

> For many of the managers and professionals involved in partnership dealings, the empowerment is clear and direct. They have increased access to top management, whereas previously they were not included in strategic deliberations. They are given information and data allowing them to better understand what drives business decisions and they can get questions answered with a single phone call to a previously inaccessible executive. They are consulted on matters of business significance to the company, before decisions are made.[13]

Eradicating traditional demarcations and buffers between company and customer – whether business or individual – is basic to making connective relationships work. Each of the stages described (Figure 4.1) have different skills associated with them which build upon one another, all containing elements of the others, with connective relationships therefore requiring all four: if transactional skills are not up to scratch, sales are compromised. If relations are not solid, market position will be in jeopardy. If the interactive side of a relationship is lacking, bonding will be impossible to achieve. And finally if the connections – be they physical, psychological or electronic – are not made, firms cannot hope to sustain long-term customer satisfaction. Looking at some of the principles of new relationships in greater detail:

● *Both parties have a vested interest in making the relationship a continuous one, because everyone is better off that way.* To make more efficient use of its card, American Express has worked towards solutions on two fronts. First, it transformed its sales offices and travel agencies into full service centres to give card holders global assistance 24 hours a day. Then, it tackled merchants, offering them such services as promotions, credit, insurance, consulting on electronic payment systems, and seminars on fraud to help them prosper in their daily business operations.

- *Since partnering is a two-way street, a win-win situation prevails rather than one with outright winners and losers.* SKF involved distributors through a joint action programme in initiating its trouble-free operations. Partly, the decision was taken to get global coverage for the sake of accessibility. But, the object also was to strengthen the whole distribution chain with both parties ultimately responsible for ensuring better services to end users.

- *A sense of reciprocity applies across the board.* Toyota and Honda – like most car manufacturers in Japan – make customer fidelity their main goal, which is one reason why brand switching tends to be infrequent in that culture. The idea is to strive for lifelong relationships with both dealers and end users. If a problem arises after the car is bought, it is fixed at no extra cost by dealers. Formal guarantees are provided by the manufacturers, but they are irrelevant because repairs are done for the life of the car anyway.[14]

- *Mutual interdependency – rather than domination or dependency – is what cements relationships.* When retail outlets began to sink under the weight of excess stock, Kao obviously suffered as well. The company embarked on a sophisticated information system which would enable retailers to order electronically on demand. Kao's retailer customers carry no excess stock at all today, yet they can still meet 100 per cent of their shoppers' demands.

- *Shared destiny is fostered and becomes the overriding goal.* At ICI, 'mutual prosperity programmes' are undertaken with key customers which go beyond legal contractual agreements. The company works with customers over long periods of time, sharing objectives, aspirations and even resources. The ICI paint division works closely with accident repair shops throughout Europe, offering these customers an array of services to promote their operational efficiencies and future developments.

- *Relationships are forged throughout the distribution chain.* Carpet mills, as well as retail customers, were asking DuPont's carpet fibre division for discounts. The carpet industry had been reduced to heavy discounting as its image and service level had gone awry: people were buying less carpeting, less often. DuPont took up this challenge, working closely with the mills, the retailers, industrial and personal users. The company now in addition to emphasizing the design and durability of the products, assists carpet manufacturers and retailers with improved services, plus such aftercare to end users as cleaning and a 24-hour-a-day user hotline.

The spirit of the times

In the industrial era time was both the key driver and management's staunchest enemy. Taylor's 'time and motion' studies had set the ground rules.

Methods were being defined and refined constantly so that seconds could be shaved from each activity to improve internal productivity, devoting as little time as possible to any single task. Of course the ability to do things quickly always has been and always will be cardinal in business, if not more so now in the 1990s.[15] This is true for all the routine transactions where the object is to to reduce customer waiting time to as close to zero as possible. But in selling solutions and results for customers, what's at stake are long term relationships and this can only happen over extended periods of time. The question is how to master the rote tasks while leaving more time for the high value activities and relationships. Then there is another challenge related to time which managers now have to tackle: how to work with time frames as perceived from the customer's standpoint? Take an example in the food industry. How was the term 'freshness' defined using industrial logic? When the package left the factory or the retailers' shelves. But this really doesn't address the issue of use, which is how much time does the customer need to consume the product. For instance how long does it take for the freshness to disappear once the package is opened?

A different approach is needed:

Then: the object was to minimize time with customers.
Now: time is being spent to develop relationships.
Then: managers focused on short-term immediate customer requests.
Now: they must also be willing and able to anticipate future, longer term and often less obvious customer needs.
Then: pressure was on firms to deliver products or services on time or JIT.
Now: they must also provide services which last over extended periods of time.
Then: the object was to get customers in and out of facilities as quickly as possible.
Now: firms also look for ways to keep them usefully engaged.

Some examples include:

● ICI's paint division has its employees 'live' in their customers' factories so that they are present and party to all application processes. Previously, the company would be called in to sell to body shops repairing autos which had been in accidents. Typically now an ICI employee can spend weeks even months with customers, assisting them with financial matters, shop layout, throughput, technology, marketing and computer systems.
● Digital no longer asks customers, 'How many black boxes do you need now or in the foreseeable future?' Today, the question is different: 'Where do you see your business going in the next five years?' Finding that answer means having to take a longer-term perspective, which may require that short-term earnings be sacrificed for longer-term aims.

- IBM recently went against its traditional grain, which dictated that discounts be offered only when and where major sales were made. Realizing for instance that Shell, one of its key customers, would need resources and support in Singapore as they developed in that area in the future, IBM offered to give Shell accumulated discounts in the form of service application centres in that region when the occasion arose.
- Airlines – like SAS and Singapore Airlines – have learned that the passenger's seat is only one small part of the total customer solution. Therefore, they now are putting more resources into various on-the-ground and in-the-air services to enhance the quality of the customer's overall experience. Simultaneously, they are looking for innovative ways to minimize unnecessary intervention which wastes customers' time.
- Hendrix Voeders' sow management system goes well beyond delivering bulk feed on demand to its farmer customers, no longer treating its products as mere commodities. In fact the feed is not delivered until after a series of services which begin even before the piglets are born; these include selecting livestock, feeding them, managing their environment and various other activities to ensure the animals' ongoing health, well-being and growth throughout their lives, and ultimately their commercial value for farmers.
- BP's initiatives at its service stations had a twofold aim. Firstly, customer traffic flow was redesigned so that time would be saved in the actual petrol transaction. At the same time, it made various office and shopping services available so that business and personal customers could benefit from a one-stop shop during their journey.

The solution is in the process

Process-based techniques, used so prolifically and so successfully by firms during the industrial era, began in the production and operations functions. They created internal efficiencies by providing managers with precise details of the transformation process. Its various proponents claim that, through this discipline, activities can be analysed step by step, thus leading to better control than would be possible by merely waiting for output and optimistically hoping for the best.[16] The trouble, say the critics, with this approach – sometimes called a blueprint – is that to become ever more precise managers began to splinter their processes down to such an extent that the overall picture got lost.[17]

So obsessed did people become with their own small part in these processes, that they forgot their role overall. This disadvantage was exaggerated because they were focused inwardly and so became more and more entrenched in the fineries of their operational details.[18] Peter Drucker talks about this from a manufacturing perspective in his book *Managing for the Future*, calling for a redesign of the core business process. His view is that unfortunately process techniques largely became a cost cutting exercise. But there's no point in making cost cutting *the* objective, he observes, if it's at the expense of the customer. The manufacturing process begins before anything arrives at the factory, and ends well after it leaves. And it's only when managers are able to see the process holistically that they can begin to compete effectively. Here's how he puts it:

> The manufacturing process is a configuration, a whole that is greater than the sum of its parts. Traditional approaches all see the factory as a collection of individual machines and individual operations. The 19th century factory was an assembly of machines. Taylor's scientific management broke up each job into individual operations and then put them together into new and different jobs. Modern [industrial] 20th century concepts – the assembly line and cost accounting – defined performance as the sum of lowest cost operations. But none of the new concepts is much concerned with performance of the parts. Indeed the parts as such can only underperform. The process produces results.[19]

The services school started using process quite early on in the 1980s. This was a good way to take an industrial methodology and apply it to their operations in order to increase efficiencies.[20] In particular what the services experts were able to do with this flowcharting was track and trace quality problems to their origins. The difference with services, however, was that managers were not dealing with a strict set of tasks based on a predictable pattern of outcomes. Nor could these tasks be kept insular, isolated from what was going on with customers.

Several writers on the subject have criticized flowcharting, citing its various advantages but pointing out its disadvantages. Or put another way they say that if this technique is used only to detect simple cause and effect relationships, spelling out every excruciating detail, it can do more harm than good in services. In effect it becomes an engineering overkill, blinding people to the customer and what is really important. Employees become over concerned with the details of what they have to do and so create rather than solve customer problems.[21]

In modern process type thinking and models, instead of tasks being divorced from customers, they become the value adding mechanism leading to customer satisfaction. The process, instead of being essentially internal, extends beyond the firm into the customer's space and activities. It begins with end users and works backwards, differing therefore from sequential industrial value chain thinking at a very fundamental level. Corporate processes don't only take the customer into consideration, they run in tandem with customer activities. In fact one might go so far as to say that they merge with customer activities, being totally synchronized with them.

The customer's activity cycle as a working tool

At this point, it's time to look at the customer's activity cycle as a working tool. Whether the industry is old or new, high or low tech, what can be observed is similar. If getting results for customers is the end goal, then the means or mechanism is the design, delivery and support of products and, to an ever-growing extent, the services that produce results throughout their activity cycle.[22] Whosoever finds the opportunity for adding the value during this process has the competitive advantage. What does this entail?

Previously, managers focused their attention on the minutiae of their own working processes. Now, they have to understand the inner workings of the customers' processes – 'seeing' things their way – with the same amount of detail. High value corporations apply the same industrial gusto to routine services in order to master and make them efficient. But this cannot be their sole *raison d'être*. At the same time, they must be more flexible in every facet of their business, allowing for variations and deviations that will lead ultimately to the right solutions applied to the correct customer problems in a timely way. And if these solutions are to be mass custom-alized to fit new customer values, they need greater depth of application and more dedicated personalization over extended periods of time. All rather different from the mechanistic approach. More and more of the enterprise's value is created during the customer's activity cycle rather than in their laboratories, factories and office blocks. In other words, whatever is known by the organization and translated commercially only becomes meaningful if it ultimately has a part to play in the experiences which customers undergo.

It's possible to divide the customer's activity cycle into three phases so as to create a framework for discussion and practical application. Most writers on the subject have talked about the customer's buying process rather than their experiences, which is a decidedly different tack. The customer's activity cycle has more to do with users and usage than with formal buying procedures which of course is one part of such a process. It is also more systemic stretching from the beginning of any customer experience through to the very end. In fact, being systemic it's an ongoing loop rather than a straight line – so characteristic of industrial models – with a series of overlapping phases which effectively have no beginning or end:

Pre-purchase phase: When the customer is concerned about '*what to do*'. This question is often either too complex or strategic in real or opportunity cost terms to be answered by individuals or official buyers, and the advanced expertise is too expensive today for customers to obtain or acquire. Hence the growing need for suppliers or third party involvement.

Purchase phase: When whatever has been decided must be executed, with all the concomitant tasks involved in actually making the experience a reality.

Under the industrial regime, '*doing it*' was mostly left to the customer to handle after the sale was made and delivery had been honoured by the firm. Now, high value firms assume a much larger portion of this role. Ideally the desired results are achieved for the customers who are then free to get on with what they need or prefer to do.

Post-purchase phase: When the customer has to '*keep things going*', and this doesn't only mean repairs. It also means making sure that an investment is fully successful – well into the next cycle, because considering the future has become more important to today's customers, who tend to make decisions with a longer-term perspective. Things should not go wrong but, if they do, support is available. Consumers expect these services from high value corporations which go well beyond the service contract. And in business-to-business relationships a larger number of firms are more willing today to outsource their non-strategic activities in the interest of focusing their attention on their end users.

Mapping the customer's critical activity points

It's just not possible to use the customer's activity cycle as a tool without a profound understanding of *who* the customers are – particularly the users – and *what* they do in their daily work and life styles. Reliant as suppliers now are on customers' activities to determine their own priorities and processes, it is essential that managers understand each critical activity point in this customer activity cycle and are able to map them out in some organized way. Thus they are able to get the overview they need in addition to understanding the details. Then the question is where the opportunities lie to provide the value added.

To do this requires a contextual shift away from some of the more rigid marketing research methods previously used to try and understand customers. In industrial days, the kind of information which was gleaned from the marketplace for interpretation and action was dependent on surveys. Though useful, this data gave feedback on sections of the market, or target groups based on large random type samples which broadly examined trends and needs often in a numbers driven and abstract way. These surveys missed the nuances which are needed today as firms work for and with customers and try to supply more personalized solutions.[23]

While conventional research techniques may still give managers an important view of the market, they are being supplemented by more discourse, face-to-face feedback and in depth examination of customers *in situ*. From this vantage point, high value corporations find they are in a much better position to create a business process which produces results that customers want. Here are some examples to illustrate:

- Information, ideas and insights are often exchanged rather than elicited. This is done on a one-on-one basis with the people who are involved in providing and supplying the services, rather than third parties who, while they may be more objective, are also more distanced. Digital executives for instance will spend time with key customers – like, say, a UK bank – talking to senior management, the branch managers and the IT people. Rather than being a formal piece of investigation, the tone of the dialogue is to listen and share respective views of where trends are likely to go and what can be mutually achieved, given the customer's direction and aspirations.

- 'Full ownership experience' is how Toyota refers to its customers' investments in its cars. This concept engenders, among staff and dealers alike, a frame of mind which necessitates spending time with customers in their homes, learning what role a car plays in their lives. The company is constantly trying to ferret out information that will improve the quality of the customer's day-to-day auto experiences. First-hand information is acquired and analysed: the number of school-age children in the home; distances travelled between home, school and work; who does the shopping, how often and where; favoured vacation sites; how frequently cars are washed and parts replaced, etc.[24] Honda, which targets the businessman in Japan, thoroughly dissects every transporation requirement for this group. But then, to avoid 'averages', they go to see customers personally and ask: how often they travel on business and where? What added business-related features – from faxes to financing – do they need so that they will use the car more often? Do they travel outside Japan by car? Where do they tend to park? How often do they prefer to service their autos?

- Instead of just studying statistics at their desks, representatives from Universal Underwriters, The Maryland and Zurich Australia visit retailers and factories to understand exactly where their operational pitfalls may lie and, hence, where potential accidents may occur. Data is collected in the customer's own setting on the small, unreported, minor uninsured incidents that have taken place. Such incidents typically can lead to the more serious accidents and disasters that cause ultimately the really big losses and grief. So, if they can be discovered and obviated, a great deal of expense and the associated ripple effects on customers' staff can be eliminated.

Several examples follow to demonstrate the customer's activity cycle at work. Figure 4.2 shows how pig farmers in Holland go through a series of activities to attain productive results. The process no longer ends for feed supplier Hendrix Voeders when the piglets have been provided with food, or for the farmer when the livestock is delivered to the slaughterhouse. Success hinges on seeing the entire process through satisfactorily, all the way to the

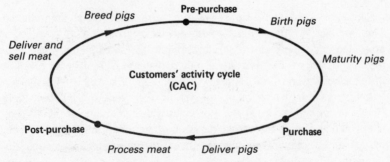

Figure 4.2   Pig farmers: Hendrix Voeders customers' activity cycle

householder's table, taking what is being learnt and incorporating it into a new cycle.

A quite different example is shown in Figure 4.3, the activity cycle of a typical car or tractor customer for Mandelli. As they are updating their models continuously, these customers must design new engines constantly. These engines must provide two things: enhancement of the new product and effective manufacturing possibilities for the plants. The process is an ongoing one: first, the new model vehicle is designed, followed by the engine design and development. Then, a new flexible automated factory is designed, or an existing one is revamped, set up and made operational – until a new model comes off the drawing board and the cycle repeats itself.

A third and expanded example of the customer's activity cycle comes from Rank Xerox clients – typically corporations or professional print shops. Any new or improved document management system begins with an analysis of the existing document processes within the firm. A new or better system is then designed, purchased, installed and set up, integrated into daily routines and maintained. Figure 4.4 examines one of the critical post-purchase points in more detail, in this case application. As soon as the customer plans to print or publish a document – say an invoice or newsletter, this sub-process goes

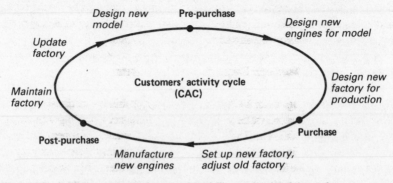

Figure 4.3   Car and tractor manufacturers: Mandelli customers' activity cycle

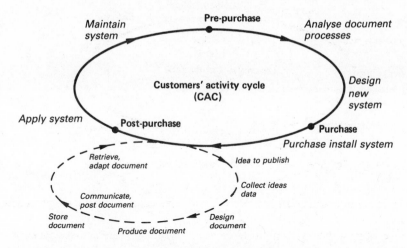

Figure 4.4 Corporations and print shops: Rank Xerox customers' activity cycle (expanded)

into action: data is collected and assimilated from a number of sources, the document is designed, produced, stored, distributed and, subsequently, retrieved and adapted for further use.

A tale of seven case studies

An assortment of seven case studies is presented in Figures 4.5 to 4.11. The pre-purchase, purchase, and post-purchase stages of the customer's activity cycle are illustrated with the respective solution module responses offered by the firm. Each one has its own particular context, although they are, of course, more simply sketched here than is the case in reality. Common threads run through each example. They highlight the connections between what the customers experience and the corporation's value creating potential; they demonstrate that the customer's ultimate results can only be due to an ongoing and continuous process and, perhaps most significantly, the crucial role played by services in creating one seamless flow of activities.

Case 1: Hendrix Voeders: From feed to fat piglets

Anyone can fatten up a pig by feeding it more, but this is not the sole object. While more bulk feed might be sold that way, pig farmers won't get the results they want – the nutrition and well-being of their animals. Pigs need to be fed and looked after in a way that is acceptable to end users as well as commercially viable for farmers, distributors and retailers. The major services in the solution system offered by Hendrix Voeders to its customers can be seen

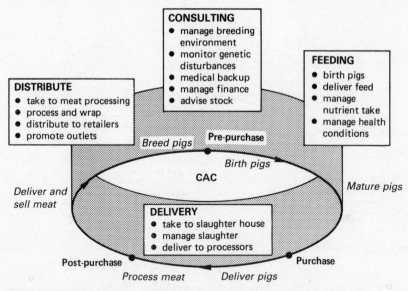

Figure 4.5   Solution modules over Hendrix Voeders customers' activity cycle

in Figure 4.5. During the customer's pre-purchase phase, consulting on stock and sow management is provided so that breeding conditions are optimal. During the purchase phase, the piglets' feed is customized along with their individual supplements and medication needs. In the last phase, the pigs are taken to the slaughterhouse, then the meat is delivered to processors who wrap and distribute it to the retailers for sale to the ultimate consumers.

Case 2: DuPont: From carpet fibre to floor covering enhancement

Homeowners had doubled their repurchase cycle time for buying carpets to almost 12 years and were taking up to 10 weeks to make a decision. As well, this decision was made reluctantly, as they greatly disliked the buying experience. Then DuPont decided to take the lead in improving this situation. Management assessed the critical activity points during the end users' experience, starting with the moment the potential buyers decide to get floor covering through to the replacement decision. At each part of the distribution chain – including carpet mills and retailers, for home, office and key institutional users such as hotels and hospitals – DuPont is involved in value added services to solve the respective problems, as shown in Figure 4.6. Some examples include: providing information and advice about decoration for end users; applying fashion designs and forecasting to the key carpet manufacturer clients during the pre-purchase phase; training, merchandising, store layout and credit for retail stores; and a variety of post-purchase services including maintenance, repairs, refurbishing, and emergency help for spills and disasters.

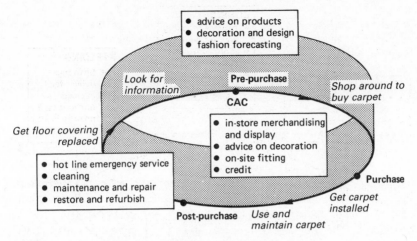

Figure 4.6 Solution modules over DuPont end user activity cycle

Case 3: Digital: From 'plumbing' to profits

Much like plumbing, IT had always been there, not highly visible but necessary to channel and process data. Now that companies like Digital have to help customers increase their viability through IT rather than merely sell more 'black boxes', its emphasis has had to shift from the technical quality of its wares to adding services which lead to more effective client applications and information network use. Digital covers the entire gamut of solution modules needed to mesh its customers' IT infrastructures and strategies with their goals. Figure 4.7 includes details about Digital's offering for the pre-

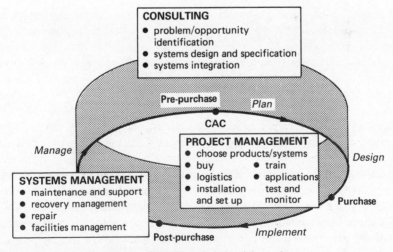

Figure 4.7 Solution modules over Digital customers' activity cycle

purchase, purchase and post-purchase stages of the customer's experience, beginning with consulting through to systems integration, project management, maintenance, repair and, finally, the management of total facilities.

Case 4: InterForward: From loading to logistics

InterForward in Germany handles the European logistics for Harley-Davidson, the American motorcycle manufacturer, and for Denon, the Japanese stereo speaker maker. InterForward prepares the customers' products for the various countries, distributes JIT to retailers, and maintains them for end users. As shown in Figure 4.8, InterForward takes responsibility from the moment the bikes and stereo sets arrive; the products are inspected, modified and reassembled, and sometimes repaired, then delivered to their final destination. The company also follows up by providing maintenance, as well as updating – adding the latest features to products already delivered – to end users. In this way, each critical activity is handled with an expertise which the company either already has or then acquires.

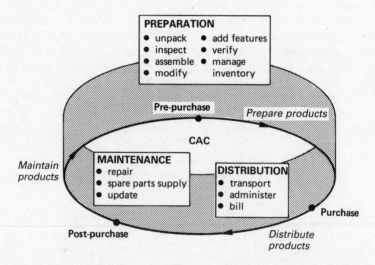

Figure 4.8   Solution modules over Interforward customers' activity cycle

Case 5: SKF: From bearings to trouble-free operations

SKF's object is to avoid unscheduled downtime for the aftermarket, as it costs a fortune compared to the price of a bearing. A bearing's life expectancy depends only partly on technical quality. The rest hinges on the environment and how the bearing is handled and cared for. SKF factory aftermarket clients

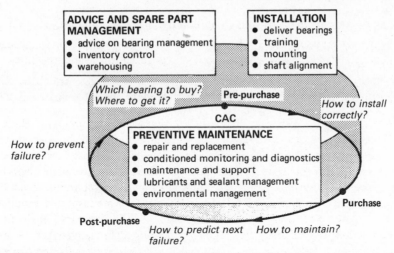

Figure 4.9 Solution modules over SKF (after market) customers' activity cycle

need the answers to several questions related to the process of maintaining their machines, as in Figure 4.9. Which bearings do they buy, from where and when? How do they install and lubricate, clean and configurate them? How do they anticipate, prevent and plan for a failure? How do they prolong the useful life of a bearing? The answers to these questions form the basis of a whole new set of value added services which SKF now offers to customers during the pre-purchase, purchase and post-purchase phases of its activities.

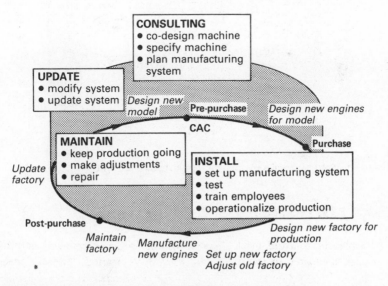

Figure 4.10 Solution modules over Mandelli customers' activity cycle

Case 6: Mandelli: From iron to automotive factory management

Right from the outset, when the first ideas for new car or tractor models are being formed, Mandelli works with customers in their laboratories. The company provides know-how about the specifics of engines, machinery for the automated flexible factories that will produce these engines, and the design of the factory where they will be made. These steps, as shown in Figure 4.10, take place up front, so that by the time the client – say Ferrari or Caterpillar – makes a decision, they've been through all the scenarios. Once a decision is taken, Mandelli sets up the factory, trains staff, gets production going and maintains the lines, recommending updates when needed. So as to minimize expense and disruption, each factory is configured with the next engine models in mind, modular style.

Case 7: Rank Xerox: From single boxes to in-house publishing

Rank Xerox, shown in Figure 4.11, can take between two to five weeks to analyse the flow and volume of all the documents within a customer's firm – their content, their origin, and their destination. Once this is done, an integrated solution can be designed for both paper and electronic documents throughout the firm that will capture the operational synergies within that specific milieu. Before installation, the site is checked and the system fine-tuned to avoid holdups. During installation, applications are developed, the system is set up and employees are trained how to combine ideas and data in order to get the best technical and creative results. Rank Xerox also manages

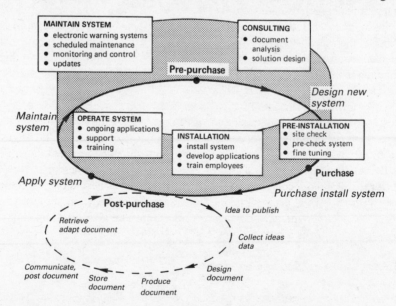

Figure 4.11   Solution modules over Rank Xerox customers' activity cycle

post-purchase applications, ensuring that the latest technologies are integrated into the system, as well as electronic diagnostics, monitoring and maintenance control.

Putting the value added in: and taking the non-value added out

In understanding the customer's activity cycle, the manager is best able to judge where the added value can take place at each critical point. Being present at one stage of the cycle provides an entrée to the others, which is one reason it's so important for firms to be involved in some way during the entire flow of activities. Back in the industrial days, this issue did not exist, as corporations were involved in their own processes – making and moving finite 'things' – repairing them if they went wrong. Today, any firm which confines itself to one activity in the customer's total experience, especially if it is in isolation from the rest of the distribution chain, must risk eventually becoming a commodity supplier and having competitors gnaw away at its markets.

As the examples demonstrate, the service ethos means establishing relationships with customers that start sooner, last longer and cover more ground. The same amount of effort and resources now go into the pre-purchase, purchase and post-purchase services as went into making and selling things before. Above all, a firm must be there for the customers, visible and accessible throughout the activity cycle so as to influence and activate important decisions and facilitate results. More than just getting a foot in the door, however, real value adding must take place to avoid having a rise in cost without the commensurate rewards.

To be everywhere at all times is the object. Ultimately, corporations need to think of their own and their customers' value creating chains as the same, not as distinct and sequential. As partners they must organize their firms so that they run in tandem, concurrently, compressing time and distance, and sharing space.

Only then can managers also begin to know where the non-value adding costs are taking place. And how to remove them. This is rather different from what took place only a couple of years ago, when firms sought to ply customers with as many 'things' as possible. Now through its expertise, a high value supplier attempts to find a way to eradicate unnecessary activities. Since the process between company and customer is viewed as best as one, or at the very least together, each party has to do less. This eliminates redundant overlaps, obtains synergies and thereby increases value all around. Examples of what some firms are doing include:

Taking out non-value adding expenses

- All soft drink manufacturers need carbon dioxide (CO_2). This product used to be kept by them in large expensive storage tanks because an out-of-stock position halted their flow of production. Customers spent vast amounts of time on tasks associated with this, like checking stock levels and ordering. ICI, the major CO_2 supplier in the UK, has developed an electronic 'stockmaster' system which automatically reads a customer's inventory situation and delivers the product JIT. The onus is now on ICI, not the customer, to assess the stock position and make certain there is always an adequate supply. Because many activities are eliminated – such as monitoring, phoning, ordering, checking, invoicing, receiving and paying, as well as the cost of the tanks – the customer is more than compensated for the fee being paid.

● Canon has eliminated warehousing and distribution for half of its dealers; over 30 per cent of their time used to be spent on this activity. The delivery of copier and office spare parts, components and supplies was complicated because, being small operations, end users typically did not keep track of what paper, toner or cleaners they bought. Additionally, this exercise was also costly, space being extremely expensive in Japan. Now, as soon as a dealer receives an order from a customer, Canon is alerted through its on-line system; the company expedites the order directly to the customer by courier, which takes only half a day and costs much less. Customers are debited automatically, and this too is less expensive for the dealer.

Removing unnecessary duplications

● When Hoechst sold paint to car dealers – such as Peugeot in Socheaux – the customer would have to follow all the usual procedures from the time the paint was received to its modification for a specific production line and application onto cars. Now, Hoechst has built a warehouse in a nearby location, thus eliminating storage duplication and other activities both parties had to do. Hoechst also customizes the paint mixtures before delivery, thereby saving time for its customers, who now simply have to apply the product.

● To get custom-designed cars to dealers and customers within five days, Toyota eliminated a whole series of redundant procedures which the company, the dealers and the customers previously had to go through. Now, customers go to the dealerships where they send in their orders electronically, which are transmitted directly to the factory and simultaneously picked up by the suppliers. No billing is done between the factory and the suppliers; payment is made automatically by Toyota to them when the goods are used.[25]

Eliminating activities intended to control others

● Between the moment an order was given to DuPont from a carpet mill and the carpet fibre manufacturer was paid, several activities transpired, many of which essentially served only as a double check. Had the carpet fibre arrived? Was it correct? Had it been ordered? Had the invoice been sent? Had the payment been received? Was the amount right? As these activities have become increasingly intertwined, many of these controls have begun to disappear. Customers are able to save even more time by billing themselves, all benefits are shared, and any risks are more than offset by what is gained.

● Zurich Insurance Canada used to demand two or three quotes for home or motor repair claims. While the paper floated to and fro – from the company to the customers, on to the contractors, back to the assessor and, finally, again to the customer – valuable time was lost. The more each detail was conscientiously itemized, the larger the files became, with correspondingly longer delays for customers. Today, only one contractor is chosen, and it is given the green light to proceed with repairs on the same day. Other sorts of redundancies between The Maryland and its agents have been removed. As previously, these independent agents would call in for information about shared clients and then phone customers back. Now, service centres handle the entire procedure and customers can call in directly to get information, requests and claims handled.

Not surprisingly, adding value is an effort shared by customers and corporations today. What is the point of a partnering relationship unless this kind of mutual benefit can take place? Having an activity-based outlook is the way of the 1990s. The difference now is that managers ask: where can value be added to the customer's activity cycle instead of to their own? What problems need to be solved for customers, what opportunities should they explore together? After considering these questions, the management determines what has to be done or undone. They also acknowledge that they must focus on the immaterial aspects of their business to achieve applied performance. In this way, they can strive to avoid potential vacuums in the customer's flow of activities and thus firmly entrench long-term customer relationships.

5 Building service-intensive networks

To see a World in a Grain of Sand
And a Heaven in a Wild Flower,
Hold Infinity in the palm of your hand
And Eternity in an hour.

William Blake, Auguries of Innocence, c. 1802

With no top or bottom, the brain is a skein of interconnected parts, each one linked to hundreds of thousands of others. Consisting of tens of billions of individual cells, its structure is, to say the least, complex. One small part of the brain the size of a walnut contains over ten miles of human wire too thin to see under an ordinary microscope. Each link in the chain is only a mere fraction of an inch long, intertwined in such a way that it is difficult to tell them apart.[1]

What is so marvellous about the brain is not the structure itself so much as the way in which the structure works. What makes it exceptional is the uncanny stringing together of the bits, which endows it with an enormous capacity to interact with the world around it. Without having to concentrate on anything in particular, it can pick up an inordinate amount of specific stimuli. So interlinked is it, that one job can be done well despite distractions.

The brain is the archetype of network structures that scientists have observed elsewhere in living systems. Independent of any central command, it can react immediately when the unexpected happens. In most sections of the brain, if a part is damaged other bits quickly take its place. Its cells reorganize themselves instantaneously when confronted by a disturbance or some unusual task. Brains are able to adapt to changing circumstances for many reasons. The first is due to the the redundancy built in, which is what enables a damaged part to be renewed. Second, every region distributes what it knows to every other and this keeps the system functioning always. Third, activating one part of the brain such as memory or movement doesn't shut off the other parts, so while each region specializes in something independently, the brain is working as a whole in a generalized manner.[2]

It was the computer wizards who first applied these ingenious principles to the commercial world. Previously, computers had had one central processing unit from which all control emanated. That unit was the locus for any action; if it malfunctioned, the whole system shut down. But, in the modern neural networks that have been modelled after the brain, each part is able to act autonomously, learning as it goes along, through trial and error. Its intelligence is gained incrementally so that, instead of sticking to a fixed and programmed set of responses, it updates continuously its know-how bank and adapts its reactions accordingly. Like the brain, its structure is a mixture of hierarchy and network, with a central panel to coordinate the various interdependent pieces.[3]

Could the brain, nature's own, also be a template for the modern organization? Such an idea was nearly impossible to imagine a decade ago. But, today it seems clear to most contemporary managers that building organizations which are more relevant to prevailing values and conditions must be of the highest priority. How this goal can be achieved is not altogether clear, except that any new architecture should more closely resemble living organisms than industrial bastions, be more akin to Russian dolls than tin soldiers.

The brain does have many of the necessary characteristics. It is, after all, malleable, quick and adaptive. It is also stable without being static, and it can absorb new experiences at once – all these traits are more in keeping with service environments than with assembly lines. The brain is also a living example of the fact that what matters is not just substance but how things are put together. Because they produce the knowledge to solve problems, the interconnections and interactions of the brain are as important, if not more so, than the specialized neurons. When some 'intelligent' action is needed, be it simple or complex, the real value comes from having the flexibility to assemble the correct pieces at the correct time and place.

At last, modern managers are changing structures, unshackling strict hierarchies to suit the service ethos better, placing customers at the top of their corporate structures and agendas. In the interest of learning and harnessing the immaterial – which generates the value on which their organizations now depend – they allow and even encourage experimentation. As they leap forward, managers are freeing themselves from unwavering rules, rigid reporting lines and central command posts, replacing these impediments with fluid channels of communication that can span the globe. They are also mobilizing individuals and teams, empowering them to make decisions about customers. In this way, specialized expertise and skills are being transformed into more general value-adding business solutions.

Seeing the whole, yet understanding the processes by which the parts are linked together, is what makes high value corporations special. Within them, boundaries have faded. No longer do they separate one function from another, one firm from another, one country's operations from those of others, and keep competitors outside their own clearly demarcated area. Now, they foster interdependence between members in the network and, through a new culture and creed, make organizations permeable while, at the same time, knitting people, functions and firms more closely together.

Networks, or taking a cue from nature

An organization's structure is the manifestation of prevailing managerial priorities and sentiments. And the classic hierarchical pyramid that neatly laid out three strata – top, middle, and bottom – was deeply ingrained in mechanical thinking and practice.[4] Like an electrical circuit, it operated in serial format; if one part blew, so did everything else. If its top were cut off, everything else ceased to function.

By contrast, the network model works in parallel: everyone knows what everyone else is doing at any moment. By virtue of its interconnections, the network is able to sense and react to changes in conditions. Because it is a dynamic living system, it can transform itself endlessly. It is an antidote to alienation that is more relevant for partnering and activity-based notions than was the bureaucracy. As Marilyn Ferguson puts it, the network is the institution of our times. The futurologist who looks at how to develop human potential in the years ahead, expands on this in her book, *The Aquarian Conspiracy*:

> This organic mode of social organization is more biologically adaptive, more efficient, and more 'conscious' than the hierarchical structures of modern civilization. The network is plastic, flexible. In effect, each member is the center of the network. Networks are cooperative, not competitive. They are true grass roots: self generating, self organizing, sometimes even self destructing. They represent a process, a journey, not a frozen structure.[5]

Although the hierarchy has faltered in favour of the systemic network model, this doesn't mean that its good points can't be preserved. Indeed, in creating flatter, more agile, less cumbersome structures, the need for coordination of autonomous pieces should never be underestimated. But most real systems – from the body or oceans to the solar systems – are a mixture of hierarchies and networks: the pieces can act independently, but some unifying mechanism must be in place to avoid anarchy. The brain has elements of both: autonomous pieces, self-organization and self-renewal, as well as a hierarchical organization meant for cohesion, though in truth no master control system has yet been discovered. Why can't organizations be this way too?[6]

Among nations, it is the Japanese who seem to have been most successful at marrying tight and rigorous structures with lighter, more collegial, entrepreneurial frameworks.[7] Western managers are now also having to deal with the obvious and sometimes not-so-obvious contradictions associated with this. They have no option. For current structures cannot cope with new customer relationships. Indeed, observers exploring this question are unanimous that most companies today have structures which lag behind their thinking. [8]

The question still remains: can we realistically use the brain as a metaphor for the contemporary firm? Gareth Morgan, Canadian organization academic, looks at this in his analysis of current organizational dynamics. According to him, the brain stands supreme as *the* metaphor for modern firms. Mechanistic models were fine, he says, when fixed tasks had to be performed in stable circumstances. These conditions don't apply anymore. He makes this point in *Images of Organization*:

> Many managers and organization theorists have readily grasped the point. But for the most part they have limited their attention to the idea that organizations need a brain or brainlike function – e.g. in the form of corporate planning teams, think tanks, or centralized research and decision-making units – that will be able to think for the rest of the organization . . . it is far less common to think about organizations as if they were brains.[9]

It's easy to see the connection between brains, networks and services. When dealing with interactions between people, results are often unexpected. Because of this unpredictability, modern organizations need a structure capable of constant learning, adjustment and re-adjustment. If they are to provide solutions over extended time frames, they must consistently be responsive and adaptive. While services are being performed, expertise is being acquired organically. Individual parts of the system learn while doing, but then the know-how they have attained must somehow be distributed to equip the whole better. Some degree of redundancy enhances the likelihood of a seamless flow of service because, if things do go awry, the system is able to self-renew: something or someone can and will take over. Dealing successfully with the customer face to face means having frontliners who are both willing and able to act and react. But, since results cannot rest realistically with one person or unit, each interaction is backed up by the input and the active participation of the entire service delivery process. In sum, highly interdependent and interconnected, the network can achieve as a whole much more than the sum of its parts.

The syntax of service network structures

How new service structures are arranged helps present-day managers deal with some of the paradoxes involved in combining the best of both worlds. They need the specialization in technical skills provided by individuals and units, and generalization in the way customer problems are tackled and solved. A happy balance has to be found between decentralization – so that people at critical customer interface positions have the autonomy to respond as they see fit – and the centralization of activities needed to synthesize know-how and effort. While the structure is set up to handle the unforeseen, it must also be organized so that checks and balances prevent undue breakdown. Free from the confines of bureaucracy, people must be self-directing, able to act spontaneously to customer requests both internally and externally. And a way must be found to engender individual judgement yet somehow institutionalize what the organization as a whole has learned.

In service network structures, upward mobility achieved by the few who are responsible for the bottom line results is no longer the driving force. Command doesn't come from the top, leaving those in the middle to control those down below. As Mary Anne Devanna and Noel Tichy, experts in the characteristics of new organization structures explain, the network has no top, middle or bottom. Control is primarily self-control and anything else is not only undesirable, but extremely expensive. These authors expand on this idea in their article, 'Creating the Competitive Organization of the 21st Century: The boundaryless corporation':

> There's less constraint; the emphasis is on learning with as few rules as possible. Errors are embraced. People admit mistakes, examine causes, and learn from them. There is an emphasis on risk taking and innovation; responsibility is realistically accepted and shared. Goals are set and constantly revised. Decision-making processes value intuition and creativity; there is less emphasis on purely analytical approaches. People perceive power as a nonzero sum game; there is expansion in sharing. Uncertainty is confronted, not denied. Interpersonal relationships are open and there are high levels of trust.[10]

Networks dispense with the notion that stability is the only desirable state for a business. Previously, we believed that if tasks were done correctly and people behaved rationally, a certain output would ensue. What is more realistic today is to say that the correct outcome is the one that is appropriate and that this is what should dictate behaviour. Richard Pascale, a professor in this field working in California, suggests that it's far better to arrange structures today so that they are resilient rather than stable. In his book, *Managing on the Edge*, he talks about the need for stability being a signal of the 'failsafe' industrial mentality in which things work like clockwork. A 'safe-to-fail' structure, on the other hand, is one where managers expect and accept unpredictability, and can cope with it because the structure is built to be resilient.[11]

Figure 5.1 summarizes some of the differences between old industrial and modern service structures. The vertical 'stovepipe' setups which reflected mechanistic and formal controls with fixed and permanent arrangements are contrasted to networks, more concerned with the binding and bonding of relationships where capabilities flow across functions, dependent on the freedom of people rather than the power of the organization. In these service structures, whosoever can participate competently in the design, delivery and support of solutions is accountable either in an individual capacity or as part of a team or project. More often than not, neither time nor geography are fixed, nor are links set in concrete, made permanent. People are part of

Industrial structures	Service network structures
Competitive entities	Collaborative entities
Hierarchy	Hierarchy and network
Vertical functions	Horizontal relationships and flows
Lines control, fixed	Lines coordinate, flexible
Centralized or decentralized	Centralized and decentralized
Formal matrices	Flexible and floating matrices
Strict organization	Self organization
Specialization or generalization	Specialization and generalization
Accountability function	Accountability individual/team/projects
Permanent units, fixed	Temporary links, not fixed
Time fixed	Time not fixed
Geography fixed	Geography free
Organization power	Freedom people

Figure 5.1 Service network structuring

flexible matrices which 'float', and they are accessible to other members of the network engaged in the service delivery process.

Networks seem to be more informal than hierarchies. So much the better. Christian Grunroos, a Finnish marketing professor, is one of several writers to point out the disadvantages and risks associated with bureaucracies trying to deliver services effectively. Specializing in analysing what makes service operations work well – particularly in Scandinavia – he says that the more complicated and formal the structure, the greater the problems in giving customers high-quality. In his book, *Service Management and Marketing*, he elaborates further:

> Good service means, among other things, easy access to service and quick and flexible decision making. If the organizational structure does not allow employees to perform in this way, the norms and values characterizing a service culture cannot be developed. Good intentions, even when they are based on a strategy, just cannot be implemented. This makes people frustrated and may have a countereffect. Employees easily feel that management's demands are impossible, and the effects, as far as services are concerned, will be negative.[12]

The ability to succeed in the world of immaterials is based on the premise that people, information, and technology can be brought together to do whatever is necessary rather than what the book of rules or job description decrees. People keep an eye on what they can do, as well as what is useful for others, to enhance either their capability or that of the whole system. And previous methods and decisions can be reversed when it is in the interest of better customer responsiveness.

While it is a service ethos which gives the high value firm its focus, its ability to perform comes from the syntax of the network and how it functions as a whole. As one executive from Digital says, the concept of the network not only holds the various facets of a company together better, it also becomes its key selling tool – part of its differentiating apparatus. In his words:

> We not only sell networks but we also think and behave like networks. We tell our customers, we can serve you better because we are a network. We can respond faster and react more flexibly to your specific needs because of the way we organize ourselves.

Putting the power where it matters

As for power, in industrial firms, it stemmed from the amount of resources owned and managed. This power was guarded, limited to 'high' places in large amounts, by and for a chosen few. Wherever this power was located, it certainly wasn't with customers. On the contrary, the higher that employees were on the organizational chart, the further away and more distant they inevitably were from the client. Status distinctions between top and bottom, together with steep layering and ladders, hindered any serious idea of a high-level person being close to customers, and being revered within the firm simultaneously.

Power is not crammed into administrative rungs in the modern enterprise. The ability to administrate doesn't determine the fate of a career. Those who know how to achieve success in the customer's terms and in their space hold the key. If it is this kind of expertise that counts and will determine the competitiveness of a corporation, then no single person or group can control a firm today in the conventional sense of the word. Robert Reich expands this theme in his book, *Work of Nations*:

> The formal organization chart has little relevance to the true sources of power in the high-value enterprise. Power depends not on formal authority or rank (as it did in the high-volume enterprise) but on the capacity to add value to enterprise webs. . . . The most skilled and talented problem-solvers and identifiers, on which so much depends . . . will have considerable discretion over what they do and how they do it. Routine functions are, increasingly, contracted out. Thus power is diffused.[13]

Frontliners were at the bottom of the pile in old structures, far from the power and the glory. They had to play by the book of rules – their guide in any customer interface situation – particularly if it involved an unusual request. A lack of power went hand in hand with a lack of information. How could they be responsive, therefore, to customers? On top of everything else, frontline jobs, with the exception of some high-commission sales positions, were also the worst paid. And, those jobs that dealt with customers were of lowly status and poor potential. In almost every kind of industry – both product and service, the consequences for firms were devastating. Karl Albrecht takes up this theme aggressively in his work on service cultures, *Service Within*, where he says:

> It's a curious fact that in most businesses the lowest quality people in the workforce are the ones placed in contact with the all important customer interface ... At the same time those not involved in the interface scatter their energies and have their behaviour driven by all manner of internally generated demands on their time. It's almost as if the quality of the customer interface and the degree of support for that interface are left to chance. And yet everything we know about competitiveness in the service market tells us it should be the other way around.[14]

Putting power at the point of customer contact is one way to instill an outward-looking frame of mind into a firm's culture.[15] As for middle management – sandwiched between the top which made the decisions and the frontliners who dealt with the client – they must now be supporting and facilitating to those around them. Staff positions, general managers and strategists, who once did the thinking and made the decisions carried out by others, are now an integral part of the network drawn into the service delivery process where and whenever their expertise is needed.

Power is expanded on the front line by placing more people there with more clout, but perhaps with fewer customers to handle, so these customers can be given more attention over longer periods of time. High value corporations go even further, making radical alterations to the frontline position: redefining it, making it fit with customer philosophies and structuring the network so that value is channelled through these critical employee points to end users. The following examples illustrate the point further:

- An average of 750,000 enquiries a year were never answered because employees at British Telecom were loaded with administration. Now there are nearly twice as many people in customer-facing positions than a decade ago. Frontliner jobs have been enhanced, giving employees new, more customer dependent responsibilities. The highest priority is given to spending time with customers either face to face or through a telephone account system. Employees who were previously in back office and staff positions – such as billing, installation and engineering – are now able to respond to customers and handle queries directly.

- The impetus for IBM's restructuring was to move the monolithic giant closer to customers. Stripping away layers and decentralizing power so that more people could be at the front line began in earnest during the late 1980s. By the early 1990s, the heavily centralized product-based structure had been unhinged. Tens of thousands of jobs exclusively dedicated to dealing with the company's problems were eliminated, converting the classic pyramid into a hub-and-spoke network squarely focused on the customer's activity cycle.
- ICI has reduced the number of customers using refinishing paints that the company's frontline employees handle, so that they can devote more time and provide better business solutions to these auto body shops. Some executives now have only one-eighth as many customers as they used to have, yet they achieve the same if not more revenues. Instead of diffusing their efforts, they grow existing business. Instead of chasing new customers – which invariably ended in price competition, they concentrate on sustaining existing relationships.
- DuPont has taken office workers, such as secretaries who were previously doing administrative work, and turned them into hotline-telephone service bureaus for end users to handle questions and problems about carpet maintenance. Their knowledge of the business and the customers, plus intensive training, enables these employees to deal with incoming queries and to know when to pass them on to technical staff.
- There are two reasons why Zurich Insurance Canada uses legally qualified brokers to settle claims on homeowner policies. First, customers are more accustomed to dealing with a particular broker and, second, it saves time. Now that car repair shops and home contractors make repairs on cars or homes immediately, Zurich's clients no longer have to wait 7-14 days to reinstate their activities. Employees who were previously back office claims people now manage this process on the front line, in a highly visible way.
- Digital in Ireland is transforming parts of its manufacturing plants into 'reference sites' for customers. What was previously just a factory, seldom exposed to customers and isolated from real-world applications, is now abuzz with customers who are invited to observe the company's wares in action. Manufacturing experts are now part of the customer interfacing web, not only directly exposed to customers but also participating actively in the design and execution of their offerings.
- The whole idea behind Ciba-Geigy's organizational change was to eliminate the endless layers at the head office, which had been hampering market responsiveness because the people there made all the decisions. Until recently, these central functions – as the firm called them – comprised a fifth of all employees worldwide. Now, only one in 20 work there: the rest are out in the field with units directly interfacing with customers or supporting frontline activities with their know-how in the various countries.

● There's no room in Citibank's world for junior level relationships with corporate customers, especially the multinational accounts. The banking clients, in fact, resent having to 'train' people to become senior bankers. Dealing in relationships and trust, they want people on the front line who may not necessarily always have the right answer, but they know how to make the bank work for them because they have clout, know-how and experience to take decisions without having to check with the boss.

Structuring to de-structure around customers

Boxes on charts put boundaries around people, functions and firms. They also created a state of mind about running a business. Who should do what? Who reported to whom? Who was important? Who wasn't? When, in the early 1980s, SAS's Jan Carlzon made the inverted pyramid popular, it gradually became a symbol for structures more in tune to customers. It gave prominence to the frontliners who actually faced them and made some important service principles clear in a very graphic way. This upside-down approach had a considerable effect on managers because it gave them a new mental model for viewing relationships with the market. For some, it reinforced what they already knew, but to the majority – who were still living in their rather stilted, well-ordered, inwardly focused world, it gave a powerful nudge.

But what was to take place was a much more complex process. Instead of just turning pyramids upside down to make them flatter and reshuffling existing structures, by the late 1980s and early 1990s high-value firms were 'de-structuring'. Management literally began to peel away at the functional and corporate barriers which had beset them, clearing the blockages and so allowing competencies to flow more smoothly among themselves, their customers and other businesses.

One of the most daunting challenges to be faced was how to make the transition from functions to multi-functional processes. Functional addiction – which had led to patchwork specialization within firms – had been perpetuated for so long beginning with Adam Smith. By contrast the Japanese had always somehow thought more holistically, and it was partly this difference, according to some experts, that has made them compete so successfully on a global basis.[16]

A product of industrial minds, functionalism reinforced the insularity which reigned during the 1960s, 1970s and 1980s. It began at the research or design stage within corporations and conscientiously worked its way through the entire system. Could this functional approach have been at the root of the commercial and technological decline of some of the leading western economies? ask Richard Florida and Martin Kenney, two American writers. They maintain in *The Breakthrough Illusion* that this is more than a distinct possibility. The hoarding of information by functions, the maze of bureaucracy and individual turf protection stalled decision-making and got in the way of good customer strategy, leading to huge blows from competition and the environment.[17]

In industrial firms, rules were allowed to take precedence over individual reasoning; the sanctity of internal procedures outweighed individual talent and creativity. Firms left customer relations helplessly and haphazardly in the hands of low-level employees designated, often despite themselves, to that not-too-popular task. The fixation on pleasing the boss and head office reinforced insular behaviour. Since much of the dialogue, language, interest and indeed rewards revolved around a firm's internal workings, employees effectively looked inward and upward rather than outward and across. Internal politics drove the momentum, sapping managerial time and energy dry. Functional disputes raged. As just one example, an IBM executive comments:

> Before, our whole system was built on contention between the functions: if you wanted anything as a product function or local branch, you had to argue your way there. Finance looked at numbers and wanted volume sales, marketing was trying to hold customers and make them happy. Marketing liked lead times that production couldn't deliver. It was a struggle for each function to optimize their own area and now we see it was sometimes at the expense of overall business. Today we say to the functions: compete with the outside world, not with each other.

High-value enterprises think in terms of activities, not functions. The corporation is seen as a series of these activities, instead of a series of layers. Structures are designed based on the processes needed to create value for customers over the period of their experience. Managers seek the connections within and without their corporations that ultimately lead to the design, delivery and support of mass custom-alized solutions. Preoccupation with 'upstream' and 'downstream' switches into concern for what goes on 'instream' – within the interfunctional and intercompany spaces which form the service delivery processes.

This dispenses with the sequential passing of the baton – and 'the buck' – to the next function. Instead of people cramped inside vertical silos, dealing in categories of 'things', those with relevant skills come together from various parts of the network and, through their webs of professional and social relationships, disseminate know-how and services about things. It is the constant and simultaneous interplay between members of the network – those mutually involved in solution processes from start to finish – that counts. These multi-disciplinary groupings of people become 'partners' devoted to projects and processes. In their synergy and synchrony lies the key to a firm's success or failure, setting new criteria for organizational design:

- IBM has reconfigured its massive company so that now about 15 process streams make up the whole business. The new approach clearly articulates the entire path of the three major activities which jointly constitute the company's performing systems for clients: defining the solution, building the solution and delivering the solution. Job descriptions no longer dictate who people are, to whom they report, and what they have to do. What drives people is the implementation of a common customer goal and set of objectives.
- The SKF organization no longer operates on an exclusively functional basis as it did formerly. The business is now built around the activities of the 'before' and 'after' market, which more accurately reflects the way customers buy, use and replace their bearings. Bearing Industries caters to customers who buy the components for their machines and cars, while Bearing Services provides trouble-free operations to end users of the vehicles and machinery.
- Three watertight functions – sales, services and spare parts – at Volvo Truck dealers once served customers. Each focused on its own particular task and they seldom interacted. Restructured around processes, the company is now geared to cost-per-mile solutions. Multi-functional teams follow the flow of customer activities in the entire fleet management cycle, from planning a new purchase to the leasing contract through to its use, maintenance and repurchase. Within Volvo Trucks itself, the classic functional structure has also changed to mirror this activity-based customer approach.
- To have customer linkage throughout the organization, Matsushita has a 'customer satisfaction' division which, according to the company's chart, belongs everywhere. It permeates the entire company, linking together all the customer value-adding processes. The object is that every operation in the design, delivery and support of its human electronic solutions should be connected to each other, as well as to the dealerships and end users.
- At Zurich Insurance Australia, Universal Underwriters and The Maryland, certain divisions – sales, underwriting, claims and risk engineering – have been joined. Specific technical expertise, combined with an in-depth understanding of each customer's operations, straddles them all. The sales role is seen as the beginning of a process rather than as a separate function, and the sales contact is the means to a solution rather than an end in itself. Formerly, sales, claims, underwriters and risk engineers had distinctly different roles and objectives – which hampered relationships both internally and with customers, whereas today they align themselves to customer activities. Describing this change, an executive from The Maryland says:

We are used to seeing our companies as vertical, but our customers like to look at us as horizontal. They want to get all their queries and requests attended to together. They couldn't care less how we are structured or why. Now we've had to learn to organize in a way that makes sense to them.

Making the walls between company and customer into membranes

Why was it that managers thought of themselves as extensions of their organizational charts? That the physical and commercial limitations of the firm was determined by where the chart ended? The energy and influence of an employee went only as far as the boxes on the chart allowed. The lines connecting one box to another dictated the relationships between people and, they didn't dare to trespass over a set boundary.

By the 1990s managers running high value corporations had a new managerial dream.[18] Could they make the mechanistic boundaries that had been interfering with their firm's ability to serve customers dissappear? Of course, the 'boundary-less' company, as it was called by some people, still has functions. But the vertical cuts which had separated them no longer exist or, if they do, don't get in the way of transferring expertise, particularly when destined for customers. The walls between people or groups of people engaged in particular activities become permeable. Horizontal relationships flow between them, bridging boundaries, because there is no other way they can achieve their common goals. And, the clear demarcations which existed between producer and consumer are vanquished. Borders stretch and overlap, they become elastic. They are thin enough to penetrate, porous enough to get through, and transparent enough to engender the kind of sharing and trust that partnering demands. Unfamiliar terrain becomes a mutual working space, schedules become interactions and, last but not least, independent consumers and producers of products and services become interdependent. During the first planning stages for a new Toyota factory in the UK, Hoechst became involved in the computer-aided design of the polymer material and moulding process needed by the Japanese firm to make central consoles for its autos. At the outset, it, together with the injection moulding subcontractors and the automobile manufacturer, began working together in teams, sharing information and making prototypes at the pre-purchase phase of the activity cycle. This joint endeavour was undertaken by Hoechst to ensure that ultimately their polymer would perform when it was used, first by the subcontractor and then by Toyota manufacturers and finally by end users. This sort of interdependence is achieved in several ways:

- *By physically co-locating people inside the customer's space and vice versa.* The self-help desks that Digital have put into their customers' offices and factories to keep the business system going is one example. Another is InterForward which, in its Swedish operations, has located its own staff inside IBM's printer plant, from where they handle all material flow. This group appears on local IBM organization documentation.
- *By creating common teams composed of people that come from both the company and the customer.* Digital's self-help desks are staffed by

individuals from the client corporations as well as from Digital. These teams work jointly to solve daily business system problems as they arise, for the technical problems are not the major culprits. Mandelli sends its R&D experts to automotive customers, thereby creating joint project teams that work together from the inception of the first idea for a new model through to setting up the production plant. This saves both time and money, with good ideas being harnessed early on.

● *By forming new project entities that combine the resources of the 'partners'.* In this way, customers and producer are able to achieve a feat which almost certainly neither could do alone. The large air traffic control facility at Heathrow Airport was either idle at non-peak times or overloaded at rush hour. So British Airways and British Telecom joined forces and together formed a team which developed a traffic control system able to operate at optimum capacity at all times.

Needless to say, it is a complex process for firms to extend boundaries further down the distribution chain than would have been done some years earlier. The delineation of what belongs where and to whom, what is within and without, becomes fuzzy as structures between company and customer overlap and begin to converge. An interface zone between firms develops, taking on its own shape and culture. New questions have to be answered like: Who owns what when innovations are jointly discovered? What part of that discovery is kept exclusive for that customer? Who pays for what?

Some of these questions continue to hang in the air. The most awesome barrier seems to be the human factor. As managers move boldly to dismantle physical barriers between themselves and their customers, they have to get people to open up, share information and trust each other. While shared interests and common goals may be the fuel that drives the engine, trust is the oil that keeps the parts moving without friction.[19] The only way to achieve this trust is by visibly demonstrating it say managers. To make this point:

● Zurich Insurance Canada no longer checks and double checks every single detail of a claim or repair quote before work proceeds for a customer. In any event it says contractors can never know in advance exactly what to expect behind damaged walls and, in the past, they typically would just make a guess, often cutting their quote in the hope of getting the work. Now, the insurer gives these contractors leeway and freedom to do the job thoroughly and, if they need funds up front, they get them.

● There is no substitute, says DuPont, for face-to-face contact and discourse with customers to get the level of trust necessary for new relationships. Through dialogue, people on both sides shed their defences. For not only must customers be convinced that a genuine partnership exists, so must the firm's employees. A remark by one executive from the carpet fibre division of DuPont provides an interesting insight:

We are all (carpet mills, manufacturers and retailers) interested in our mutual success so we all have to do whatever is necessary to make this possible. But it's tough. We deliberately go to a customer, talk to the management and give away information we would previously have regarded as confidential. Our sales people are amazed, as are our customers. But, by the end of the discussion they can see we are serious. And it's the only way to get real trust going.

Specializing in separating and integrating services

In their efforts to build networks, managers must make decisions about where to put the new services. Here too lies a paradoxical situation. Can these intangibles be separated out while at the same time be fully integrated into the delivery process? Where is it prudent to place services? Should they be grafted onto existing activities? Or made into distinct units? Should they be part of the overall revenue generating power of the network, and when should they stand alone?

A comparison between industrial and present-day approaches helps put these questions into perspective:

Then: the pre-purchase services were typically bundled onto the sales function taken into the promotional and selling budget. It was easy for one person to accomplish this task, for offerings were less complex.

Now: given their level of sophistication, several experts from within the network need to be pulled into the customer satisfying process. These individuals or groups, each with a particular brand of expertise, often need their own identity and credibility.

Then: what customers expected from an enterprise was its core product or service.

Now: they expect firms to find the best solution possible, which may include outside services or products. Cardinal is that the advice given is objective, which often makes it more appropriate for services to be separated from routine transactions.

Then: customers took value-added services, if offered, pretty much for granted and, if they paid for them, it was through a premium on the goods.

Now: these intangible activities hold so much of the revenue potential that separating them out helps establish their value both inside the company and with customers.

Then: services were considered marginal tasks and so received little corporate attention.

Now: with services so substantive in customer relationships, managers must give them status and credibility once accorded to the transformation of 'things'. This is often easier when services are distinctive organizationally, especially if they are new to the market or firm.

Then: value-added services had less commercial value than the core goods within firms. They featured as neither an investment nor a source of revenue.

Now: since they are the value creators, they must be treated like any other investment. If services are separate, it is often easier to substantiate their true profit potential and allocate them the R&D funds needed to become and stay competitive.

A number of firms are separating their value adding services out:

- Both IBM and Digital have put their consulting, maintenance and facilities management into separate divisions. Before, they typically provided everything themselves, and what they didn't make or do, they just didn't sell. Now, if a product or service is needed by a customer it is provided by one of their distinctive service units. If for some reason they don't produce a desired product or service, employees go wherever their search may take them.

- Until recently, American Express only offered consulting services to merchants on their own electronic payment and data transmitting systems, including this activity as part of sales and promotion. A special consulting unit now provides expertise to retailers on a wide range of supplier options. Its electronic showroom, situated in Frankfurt, enables customers from retailers, restaurants, and hotels to see a demonstration of terminals in action from all leading manufacturers.

- Nokia-Maillefer, as a traditional manufacturer, never really took services very seriously until it moved from selling machines to productive capacity. Separate divisions were then created for its consulting, project management and maintenance services. Nokia-Maillefer had twin sights in view: to gain credibility among highly price-sensitive customers unaccustomed to services and, equally, to give more clout to services internally so that the right people would be enticed into the unit.

- Companies in the consumer trade have had the same experience. A whole range of value-added services is offered by Nestlé to restaurants, hotels and hospitals in order to improve the utility of food and drink products. Nestlé deliberately set up a specialized food services division to handle this activity so that these services would not be perceived as just another promotional device.

- The trend towards separating out services can be detected in classic professional services enterprises as well. There was a time when Price Waterhouse, the international accounting firm, put all its services into one pot. In fact, some of the more lucrative services requiring deep levels of specialized know-how were simply given away as part of a routine audit call. Today, corporate finance and tax consulting are self-standing revenue generating units as are other specialized services, each with its own skills and pricing mechanism.

● Hendrix Voeders has created an independent consultancy function, separate from the salesforce. These nearly 150 professionals have no direct sales tasks. Without their objectivity, the entire concept would collapse, for they are the source of the data which must be collected – both positive and negative – in order to make the expert system pertinent. It is from this data that decisions are made to achieve the desired results.

Giving the value-added services their own identity in the network has its advantages and disadvantages. It provides the focus they need to be state of the art in their field, but can diffuse efforts and dissipate energy. How well they fit into the overall structure determines the cohesion of the offering and it is this which management must strive to achieve without interfering with their stature, objectivity or quality.[20] To ensure integration, some counter-balancing mechanism must be put in place otherwise the different parts of the solution can become disjointed and some serious 'we/they' divisions within the company can form.

Corporations cope with this in several ways, by either getting tighter integration at the strategy making level or on the front line. Here are examples of each approach:

● After a while, the two divisions at SKF – Bearing Industries and Bearing Services – began to drift apart, each dedicated to its own tasks. Certain duplications in procedures and functions – like warehousing – increased overall costs because the two cultures worked side by side without fully integrating. To counter this, some head office activities have been re-combined so that resource planning coincides better and strategies can be jointly formulated.

● AT&T's General Business Systems division, which deals with the giant's small and medium-sized business customers, had always kept traditional installation, maintenance and repairs separate from sales. Management maintained that the skills and culture of the people were different enough to warrant it. The problem, however, was that with no integration of these activities, customers were left dangling. Now, this division's services are attached to retail units handling clusters of customers which results in a better coordinated process.

Mirroring customer activities through structuring

The major features of the network structures being developed by high value corporations mirror the customer's activity cycle (as shown in Figure 5.2).

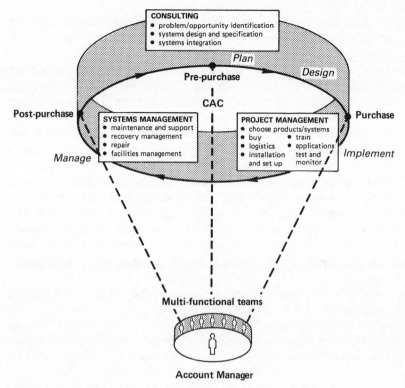

CONSULTING
● problem/opportunity identification
● systems design and specification
● systems integration

Plan

Pre-purchase

Design

CAC

Post-purchase

Purchase

SYSTEMS MANAGEMENT
● maintenance and support
● recovery management
● repair
● facilities management

PROJECT MANAGEMENT
● choose products/systems
● buy   ● train
● logistics   ● applications
● installation   test and
  and set up   monitor

Manage

Implement

Multi-functional teams

Account Manager

Figure 5.2   Single customer account management structure: Digital

Instead of the one-dimensional buyer and seller contact, reminiscent of industrial days, connections are multi-faceted and they take place throughout the customer's experiences.

Figure 5.2 is one example to demonstrate the point.

New structures make fresh demands on the corporation. Only if the account management system pulls together the various pieces of the network is it a workable proposition. Account management has been used in the sales area for years, but it is being elevated to a much higher level these days. For mainly through this medium resources can be sourced, mobilized, coordinated and funnelled into the customer activity process.[21]

Most customers want 'one contact/one contract' type relationships from the firms they deal with today. This should not be confused with the 'one-stop' marketing concept, where everything was offered in one go. They want a single point of contact or reference, preferably only one person who is engaged with them over extended periods of time. Not primarily concerned with how their contact obtains the various bits and pieces that make up the solution, what they want is cost-effective results. Take bearings. Does any auto repair shop or factory manager really care where the bearings come from? Or are they more concerned about someone making sure that things are going according to schedule? Are policy holders particularly interested in knowing who supplies the various parts of their risk investment portfolio? Or are they more concerned that someone is there to help them when necessary?

Customers simply refuse to be shuttled around from one department or person to another anymore. The account management system provides the vehicle for coordination, and the account manager becomes customer integrator, champion and advocate. They may be on the end of a wire or telephone – as many are – at a retail branch, or living in the customer's space. They may only act in an account management capacity or be feeders to colleagues also doing that job. But, what they dare not be are glorified sales people or troubleshooters. For all intents and purposes, the account manager – or whatever other terminology a firm might use – 'owns' the corporation's relationship with its customers. This is the person who is ultimately accountable for the clients' long-term satisfaction and, thus, the company's profitability.

The account management system may operate on different levels depending on the size of the account. At British Telecom, a telephone account management system enables individual customers and members of small businesses to be in personal contact with the company at all times. Each account manager works with a cluster of a few hundred or thousand accounts to coordinate all enquiries, requests and needs. But, multi-level links are also established with key corporate customers at very senior levels. In addition to an account manager for a prime customer, every executive – including the chairman – has responsibility for an account portfolio at that company. These 'calling directors', as they are known, visit their counterparts in the customer's firm, regularly feeding the discussions, requests and suggestions back into the system.

Account management is also being used with dealerships today. Matsushita has such teams for geographically-defined areas, with large operations allocated an account manager of their own. These teams assist the dealers with all customer-related issues, including providing the value-added service of helping end users make human electronic solutions work. Similarly, Canon has set up a local account management system which supports dealers as they provide solutions to their 30,000 small and medium-sized customers. Together, they handle the value added services that go into making information and documentation systems. The following examples illustrate some of the critical facets of making account management work:

● *Account managers must have the power to make decisions about customers without having to go through red tape.* The Royal Bank of Canada has personal bankers who handle the entire spectrum of retail customer needs from start to finish. Decisions which used to take a week are now made on the spot. They skirt organizational bottlenecks and rally anyone they need with specialized skills – say offshore tax consulting – to serve their particular set of customers.

● *Resources within the network must be accessible to account managers.* Especially important is that they are able to source expertise when and where they need it. This means they must know where such expertise is located at any moment. When dealer customers require sophisticated technological advice, account managers can call in experts from Canon headquarters. What this means is that all parts of the network – including top management, other staff or centres of excellence – are effectively 'on call'. One DuPont executive explains the policy this way:

> We say to our account managers, you and your customers take priority. No matter what the internal matter happens to be that we're dealing with, we'll drop it if you need us to see a key customer. And we do. This is now our number one priority.

● *Account managers must have access to clients.* The Digital account team will typically interact with various sections of the company's key client corporations. In a bank, for example, this would include the chief executive, the chief information officer, business branch managers and IT operators. In other words, there is contact and discourse at both strategic and operational levels wherever the IT is being used. Without this entrée, open and regular, they could never fulfil their role.

Increasingly, firms are dedicating account executives to key customers on a permanent basis. They are supported by multi-functional teams and jointly

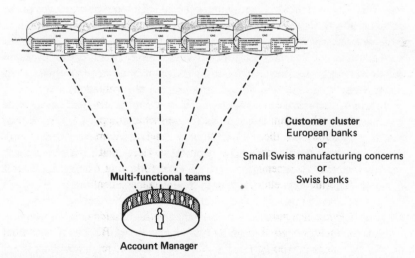

Figure 5.3 Multiple customer account management structure: Digital

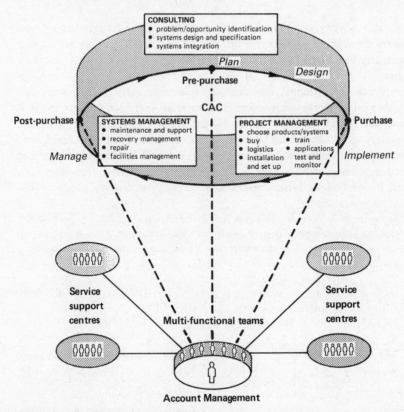

Figure 5.4   Remote service centres: Digital

they are responsible for delivering the value added at each of the stages of the customer's activity cycle. Account managers may have one client – if it is large or strategic enough – or several hundred. Let's go back to Digital. An account manager could conceivably have a cluster of European banks to handle, alternatively, several small Swiss manufacturing concerns, or all major Swiss banks (see Figure 5.3 for a graphic representation).

Invariably expertise must be brought in from service support centres wherever they may be. These centres (as shown in Figure 5.4), rather than having any direct reporting responsibility in the traditional sense of the word, are absorbed into the customer activity process when needed. The size of these service factories could range from one expert sitting at home to several hundred people strategically located. Individuals or groups from these centres support the account manager and multi-functional teams, who in contrast are often in daily contact with customers. Connecting either on a face-to-face basis or remotely by wire – or both – they may work directly with customers or join the multi-functional team for a period. They may enter the picture during either the pre-purchase, purchase or post-purchase phases of the customer's activity cycle or make a contribution at all points in the process. Some of these service support centres may be self-standing profit units, while others may be attached to another part of the network – such as a particular region.

Unlike tangible 'things', services can't be conveniently made in one place and shipped to market in another. The nature of services being what it is means that firms must often be locally present where the service is needed, frequently on a one-to-one basis. Critical mass determines the number of service support centres any single firm can afford. Sheer cost and scarcity of expertise today prohibits any firm – no matter what its size – from having a centre for every geographical area and profession, or every industry, segment or individual customer.

Managers will have to find a suitable number and mix of these service support centres, locating them within the network so that they can get to customers speedily and cost effectively. The ideal model for making these decisions will be the one which is most flexible, where services and skills are 'mixed and matched', depending on the circumstances, and formats may be changed as the need arises.

Internationalizing services extra-territorially

The emergence of the global customer poses another set of challenges for contemporary managers in their structuring. These customers – people or firms – buy cross-border and demand local service backup wherever they happen to be at a moment in time. If the customer is a company, it probably buys solutions from central points for its world operations. But services are expected to be consistent from one country to another, and the various pieces in the delivery process coordinated around the world.[22]

Firms which operated internationally organized in an infinite variety of ways, invariably on a domestic basis, usually as a confederation of sorts of independent subsidiaries. The country from which the request or sale emanated was responsible for customers – the same customers who today want worldwide solutions. The question in structuring globally then is: who is responsible for whom and what? Previously it was clear: Hoechst for example was selling to a subcontractor in the UK. Today the situation is more complicated. The customer is Toyota in Japan and with the subcontractor Hoechst jointly provide it with a solution – in this case the central console – which is destined in some way to improve the experience of drivers. And the Hoechst people involved in the pre-purchase phase of the solution are in Japan. Who should take responsibility for what, when and where? And how should this be managed?

Today the high value firms which are experimenting with these issues are working with some basic principles. They accept the logic that an account management is needed worldwide. Many agree that an account manager should be situated at the main locus of the customer, since it is from here that key directions and decisions emanate. The concept of extra-territorial is useful in this context, especially for key global accounts. Borrowed from diplomacy and applied typically to the status of embassies abroad, the reason for this analogy is quite simple. Just as the land upon which the American Embassy in Paris stands is American territory – despite being in France – so an extra-territorial account is one which belongs to the originating country although it happens to be placed in another region's geographic space.

What does belong mean? Responsibility? Revenues? Resources? Clearly the responsibility for ultimate satisfaction and profitability of the account globally must rest with the account manager. Following on logically from this is that the revenues accrued extra-territorially must go to the global account managing country. The resources that deliver the services, most managers say, should therefore be accountable to them, although for practical, legal and fiscal purposes these employees still rely on the local country for their salary and career development.

Take this as an example: Shell happens to be an IBM extra-territorial account – one of some 100 key worldwide clients. Because the petroleum company's headquarters are in London, the account executive for Shell is stationed there. Services for Shell in the various countries are handled by individuals and multi-functional teams who may be assigned to Shell exclusively, to all oil companies in that country or to all UK firms. It is their responsibility to design, deliver and support solutions in that extra-territorial space for the global client at each critical point of the activity cycle (an example is shown graphically in Figure 5.5).

The following guidelines apply to companies in the internationalization of their services extra-territorially:

● Account executives have accountability and power in the extra-territorial area where the value-adding process is taking place. They can request that something be done in this space and can expect results.
● If something does go wrong, it's up to the service delivering country to determine why and fix it.
● Contradictions will inevitably arise as local managers become increasingly independent, yet find chunks of their customer base and decision-making removed. These contradictions must be resolved in a worldwide context.
● Options should be kept open as to where to hold the account. At certain stages of the offering, the head office country of the client may be inappropriate because that's not where decisions are being made. In such cases the relevant country must then be able to handle the account extra-territorially, even if only temporarily.
● It's important that a sense of reciprocity prevails between countries. Sometimes a country may supply services, then on other occasions be the

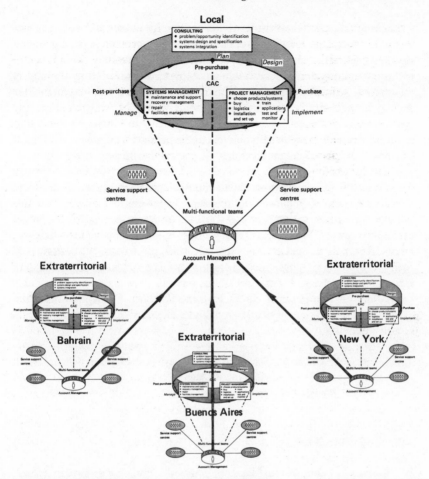

Figure 5.5   Internationalizing the service network: IBM

recipient. What each country gets and gives somehow balances out over a period of time, rather than on an account-for-account basis.
● Complete coordination is required between the countries on their human resources needs for local service delivery of these extra-territorial accounts. Countries understand and agree on each other's requirements at the beginning of each planning cycle.
● Data and systems are made transparent between countries. The only way the account executive can manage at a distance is to have this two-way information and communication flow.
● Local countries are given some form of credit to reflect their overall contribution in the extra-territorial area. This becomes part of a global evaluation system.

Looking to anchor their firms around reciprocity instead of a *quid pro quo* and to grow global service networks instead of domestic empires, contemporary managers don't all insist that a premium be paid from the receiving to the providing country for services rendered extra-territorially: costs – whatever they may – are covered by the recipient. Others believe a more competitive pricing mechanism from one country to another is the only way to realistically see where the revenues are actually coming from. One way to get round this, ensuring that the interests of global clients are always paramount, is to have one profit and loss account spanning all countries with profits per customer calculated globally.

How well a firm is equipped to handle this depends though on a lot more than its structure. A request from a partner anywhere in the world at Price Waterhouse carries the same weight as one from a colleague sitting in the office next door. Every country is dependent on the others, and the structure and workings of the network is such that serving international customers is seen as an overall corporate responsibility. The Japanese operations of Hoechst do not charge for the specialized services they supply the UK, which finally end up as a polymer contract for the British company, because their system is based on mutuality and global interdependence. As a manager from Hoechst explains:

> If Toyota in the UK gets a higher performing polymer through our contacts and design services in Japan, it will result in better sales in the home market as well. The stronger we can be globally, the better off everyone is in every country.

Learning not to do it all

When managers believed that the capability to do things was directly related to what the firm owned, they built empires based on hard assets. To control both upstream and down was to avoid the uncertainties that could upset a company's ability to consistently perform financially. With Alfred Chandler's idea of a 'visible hand', made popular in the early 1970s, came the tremendously powerful belief that, in order to succeed, firms had to accumulate and control as much as possible. The notion flowed into all types of mainstream business.[23]

Was this feeling of stability and control a mere edifice? As many people observe, firms which frequently practised vertical integration were often working not from strength, as they had then assumed, but from weakness. Much of the motivation behind backward and forward ownership came from having to do things themselves that could not safely or satisfactorily be left to anyone else. To be saddled with these problems hardly seemed to warrant the assets though. They never quite solved the problem. In fact in many ways, massive acquisitions left firms sluggish and rigid. Ironically, managers had made these moves to secure the viability of their corporations. But, so much attention went to managing the huge conglomerates, that too little went into building the vital value-adding service capabilities they needed to survive in the decades that followed.[24]

Already in the 1970s, beginning with the publication in 1973 of E.F.Schumacher's *Small is Beautiful: Economics as if People Mattered*, many people began to talk about and see the downside of owning too much. What Schumacher and others like him detected was the first signs of diminishing returns from being too big. The 'visible hand' theory was going flat. By the 1990s, great thinkers and writers were making the case that managers should let those firms that could do the best job do it without being compelled to own or financially control them. As IT gave firms greater access to each other, this prospect of driving down activities to smaller and more flexible firms, units, teams or individuals became more practical.[25]

A smaller fixed core – but with a large set of interconnections and ties – was entirely in keeping with the development of new thinking and partnering arrangements. Here are some of the underlying tenets for making this work practically:

- *Firms switch attention and resources from owning the assets, to owning the customer.* This doesn't mean simply delegating critical customer activities to outsiders. On the contrary. A new IT installation needs resources to tear down walls, put in new wiring, rebuild the structure and repaint it. Digital uses outside contractors for this task, but the company carefully preserves its contact with customers throughout the process. Sprinks serves as the centre of a complete insurance assistance network for French customers, from home security teams to doctors, from car repairs to tow trucks, from factory inspection to services for leasing temporary premises. Sprinks doesn't own any of these assets, but it coordinates all the activities and is paid by its customers directly.
- *Instead of owning the assets, firms concentrate on owning the concept that makes them special in the eyes of the customer.* SAS sold its stake in AMADEUS, the global reservation system that it, together with British Airways, Air France and Lufthansa, helped launch and finance in the early 1980s. Why? Because AMADEUS did not add to SAS's ability to differentiate itself as a provider of travel solutions for the business passenger. For the same reason, the company gave up its share in Intercontinental Hotels when, after the Gulf War and a market slump, it decided that satisfying customers did not necessarily entail owning the entire infrastructure.
- *Emphasis goes to owning capabilities for a desired customer outcome, instead of assets to control input and output.* InterForward has avoided buying companies merely to possess such hard assets as the lorries, warehouses, freighters and aircraft which anyone, the company says, can

own and manage well. InterForward's unique ability comes from matching the capacity of these various transporting assets to customer demand and combining these commodities with the several hundred other services its enterprises perform expertly to provide customer solutions. An executive put it this way:

> If we own anything, it has to be the things that help give customers what they can't get elsewhere, not the infrastructure. Our balance sheets are used to reflect commitment to what we can deliver better than anyone else, rather than to show the world what assets we have managed to accumulate.

With value enhancement for customers as *the* core business concern, building capabilities to do so, rather than the acquisition of hard assets becomes management's major preoccupation. For therein lies the firm's differential advantage. In theory, any part of the customer delivery process can be outsourced if it can be done more quickly, cheaply, or better by someone else. Provided this move doesn't interfere with the relationship between the company and its customers. And firms may not need to turn to outsiders for all their outsourcing. Many make contracts with their own internal units or staff sections, which have become independent businesses to provide services more entrepreneurially both inside the firm and to others in the marketplace.[26] Either way corporations need to choose partners well, favouring firms or individuals who uphold the same customer ideals, and from whom synergies can be extracted to augment the strength of the network as a whole.

Competing and collaborating simultaneously

Competitors aren't off limits for high-value enterprises. In fact, making them partners in the network structure is very much in vogue. With systems so interconnected, few firms can or indeed want to provide customers with all the modules of a solution. So they look for others with whom to share costs and collaborate in their efforts to give customers a complete offering. And with whom do they often find they have the most in common? Their competitors.[27]

But, the fact that firms in the same business increasingly collaborate doesn't mean that they no longer compete. They collaborate some of the time and on some activities, but the rest of the time they compete as vigorously as ever. As we can so often see today – take the computer industry as an example – firms like IBM and Digital may be rivals during the pre-purchase phase of the customer's experience, when the system is being designed, and then be partners afterwards, co-supplying hard and software. They may provide and install the machines and applications jointly, yet be intent on doing the maintenance and facilities management of the system themselves. Some firms are fiercely competing on one activity while they are simultaneously collaborating on another. Typically, Swissair and Singapore Airlines, which compete for many of the routes, nonetheless jointly share others – for example from Zurich to Singapore.

In many cases, firms may not have an option. With every new technology generation, the cost of the capital investment to compete doubles. Customers may insist on having more than one supplier working on their particular deal. And, given the complexity of systems today, some firms may simply be forced to work closely with competitors if their customers are truly to get a total solution. Although firms like Volvo will fight furiously for their share of market, few truck fleet owners will buy one brand only. But Volvo's fleet monitoring and mobile communication system – aimed at optimizing truck usage capacity – can only work if all vehicles in a fleet are equipped with the interconnecting apparatus. So Volvo collaborates with Mercedes, Ford, Fiat and others to make dashboards and circuitry compatible. Each car manufacturer has to give a little, as far as design is concerned, so that the fleet owner ultimately has a practical solution.

One way of looking at this phenomenon is to say that firms compete and collaborate at different levels, some more preferable than others. For instance:

- The most difficult level is a single transaction, where partnering and competing simultaneously is almost impossible: major conflicts are likely as is a weakening of the overall bond.
- For a single account, this kind of arrangement is sometimes necessary – even desirable, but it works best when one party is recognized as the prime supplier and this understanding is respected by both parties.
- It is possible and sometimes inevitable that competing and collaborating takes place inside a market, but it should be done fairly selectively.
- On an industry level, competing and collaborating is entirely possible today, especially if the industry *per se* gains, provided that some differentiation can be retained by firms through the value-adding services.

All of this is in constant flux. While some firms are learning to collaborate with competitors, others are having to do the reverse – compete with customers. Either way, some ground rules must be established for these new working relationships. Managers make these suggestions: each party must know the present and future potential of the other, so that feelings of dominance can be replaced by equity in respective gains. While each strives to be the prime supplier and number one choice with customers, everyone acknowledges that winning all of the time is no longer a feasible goal. People within firms have to understand that if they don't get every single deal, they haven't necessarily lost. There must be some balance with neither party totally vulnerable. Each side has a healthy respect for the other's relationships with its customers. Harmony may not always be possible; some conflict, managers say, is inevitable. Employees must learn to wear two hats if they are to compete and collaborate simultaneously. They must work within the contradictions that abound, seeing the whole picture rather than the bits, the longer rather than the short horizon. It can happen, contemporary practitioners say, with a strong sense of fair play.

6 *The soft side of know(ing) how*

As the workman, so is the work.

Thomas Fuller, *Gnomologia,* 1732

When Copernicus, in an attempt to find a new model of the universe during the 16th century, declared that the Greeks had been wrong about the position of the earth, he did more than make a scientific statement: he rocked the status quo. Our planet, the Italian astronomer revealed, was not the centre of the universe as it was once assumed. It was but one of many planets rotating around the sun, all of which depended on the others to survive.

This announcement shattered the philosophical ideas of the time. Until then, it had been generally accepted that the earth was *the* sovereign of the galaxy, and that those who ruled this all-important sphere – like the church and the nobility – had divine authority. Because of the way society was organized, these powers reigned supreme, governing the masses and leaving them no choice but to obey. The common people, dependent on the lords who owned them and whose land they worked, continued to do as they had for generations – what they were told.

Copernicus's discovery was part of the process that dislodged the way of life which had frustrated the attitudes, abilities and aspirations of the people for so long. Through the much-awaited European Renaissance, individuals became freer to question, to open up their creative powers and have more control of their own destiny. This beginning enabled Western society to set out on the road to the several social and economic revolutions which led ultimately to a more humanistic conception of man.

Of course, Copernicus happened a long time ago. Four centuries later, Stephen Hawking, the British theoretical physicist who has achieved international prominence as one of the great minds of our day, has taken scientific ideas about the cosmos to new, only just observable limits. In his popular work, *A Brief History of Time*, he presents a modern picture of the earth as a mere medium-sized planet orbiting around an average star in the outer suburbs of an ordinary spiral galaxy, which is itself only one of some million galaxies in the observable universe. What he made the layman understand is that the earth is part of an infinitely bigger system than we had ever imagined, even less significant in the total scheme of things than we originally thought.[1]

While the astro-physicists have distanced the earth from the centre of things over the years, the individual has become more paramount it seems. For, as these scientists learn more about the galaxy, they de-mystify the omnipotence of any single body over and above a wider planetary system, which can exist only by virtue of the relationship each part has with the others. In another arena, we find the corporation; it too had lately been yanked out of its all-important centre spot around which everything and everyone previously depended. By the dawn of the 1990s, a great deal had been said and done to make sure that the corporation would no longer be sufficient unto itself.[2]

Increasingly, corporations have become more reliant on brain skills and the interactions and interconnections among people. It is here that companies are rapidly discovering their chief source of market power, or their most dangerous restraining factor. The organization was often a place for accumulating machines, muscles and matter. More and more frequently, it is a way of bringing together individuals and ideas to either create the immaterial value that adds to what machines can do or, alternatively, do what machines can never do.

Thinking of organizations as all powerful gigantic pieces of engineering, with people easily replaceable, is incompatible with the service ethos. As Charles Handy, a London-based organization specialist, observes in his book, *The Age of Unreason*, managers are suddenly waking up to the fact that organizations are made up of people, not just hands. These managers used to talk about their firms as if they were one large factory with inputs and outputs, with control devices in place to manage men and machines. Now, they speak of know-how and social relationships, small team coalitions, individual contribution and influence.[3]

The ways and requirements of the people with competitive know-how inside their heads are hugely different from those of previous generations. So are their roles. Making these roles harmonious – including how they fit and belong into the overall organizational scheme of things – is a theme which is bound to run throughout the decade. Managers will need to learn better ways to capture the know(ing) of individuals and teams, to make both their single and collective learning part of the institution's competitiveness. Those in charge of contemporary corporations will have to harness the immaterial soft assets within their firms with the same sense of urgency that they formerly used to accumulate the hard. They will have to build 'capability portfolios' as professionally as they previously did 'product portfolios'. It is only by mobilizing and combining people's know-how that they can hope to become good–better–best at doing things for and with customers. Which might seem a lot easier if there were not so many contradictions to resolve. For example, can the needs of the organization and the aspirations and inspiration of contemporary workers be made to fit? Can the individuality within each person be preserved while at the same time projects and processes operate at optimum performance levels? Can the learning acquired by individuals be passed on to others? For if not, neither the organization nor the individuals within them can prosper and forge ahead.

The employee as 'partner'

For most professional service and small high-tech companies, the employee as a partner is a well-known concept. In principle, if not law, what it means is that an assembly of people on relatively equal footing work together to take co-responsibility for achieving some desired results. Typically, partners don't consider themselves as senior or junior to each other in the command and control sense of the words. They treat each other as peers, acknowledging that all individuals at any given moment will have some kind of superior knowledge which gives that person the lead role to play. Given industrial traditions, can this concept, or something akin to it, realistically be incorporated into present-day organizations?

When all is considered, none of the great corporate industrial theorists ever really asked workers what they thought. They were, as critics point out, regarded as dumb oxen. Taylor never once asked the people to recommend how their jobs could be improved; rather, he told them what to do. Mayo, 50 years later, known as the father of human relations because of his Hawthorne experiments, tried to see what could be done to improve worker productivity. He and his team concluded that employees could not be bullied into working smarter. Managers had to appeal to their psychology, talk to them, ask their opinion and give them more attention. But in truth, according to some scholars, his theories were yet another way to express the organization's authority over individuals, asking them for suggestions but not necessarily listening, still making it clear in every conceivable way who could make decisions and who had to obey.[4]

As many business writers have discussed, the Japanese demonstrated another approach – having lifetime bonds between companies and employees. This strong sense of mutual identity and reciprocity between Japanese organizations and the individuals who work in them can in many ways be seen as a spirit of partnering, making them distinctly different from conventional Western firms.[5] In the Japanese language the words 'worker' and 'employee' don't exist – everyone is a *sha-in*, or 'member' of the organization. This difference in how employees are regarded in Japan is a threat to Western competitiveness according to some commentators, including Konosuke Matsushita, the late chairman of Matsushita, who, in the 1980s made this statement:

> We are going to win and the industrial West is going to lose out; there's not much you can do about it because the reasons for your failure are within yourselves. Your firms are built on the Taylor model. Even worse so are your heads. With your bosses doing the thinking while workers wield the screwdrivers, you're convinced deep down that this is the right way to run a business. For you the essence of management is getting the ideas out of the heads of the bosses and into the hands of labor. We are beyond your mindset. Business, we know is now so complex and difficult, the survival of firms so hazardous in an environment

increasingly unpredictable, competitive and fraught with danger, that their continued existence depends on the day-to-day mobilization of every ounce of intelligence.[6]

The intelligence within firms that Matsushita was talking about is found throughout modern organizations, from the high-powered systems engineer to the telephone operator. Everyone has know-how which can contribute potentially to the customer satisfying process. Although the know-how worker is in an entirely different league from a less qualified person, together they comprise the new service workforce. Jointly, they carry the value adding capabilities which lead to the sum effect of providing the applied performance customers seek.[7]

Regarding employees more as partners is pretty fundamental in a world of value adding through services. And almost antithetical to the industrial approach (for a comparison see Figure 6.1). Most importantly in those days workers, who ever they happened to be, were seen as a cost. Responsibility was always confined – it was just a question of degree – with efforts to improve productivity centred on doing the same tasks, as found in job descriptions, harder or smarter. Since tasks and timing could always be pre-defined and controlled, this worked well at that time. Today, there are too many unknowns, too much uncertainty, too many questions about what to do

Industrial	Services
Worker responsibility limited to what can and must do	Employee free to be co-responsible for results
Workers must do things harder and smarter	Employees must learn creative ways of doing things better and new things
Management sees labour as cost	Management sees employee as contributor
Workers' input management's primary aim	Outcome for customers organization shared goal
People expected to obey without question	Employees empowered to figure out own solutions
Management tells employees how they performed	Employees tell management how their respective performance was
Workers are part of a broader stakeholder group	Employees are shareholders by virtue of incentives and even shareholding

Figure 6.1 Employees as partners approach

and how. The manuals don't always work at the facing positions where decisions have to be made to suit individual customers in real time. Employees have to figure out for themselves, there and then, how to solve problems, constantly on the lookout for opportunities to please. They can no longer be managed or judged by traditional methods, so now they tell management how they think they did and in what way the firm can facilitate them better.

Increasingly, some European countries – most notably Germany, Switzerland, the Benelux, Scandinavia (especially Sweden) and, to some extent, France – have instilled a stronger sense of collegiality within their firms. The traditional divisions separating people have given way in these countries to more voluntary communication and social dialogue, as Michel Albert, the French socio-economist so expertly explains in his book, *Capitalisme contre Capitalisme*. As he sees it, there are two kinds of capitalism: the 'neo-American, Anglo-Saxon' version, based on the abilities of few people and a shorter-term perspective, and the 'Rhine' version, as he calls it, practised in the European countries and Japan which are more collective by nature, have longer-term goals and where effort is made to include more people in decision making. Acknowledging every individual's contribution to the overall success of the organization, and viewing everyone as a long-term investment can lead, Albert says, to higher returns, lower turnover and more enduring results.[8] This trend – regarding employees as 'partners' – is increasingly being felt in high value corporations worldwide:

● It used to be perfectly acceptable for IBM to announce a 12-month plan to its employees and the way it was to be implemented. Employees were evaluated on how well they executed these instructions. Now, there is dialogue with employees about what should be done and how. Restrictions as to who can and cannot do a task have fallen away, including the signing of letters to the outside world, which had always needed several signatures but now can be done by anyone in contact with customers.

● Federal Express has a practice whereby employees are asked to give feedback on their working relationships with their bosses. Known as the 'leadership index', it consists of a series of questions which employees fill in annually. Most importantly, this feedback is actually used to make changes which lead to better performance for customers on the facing and interfacing positions.

● At the Royal Bank of Canada, employees are treated as partners in an effort to work more closely with customers. So as to identify the blockages in daily customer activities, there are regular staff focus group sessions where employees discuss ideas and implement them directly. Of the firm's stock, 5 per cent – a figure expected to rise – is now owned by employees: for every dollar they put in, the bank adds another 50 cents. Eighty per cent of the staff have some shareholding.

● The Commercial Market Group division at AT&T allows sales managers to set their own targets today. They receive assistance with tools, training, and resources to meet these targets without supervisory control, connecting with whomsoever they need in the organization. They can work from a home workstation to eliminate unnecessary time spent at the office writing memos, office reports and doing other administrative chores. They set their own patterns and methods of work for as long as the twin goals of sales and customer satisfaction are met. Here is how one executive from AT&T explains the thinking:

> This way our people feel they 'have' a piece of the business instead of simply 'being' a piece of the business. It's one thing to tell employees they are partners, it's quite another to really make them feel they are. We've found out it requires a whole different way of doing things.

● An almost immediate increase in the quality of customer response took place recently at Kansa's regional and local Finnish sales offices after employees were given the green light to do whatever they felt would improve employee contact with customers. They set their own hours, dressing norms, and designed their offices and work spaces to enhance their ability to deal with the constant pressure of coping with customers who were usually upset, under stress or grieving.

The soft side is harder

The language tells all when it comes to soft and hard values in business. In financial circles, 'hard currency' is associated with sure value, while the soft is uncertain, unreliable, risky and prone to extreme economic swings. What are the hard assets in business if not those which are expected to gain in worth and give firms a reliable return? And hard managerial skills are formal, analytic and dispassionate, which is what most firms had sought and revered.

But now what Russel Ackoff, corporate strategist and chief proponent of the soft school, talked about is fiercely percolating within corporate circles. He took the idea, which originated with Kant, Hegel and then Jung, that people consist of both hard and soft facets and introduced it into business thinking. His point is that the distinction between the emotional side of people, believed to be biased, and the scientific, believed to be accurate, assumed a separability of head and heart, of science and values, ethics and rationality equivalent to saying that because we can look at and discuss the head and tail of a coin separately, we can separate them.[9]

But, for all the talk, the hard continued to dominate Western thinking until well into the 1990s. It made an impact on what firms did and how well they performed, especially when knowledge became *the* significant asset by which corporations began to distinguish themselves. Examining what makes certain corporations across the board exceptional, Ikujiro Nonaka's research found that much of what managers thought was knowledge was often simply data. They fooled themselves, he maintains, into believing that what must be done could be decided by gathering more and more facts and that it was nearly impossible to make a good decision using soft skills. They were wrong, he says in his article, 'The Knowledge Creating Company', where he takes the managerial obsession with hard facts back to its roots:

> Deeply ingrained in the traditions of Western management from Frederick Taylor to Herbert Simon is the view of the organization as a machine for information processing. According to this view the only useful knowledge is formal and systematic – hard (read: quantifiable) data, codified procedures, universal principles. And the key metrics for measuring the value of new knowledge are similarly hard and quantifiable – increased efficiency, lower costs, improved return on investment.[10]

They certainly were wrong for environments such as we know them today. Corporate life in general and customer relationships in particular have become too complex. Solutions require judgement, interpretation, and assessment, sometimes made irrationally, and always made with an open mind if they are to be flexible enough to adjust and adapt to situations on the front line. This is not to say that there is no use for solid hard techniques or for hard, people skills anymore. But they no longer suffice. Today we need the unique skills, not quantifiable nor related to the facts, but which capture individual insight and experience. Perhaps not explicable, packageable or even able to be written down, this other kind of know(ing) defies industrial logic, interpreting as it learns, constantly looking for the not so obvious.[11]

Combining the hard and soft sides in people is, of course, at the core of Eastern philosophies and religions. Not surprisingly, some important gains from this way of thinking have found expression in their management practices as well. Deep in the underlying principle of combining soft and hard – whether from Confucian, Buddhist or Taoist roots – is that in the complementarity, rather than conflict of opposites – yin and yang, masculine and feminine – lies wholeness, interdependence and thus effective human behaviour. Neither one nor the other works best on its own. If an individual cannot rely on one or the other, neither can the corporation.[12]

This conjuncture of hard and soft in people did not go unnoticed in the West. A good deal of research to explore the potential of intuition, creativity and pure gut feeling began in the late 1980s, but it mostly focused on skills in the higher management echelons.[13] Retrospectively, there are some wonderful examples of people in high places who used soft skills to make difficult decisions – from the move into ATMs made by the ex-chairman of Citibank, Walter Wriston, to Akio Morita's launch of the Sony Walkman.

Combining the hard with soft attributes is especially important in the delivery of value added services, where employees are dealing with customers over extended periods of time and where nothing is certain except the need for spontaneity in their relationships. Value for customers is entirely a matter of what people can do at that moment of contact, and this often embodies literally the offering itself. Also important is how employees understand the situation in relation to the values of the corporation so that they are able to act and react in an appropriate manner. For which both personal and interpersonal skills are needed which include these qualities:

Personal – curiosity and questioning, problem-solving, feelings, creativity, intuition, judgement, common sense, spontaneity, insight, empathy, ethics, idealism, reflection, capacity for criticism and learning.

Interpersonal – the capacity for socialization, inspiring, taking initiative, engaging in abstract thinking, bringing out the best in others, forging teams, adapting to unusual situations, self-organizing, self-learning, and applying and transmitting learning.

Having a balance between the soft and hard is altogether essential in making a service network a living entity rather than an advanced organigram. Corporations today need men and women who are able to grasp this principle and make it a way of life. While methods, procedures and process engineering lead to productivity, it is often the soft skills which enable the parts of the network to function as a whole. While an eye for detail is essential for producing results for customers, so too is the creativity to translate situations into customer satisfying opportunities. Neither narrow concepts nor narrow people skills can survive today's environments. In all aspects of solutions, it is the combination of the hard and soft – more difficult to find, cultivate, define or emulate – that determines how well people succeed. Looking at the solution modules:

- Enhancements for core *goods* need frequently an intuitive feel for where the market might be going – what customers need now and in the future.
- The *products* to deliver services have to be anticipated based on reflection and envisioning future trends, which may be as difficult to quantify and express as the social skills needed to transmit them to others.
- Effective *services* depend on the empathy and sociability of people so that relationships can have a long life span, and learning can take place at the point of customer contact.
- *Self-service* is a problem-solving tool to facilitate customers, enhancing their 'doing' capabilities without abdicating responsibility for the results.
- True *support* systems are those that are intuitive about customer reactions, and create harmonious environments and social networking.

● *Information* must be turned into relevant solutions using both interpretive and creative skills, insights rather than just data, as well as the ability to transfer the information to 'intelligent' use.
● *Know-how* is having a superior ability to read the environment differently and to combine wisdom with the technicalities of know(ing) what, how and in some cases from whom.

Perhaps, in the industrial days, a disparity between what was professional and what was profitable, what was inventive or implementable, sound or saleable, was justified. But how can this be so today? Maybe functions such as engineering, manufacturing, R&D and technical service could previously have been cold, distant and purely analytic, taking only numerical and technical criteria into consideration. But this is no longer workable given the critical role of multi-functional processes in serving customers. History has taught us – and research substantiates it – that these so-called 'hard' professions need an integration of both left and right brain skills if they are to contribute effectively to the customer satisfying process.[14]

Making tin soldiers into Russian dolls

Before and throughout the pre-mass production days of the nineteenth century, people had to know how to make the entire object when they undertook something. Their work life, workday or what they did at work had not yet been segmented into bits (as graphically illustrated in Figure 6.2). They were skilled at making whatever the product was – a watch, cabinet or coach wheel – from beginning to end. With the exception of work so complex that people needed to have certain specialized abilities, craftsmen in those days had an intimate detailed knowledge of the materials and methods needed to perform the entire production process. Effectively this was an autonomy all their own. When the assembly line appeared so too did the careful division of work into tasks (as Figure 6:3 shows). From the machine and paper factory worker, to the supervisors and managers who controlled them, this had become the firmly entrenched norm by the 1950s.

Following the destruction of World War II, organizations were providing the kind of security people craved. They became part of a corporate mould which defined their work and shaped what they did, when and how. This mould produced what Galbraith called the 'organization man', an image actually first conceived by business sociologist William Whyte Jr. In his epic work, *The Affluent Society*, Galbraith personified what had then become the bedrock of industrial life. He described employees who, with the growth of the organization, not only worked for it but also belonged to it, not only gained a livelihood from it but also relied totally on it for their social identity. Continuing with this two decades later, Michael Maccoby, a psychiatrist

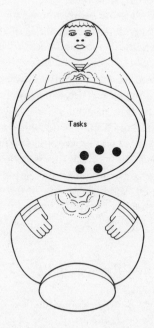

Figure 6.2 Role pre-industrial worker all tasks, some specialization

practising in America, painted a picture in *The Gamesman* of what had become almost universal by then in the Western world. He described employees who equated their personal interest with the firm's long-term development and success, who believed fervently that anything outside it was hostile and inhospitable, and who put the company's interest above their own personal lives.[15]

These workers strove to climb the corporate ladders and skyscrapers which were *the* symbols of achievement. No mingling of a person's work and personal life was tolerated, either by themselves or their corporations: they were strictly separate. To succeed was to conform: anything that smacked of individualism was rejected as going against the corporate grain. People were expected to perfect and master their jobs and all the tasks associated with them. Or, if managers, get these jobs mastered by those they supervised.

To the new generation of people that entered the work scene during the mid-1980s, born into and/or raised in an era of unprecedented wealth, the term 'corporate' had a different meaning. Even if they did fear poverty, war, or

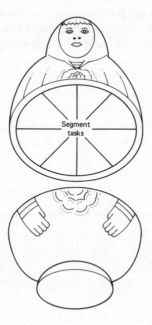

Segment
tasks

Figure 6.3 Role 'organizational man' segmented tasks

unemployment, they no longer turned necessarily to the organization as their infallible saviour. Educated, skilled, independent and less burdened by industrial traditions, they brought a new set of values into the workplace. And, as Handy writes in *The Age of Unreason*, it is only those companies which get into the heart of this issue and can cater to these people that will truly gain value from their knowledge. From his book comes this extract:

Not for them the organizational philosophies of the army or the factory or the bureaucracies of government. They must look ahead to places where knowledge has always been key and brains more important than brawn. The wise organization knows that their smart people are not to be easily defined as workers or as managers but as individuals, as specialists, as professionals. The wise organization realizes too that intelligent individuals can only be governed by consent and not by command, that obedience cannot be demanded and that a collegiate culture of colleagues and a shared understanding is the only way to make things happen.[16]

As high-value firms so clearly see today, service workers have to be treated differently from employees in the 1960s, 1970s and 1980s. In a curious twist, organizations must now earn the allegiance from employees that previous generations had to earn from firms. The question is: what goads and motivates these new workers if not the values of the post war years? Well, the experts say, first and foremost they are in search of learning. Thirty-five years after Whyte, two American writers, Paul Leinberger and Bruce Tucker, have followed up his work, interviewing original subjects and their now adult children. In their book, *The New Individualists*, the authors look at – among other things – what motivates the knowledge worker. They have concluded that they identify with their work more than with organizations – where the work is performed; they are specialists who know they know more about their own area of expertise than anyone else in the organization. Their knowledge has made them free.[17]

They want to express, use and test what they already know, as well as acquire new knowledge constantly. They want to have the opportunity to advance in their chosen field and grow in their profession. Constant retooling and renewal gives them the sense of independence they crave. Since steep ladders can't do this anymore, the momentum comes from interesting and challenging new assignments, where they can work on state-of-the-art technology with experts of their own ilk and be part of the ongoing creative process.

This does not mean that these people don't want to belong, merely that they are programmed to expect change more than their predecessors. So, ironically, the organizations where new employees excel and stay longest are those which offer them enough potential to make a switch if needs be. Paradoxically, the more know-how these new workers accumulate, the more mobile they become. As Ted Levitt points out in *Thinking about Management*, their loyalties are often stronger to their professions than to their employers. What concerns him and many others is how to keep these people, especially in high value settings, so as to retain reasonable consistency in customer relationships. This is what Levitt says:

> The more dependent the work of an organization is on the work of its professional knowledge workers (which includes its managers), the more the organization must attend to their getting their professional and personal satisfactions that keep them inspired and in place. Whether they will depart to other places is only partly a matter of demand on the outside. Whether and how well they will perform is almost entirely a matter of conditions on the inside.
>
> Two great challenges lie increasingly ahead for the modern organization: to have the requisite types and numbers of knowledge workers to do what must be done, and to have an organization in which they will thrive and with which they will want to remain.[18]

Knowledge workers are neither able nor willing to make sharp distinctions between their personal and professional lives. Similarly, the commercial and social aspects of their work lives are not clearly delineable. Essentially, what they want is a better balance than the last generation, unwilling to play the obedient cog in a huge corporate wheel. They gravitate to work environments that support their personal lifestyles and display characteristics at work which are acceptable to both situations. Having witnessed, says Peter Benton the ex-chairman of British Telecom, in an interview in *Long Range Planning*, much of the stress imposed on people by the hierarchy, they are unprepared to pay the same price. He says:

> We are looking to a future that is potentially much more attractive and human, in which the individual who is adding value at work is concerned with the value of others; of people outside the organization, and those inside too. The qualities that are necessary to do that well happen to be extremely close to the qualities that are necessary to be an enjoyable and fulfilled human being. Consequently we are moving from an unnatural and inhuman way of working to one in which the characteristics of the successful human being at work will be close to the characteristics of the successful human being at home.[19]

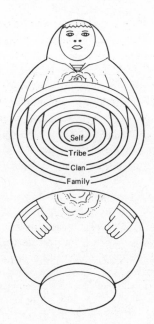

Figure 6.4   Anthropological roles contemporary service provider

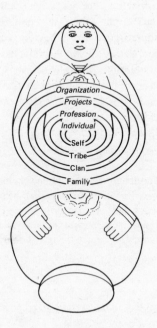

Figure 6.5   Corporate roles contemporary service provider

That workers can only be understood and handled in one-dimensional terms through a single job and set of tasks is a hangover from industrial times – today people have to play multiple roles. These roles are analagous to some anthropological typologies (see Figures 6.4 and 6.5) and, again being a more systemic model, they contain and are contained in each other – interdependent and interconnected.

The 'self', that which distinguishes one person from another, can be neither defined nor duplicated. It represents a single employee, a private and working being, unique and independent. The 'tribe' is a small group of these individuals who belong together by virtue of birth and affiliation. In managerial terms, what makes one tribe different from another is its area of specialization or profession. When individuals from different tribes come together to pursue joint interests or goals, a 'clan' is formed. In corporations, these roles are performed through the various processes, activities and projects. And, finally, there is the 'family' – the organization – to which individuals always belong and return for direction, development and sustenance, and on which they ultimately depend.[20]

Unlike industrial days, individual differences no longer run counter to corporate goals. Rather they give it its versatility and resilience. Instead of their colleagues from different parts of the organization being potential competitors and adversaries with whom they may have previously collided and contended, they are now part of the same customer serving process, accumulating and transferring know-how, both within the organization and without. Within this mutually reinforcing process, service workers are found in all of their roles – individual, professional, project-based and organizational.

Whereas the organization man put the firm first, the script today is decidedly different. Using an example from Digital to demonstrate, the contemporary know-how worker would probably say something like this:

- I'm a person with a contribution to make (self/individual).
- I'm a professional working in consulting (tribe/professional).
- I'm on a long term assignment with a client bank. (clan/project).
- ... and I work for Digital (family/organization).

No matter how one looks at it, the way that firms regard employees has fundamentally altered:

Then: people were dependent upon the organization, and their development was a means to a corporate end.

Now: they are part of the organization and their individual development is an end goal in itself.

Then: people were in one job at a time, where they could be found and easily controlled.

Now: they are involved in several roles at the same time. They work best this way, belonging everywhere simultaneously.

Then: the organizational way of doing things was valued and a corresponding behaviour was expected.

Now: the behaviour that is valued is whatever suits the role that the situation demands.

Then: relationships among employees were fixed and immutable, creating stability.

Now: relationships are both entrenched and temporary which, rather than creating stability or instability, makes the firm tenacious and adaptable.

Recipes for learning

Industrial organizations were built on an algorithmic model which implicitly assumed that, if employees could be taught to do things in a rational and linear manner, risk would be minimal, and productivity and profits high. Because it was based on a simple cause and effect logic, people were expected to continue to do what had been proved successful in the past. Individuals were trained to handle customer situations in a routine standardized manner. A picture which has quickly shifted as high value corporations have begun to transform themselves into learning organizations.

In services, learning is both the product and the process, the delivery and the deliverable. It is what the firm has to differentiate itself – what it has to sell. There is a faint line at the point of interface between what a person knows and can transfer at that moment and what the customer actually gets. Learning should therefore not be confined to any one person or any one part of the organization, as was the case previously. As Charles Hampden-Turner, British corporate culture consultant, writes in *Corporate Cultures: From Vicious to Virtuous Circles*, success today can only come from those firms which can obtain a stock of know-how from a variety of sources:

> There was a time when a company simply took whatever knowledge was available from professional bodies or research departments and put it into production. The learning was 'brought in' by hiring experts and then ground out by the factory. Employees learned up to a point but the organization simply exploited what was known, buying new expertise when appropriate. Today everything is simply moving too fast. The market environments are in ever more rapid evolution, while science develops faster than commercial applications can be generated. In such circumstances, there has to be a network of people who can learn simultaneously from changing markets 'outside' and burgeoning technology 'inside', and bring to customers the latest satisfactions which new knowledge makes possible.[21]

Service networks learn all the time. Employees add one experience to another, using the incremental learning as it is acquired. Rather than just working with a formula to produce product after product they take their observation and experience amd convert it into market potential. Their learning is a two-way flow between themselves and their customers and vice versa. What are the enabling conditions needed to make service enterprises effective learners?

People learn while doing

The high-volume company saw learning as a discrete linear event, whereas to high-value firms, it is activity-based and ongoing. A perfectly natural process, learning begins at birth and should never really end. As soon as one problem is solved, so another arrives to be solved. If, and only if, this is happening can the modern firm avoid major shocks, bending to changing circumstances rather than breaking. Before, individuals were discouraged from learning for themselves – this caused disruption. Neither was learning seen as ongoing – tasks, once taught, were expected to be carried out.

Inevitably, learning was taken out of its natural environment and made extraneous:

Then: it was assumed that learning had to be highly organized and happen at special times or on specific occasions. People were typically taken out of their work situations for this experience.
Now: the work environment itself is regarded as the learning environment, with each event viewed as a potential source of growth and improvement.
Then: corporations believed that employees had to learn the facts and procedures before applying them, only previous experience dictated their actions.
Now: they recognize that learning occurs while things are happening and, rather than being rigidly applied, previous experience may only be a guide for future action.
Then: learning was an intentional activity, with anything outside the agenda usually disregarded by both the employees and the firm.
Now: the learning is integrated into daily activities with the most significant learning – often that which is most enduring – gained unintentionally and unconsciously.
Then: it was assumed that any improvement meant something new had to be added on or be learned.
Now: managers know that when learning occurs, some unlearning may have to take place.
Then: learning was seen as a one-way progression, with feedback given after the event.
Now: feedback is on-the-spot and ongoing; it is built into the learning process with people revising methods as they go along.

Single-loop learning was characteristric of industrial firms for their mental model assumed that things would stay constant. Tasks were clear cut, perfectly definable. The people they sought got existing jobs done well, detected variations and corrected errors. Clearly, what this approach overlooked was that in services neither the circumstance nor the employee can remain constant. In double-loop learning, methods and standards still exist, but those who set these measures and those who perform them have an ongoing dialogue, and constantly ask the question: are we good at doing the wrong thing? Through enquiry and periodic assessment, they adjust and update activities.[22] These examples show how this can translate down the line:

● Singapore Airlines' cabin attendants adapt their own schedules to the passengers' body clocks. Meals and movies are planned to coincide with the sentiments and needs of passengers rather than schedules. Compared to the industry average of four times a year on high frequency flights, its menus may sometimes be changed each day, and certainly at least once a week, based on feedback surveys from customers and crew.

- SAS allows its employees to self-organize throughout the flight experience, jointly taking decisions based on events around them. If there has been a catering delay, for instance, these so-called 'horizontal teams' – people who come from different specialized areas – can decide whether to fly on time without food or wait and delay the flight, depending on circumstances.
- Rather than expect people to wait for instructions, Citibank encourages experimentation at each and every level of the organization. As an example, the mailroom – seen before as an unimportant part of the customer satisfying process – is now considered integral to getting information around the system quickly and on to customers. Since these employees are the only people who really know what goes on with mail, they are the ones who are expected to revise methods constantly and find their own ways to speed up the system, implementing ideas immediately.
- Employees at Toyota and Honda are urged to seek out learning during their daily activities, even if it leads to an interruption in the work flow which they are expected to recoup. It is considered so important that, if workers feel others can gain from their learning, they can shut down their operations and use the experience as an illustrative exercise.
- At the Royal Bank of Canada, employees are encouraged actively and even rewarded for questioning set routines and procedures. Until recently, they did what they were told, sticking to corporate policy, but now they use their experience to question and participate actively in making changes to bring about improved performance in their customer dealings.

People learn through failure

Organizations now acknowledge that since people can't always be right the first time, and learning can't happen by the book, it must take place through experimentation. Under these circumstances, failures can't always be avoided. Value is created through the person's or organization's ability to distill what has been learned, and absorb the good bits through a double-loop process of continuous feedback. For instance:

- SKF had a 'bible' describing exactly what had to be done by whom and when, which had been valid for as long as anyone could remember. As little as possible was left to chance. Then, in the late 1980s, when the company moved into trouble-free operations managers were allowed to shape their own strategies through trial and error in the forty operating countries. They tested the market, educated distributors, employees and customers alike, and adjusted strategies according to the responses.

● Suddenly, from doing routine tasks on request, Ciba-Geigy's information centre found that their internal customers wanted information solutions. A grace period was negotiated with top management, providing them with sufficient time to learn additional skills and apply them to this new situation. Having this freedom to learn motivated people to change their behaviour and aligned them to the new challenge.

In high value corporations, failure is part of the learning process and mistakes are assumed to be a natural part of this. They are seen as an ongoing opportunity – vehicles for pushing the company forward rather than back, augmenting rather than diminishing value. Of course if people are punished when experimentation goes awry, it defeats the object. Tolerance for failure is therefore high on the corporate agenda. In industrial firms, people didn't talk about mistakes, and those who made them were considered unworthy. Since trying something new meant a risk, and a risk was bound to lead to these mistakes, employees were reluctant to take initiative. It was this fear of failure which kept the organization man from learning as we understand it today. Chris Argyris, behavioural specialist, explains this problem in his book, *Action Science*. As soon as people became engaged in the learning process, it set up an immediate dilemma. It could lead to a mistake. As mistakes were 'taboo', and people feared being caught and exposed, their choice was often to ignore the learning even if it meant losing an opportunity.[23]

A culture characterized by 'permission to fail' needs both a focus and sense of trust. The focus today is undoubtedly the customer; the trust must come from working climates which legitimize questioning and self-examination. Japanese firms make this a ritual. People get together in small groups for regular meetings, share their failures and see whether some general insight can be drawn. Employees are not afraid to be singled out and, in this way, their learning is something in which the entire organization is able to share.

It's one thing to accept learning through failure inside factories and office blocks, out of the customer's sight. But, it's quite another when experimentation takes place in full view of the customer. Services are highly transparent, thus failures can be easily sensed or seen. And once sensed or seen, they become part of the customer's experience. For large-scale changes, some firms prefer to experiment with a corporate or a select group of personal customers. At least this way both the firm and the customer anticipate the need for adjustments which can be made accordingly.

People learn to transfer the learning

Learning may start with an individual, but is not worth much if it gets stuck there. Which raises the next issue: how can learning be transferred within the service network? It is ironic that industrial models tried desperately to get knowledge into their employees' heads, while service models try with equal vigour to get it out. Mechanical, administrative or technical skills that were relatively standardized could be easily learned and applied in those days. Anything to do with material things could be communicated through specifications, pictures, models, and precise methods.

Today, with high-value services, this is not easy. Only through contact and discourse can the huge reservoir of know-how acquired through learning be tapped. Service workers rely on a kind of tacit know(ing). Performing a service skilfully and effortlessly doesn't mean they can express why or how they do it. Quite simply, they often know more than they are able to verbalize.[24] But, one way or another, the learning must pass from one individual to another and from the firm to the marketplace. For this know-how is a crucial resource which results in gains only when it is gathered, consolidated, disseminated and made accessible to others. These techniques help this transfer process:

- *Rotating people* means that they are moved around so that their skills can be observed and emulated by others. At Honda, from the chairman on down, employees rotate jobs on a yearly basis for this express purpose. BP rotates people all the time. From the head office into the field, from service stations all over the globe, the company tries to capture the best ideas and practices, and get them to its vast assembly of employees.
- *Special projects* are organized to bring people together to share their know-how. What would the information division have done when working on a new fertilizer herbicide or insecticide before the restructuring of Ciba-Geigy? Probably collect information from people and departments, one after the other, linear fashion. This kind of learning would have been tedious and slow. Now the company quickly finds existing pockets of know-how, brings them together and gets people hitherto unknown to each other to share what they know and take the added learning back to spread in their own areas.
- *Reuniting people in groups* gives those who have worked together previously an opportunity to reconnect, share experiences and relearn. AT&T finds that the disadvantage to allow salespeople to spend all their time working with customers is that they can become isolated islands of knowledge if they are not absorbed back in the mainstream. Therefore meetings are organized expressly to bring them together, enabling them to exchange ideas and experiences. For the same reason, document team members at Rank Xerox meet regularly with professional colleagues, both on a national and international basis.
- *Listings and knowledge directories* make it easier to put what has been learned in the firm into some tangible, accessible and organized form. At Price Waterhouse, every technique is recorded in a knowledge directory that is given to each member of the network. These list everyone of the

3,000 partners worldwide, as well as their interests, skills, expertise and experience.

- *Knowledge networks* are similar to highbrow clubs, composed of people typically scattered around the world, perhaps a handful, perhaps many more. These associations are designed to move the know-how from one professional to another and keep individuals apace of developments in their respective fields. Digital has created a European Professional Expertise Network for its know-how workers from its service support centres. Connected by electronic mail, teleconferencing and phone, these employees are in daily contact with special conferences arranged to bring those in the same geography together bi-annually.

- *Expert systems*, being technology based, are a sophisticated method for redistributing and building a firm's knowledge bank. The data base at Hendrix Voeders contains everything that the consultants have acquired on the various stages of a pig's life: this information is then refined and spread throughout the network. Every problem and solution that Rank Xerox handles for a customer is fed into an artificial intelligence system which takes the learning, translates it, and then distributes it back to the front line for immediate use.

Institutional memory and know(ing)

Over and above the individual learning inside a firm, there is also an institutional accumulation of know(ing) and memory. The first person to talk collectively about the mind and what it knows was the French sociologist Emile Durkheim, who declared that there was a superordinate intelligence acquired by societies and groups larger than the sum of the intelligence of individuals. Because the concept was interpreted as a possible intrusion of man's free will, it was rejected initially. But the theme was taken up later by others, who since then have accumulated a fascinating body of thought on what they call collective consciousness.[25]

This collective consciousness works unconsciously to embed history within each one of us. The past is alive, researchers say, carried and contained within every person from generation to generation. From this notion came the idea – which captured the imagination of lead philosophers, historians, artists and scientists during the 1980s and 1990s – that there is an undercurrent of know(ing) which drives people from different corners of the earth to the same breakthroughs. What they suggested was that, although great discoveries and artistic works came from one specific source, inventions could, in fact, be traced to a collective know(ing) that was spread worldwide.[26]

For modern organizations – where the immaterial is all-essential – this is a fascinating thought. Can a firm think? Can it remember? How does it solidify what it knows? Values shared may persist over time, we know, even when group leadership changes.[27] With know-how streaming in at such a rapid clip and from so many sources, the question is how do corporations not only learn to collect what they know but also 'forget' what has become irrelevant? No longer, managers find, by compiling, distributing and memorizing rules, regulations and manuals. On the contrary, with learning comes constant change which neutralizes any attempts to cast it into stone.

What the organization has in its institutional memory or know(ing) is its capital. People come and go, as do their ideas and expertise. What stays is the accumulation of the learning, the way in which a firm puts together this know(ing) to produce value as one composite whole. Joseph L. Badaracco, a philosopher and authority on business alliances and know-how, makes this point clear when he says that none of the individual parties in a firm like Toyota knows what the firm as a whole knows about making cars. It takes years and years of common effort which becomes the firm's unique way of doing things. In his book, *The Knowledge Link*, he expands on this concept:

> A firm is an embodiment of knowledge; it can learn, remember, and know things that none of the individuals or teams within it know. It is, in essence, a very large team, or a confederation of teams, in which enormously complex skills and knowledge are embedded in the minds of its members and in the formal social relationships that orchestrate their efforts.[28]

It is through the know(ing) drawn from people's multi-faceted roles that firms acquire an institutional memory. From each role comes a different kind of learning (graphically illustrated in Figure 6.6). Single learning emanates from what people do and learn by such means as formal investigation or transfer, or by their endless daily encounters with customers and collaborators. Successful professions rely upon this learning to build select knowledge and application in their particular area. Much of this crucial learning gets fed into projects and activities that require knowledge too complex for one person or profession. Multi-functional groups learn jointly and eventually know more than any single person or profession does. All this experience gets pulled together by the ongoing collective process within the firm which embeds the cumulative know(ing) into an institutional memory.

A great deal of the challenge for the high-value firm is to generate the learning which enhances existing capabilities or creates new abilities to get customization for the 'markets within markets' and personalization for the 'markets of one' into their services. Equally, learning is knowing how to take this know-how and make it part of the corporate routines which go into the 'mass within offerings' for the 'mass within markets' which, through learning curves, is able to produce the economies firms need to be financially competitive.

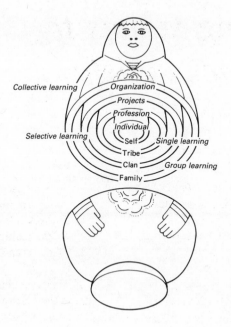

Figure 6.6 Institutional know(ing), learning and roles

Teaming for services

Even though the power of individuals is undeniable in modern corporations –
for it is they who do the learning – it is having a combination of people on or
supporting the front line that ultimately matters, as no one can satisfy the
customer single-handedly. Interchanges that occur in pairings, interactions
which take place in and between groups provoke the insights that produce the
specific behaviour which eventually manifest at the critical points in the
customer's activity cycle. Unless learning is shared, exchanged and
distributed in teams, there is little chance that a firm can build the solid know-
how base needed to provide consistently what the market now demands.

But, how groups are formed and how they stay together is quite another
matter. There is a big difference between the rather static industrial notion of
a team and the more organic contemporary version (see Figure 6.7)
Hierarchies cramped teams in several ways. They came together by decree
rather than through some spontaneous need. The composition was fixed by

	Industrial	**Services**
Origin	Decreed	Spontaneous
Form	Confined	Organic
Learning	Assumed	Evolves
Knowledge	Stock	Flow
Authority	Limited	Diffuse
Risk	Leader	Shared
Conflict	Negative	Positive
Accountability	Up	Sideways
Loyalty	Company	Group
Resources	Who there is	Who we want
Motivation	Corporate expectation	Common expectations
Judgement	Corporate	Self/Team
Background	Uniform	Diverse

Figure 6.7   Industrial and service team concepts

management, and members looked inward and upward for momentum and direction, working with their existing knowledge base within tightly defined charters.

In contrast, service-focused teams are self-organized and directed from within. They are relational, and organic – expanding or contracting in size depending on circumstance and need. Successful teams are largely propelled by their own energy. Members take their cue from each other, sharing the risks and authority as the situation demands. Common expectations bind them, and learning evolves through the free flow of know-how among them. In the industrial setting, firms avoided diversity within a team for fear that it would lead to conflict – then considered bad – whereas today tolerance for conflict, and the ability to express and deal with it constructively, is seen as positive. Moreover, the tension which arises from conflict caused by individual diversity is regarded as a good way to unlock creative powers and energy.[29]

Teams behave the way they do today in part because they are founded upon different principles, but also because they operate across traditional boundaries. As the layers and boxes separating people begin to crumble (see Figure 6.8) the emphasis in teaming is shifting from cementing the walls between groups within the firms to breaking down these barriers. High value firms also endeavour to build bridges across firms thereby creating multi-company teams. Flattening organizations is a levelling device between groups within firms and makes for stronger bonds and greater joint value creation possibilities. Mechanisms are also set up to link the firm to its customers and customers' customers, extending this bonding to add value throughout the distribution chain.

How well a team works depends to a large extent on its makeup. When teams were functional, recruiting for them concerned only management. Now, members of multi-functional teams have a say in who the members might be. If teams extend as well into the customer's space, recruiting decisions are often taken jointly with them. With industrial teams, career routes had a single track. Now they are both vertical – within the profession – and lateral – promoting people to new assignments, projects or activities. These promotions may even come through extensions of customer assignments. Multi-functional teams evaluate their own performance and, if teams work across firms, customers' opinions are included. These teams aren't necessarily composed of people who work next door to each other anymore – they work perfectly well remotely. Nor do they have to be permanently together or come from the same level within the firm. They form expressly to accomplish something; what binds them and determines their success is their common values, shared goals and how well they function together.

To illustrate:

● Singapore Airlines uses multi-functional teams all the time in its daily operations. Some teams only meet for a couple of months. 'Adoption

	Industrial Functional 'cement walls'	**Services** Cross-company 'break barriers'	**Services** Inter-company 'build bridges'
Composition	Functional	Multi-functional	Multi-company
Skills	Specific	Varied	Diverse
Charts	Layered	Levelled	Linked
Evaluation	Company	Company/team	Team/customer
Recruiting	Function	Corporation/team	Team/customer
Career route	Single	Dual	Joint
Promotion	Vertical	Lateral	Cellular
Proximity	Face to face	Face to face and remote	Face to face and remote
Duration	Permanent	Permanent or temporary	Semi permanent or temporary

Figure 6.8 Industrial and service operating team principles

teams', as they are called for example, consist of eight people who come from distinctly different parts of the firm and could include anyone from the CEO to a cleaning person. They take responsibility and joint 'ownership' for the care of an aircraft during this period, inspecting it before and after takeoff, and ensuring its smooth running and customer efficiency.

● Digital may have teams which work together with one customer for several years. They are part of many organizations and several cultures all at once, connecting face-to-face with the customers' factories or offices, as well as remotely from service support centres scattered throughout the world. Jointly, these teams are responsible for making strategic IT decisions and handling ongoing operations. The core group is chosen by both the team and the customer, and evaluation is done by both. Promotion for supplier members of the team are sometimes cellular, growing out of new projects initiated by the customer.

How can teaming be better forged? Each team is unique with its own way of doing things. With the content of know-how so high, there are only a minute number of success factors that outsiders may be able to observe, articulate and emulate. The others, such as the chemistry among people, respect, understanding, good spirits and open-mindedness may be too elusive. Not surprisingly tin soldiers were expected to keep emotions under control during the work day, as they were assumed to interfere with logic and reasoning. Today, in these teams emotions are seen as a positive part of the working relationship without which understanding, empathy and, hence, communication is impaired. Tin soldiers didn't know much about other team members and didn't really care. They avoided topics that were not work related, keeping every dialogue strictly within the social mores of the firm. Now, greater informality among team members abounds in successful service teams, considered a mutual investment in reciprocal well-being.[30] To facilitate teaming, firms are turning to new concepts:

● *Seeing the team as hero* means that winning is no longer only associated with highly select individuals as it was in Western countries. The true heroes – the number one sales person, the turnaround CEO, the new idea 'whiz-kid' – were the role models the industrial epoch understood. 'Corporations were composed of heroes who inspired others and drones who obeyed them and perspired,' says Robert Reich pointedly in his article, 'Entrepreneurship Reconsidered: the Team as Hero'. In this myth of winners and losers, the few entrepreneurs or heroes personified freedom and creativity, and they were the ones who were rewarded with fame and fortune. The drones, on the other hand, were disciplined by means of clear rules and punishment, and became lost in the all-powerful organization.[31]

More conducive to a service ethos is the notion of the team as hero. Working relationships among people in high-value companies are interconnected throughout the customer's flow of activities. Information and accountability are shared as the network as a whole searches for ways to learn, adjust, and improve offerings. So whereas everyone strove to beat their colleagues to be top car salesman at Volvo Trucks, today the attention goes to the frontline team as a whole. Where once the goals of an underwriter, sales or claims person, or risk engineer were diametrically opposed, at Zurich Insurance today they are one team, and it is this one entity which either succeeds or fails. Likewise, the old view – that being on a team was a burden because it added hours, distracting and diverting the employee from his real task – has been vanquished. Today, at a company like Citibank, every internal communication refers to 'the team' rather than individuals or functions.

- *Rewarding the team* entails an incentive scheme for joint accomplishment and performance systems based on the quality of the customer relationship rather than the quantity of 'things' produced and sold. While it doesn't discount what individuals do, or the need to recognize them, it switches the emphasis to collective contributions, acknowledging that having people so intertwined in delivering solutions can make it difficult to single out the know-how and effort of just one person. As handling customers on a global basis becomes more common, collective contribution becomes even more significant. When a company in one country – like Hoechst in Japan – provides know-how to Toyota in the UK to enable that company to offer advice which may or may not end up in sales and profits two years down the road, the final outcome is comprised of contributions from all parties.

Today, many firms employ a hybrid evaluation and reward scheme based on both customer satisfaction and financial success. The Volvo teams are rewarded for revenues on sales, spare parts and service over the lifetime of the client company's truck investment, an aim directly related to cost-per-mile targets. It is no longer the profit on each individual product which receives the sole attention at corporations such as IBM or Digital. Organized as they now are in teams which deliver a customer satisfying process, the focus is on profit per customer. Classic professional service firms, like Price Waterhouse, also look to their teams for both the satisfaction and profitability of their clients. Partners are rewarded with shares based on their contribution, with profits annually distributed from one single worldwide profit and loss account.

- *Adjusting the terminology* helps revert attention from select individuals to teams. The profusion and importance of titles, branding some people heroes and others drones, and keeping people well apart is falling away. Language in this context is also changing. Take the word 'boss' as an example. In one situation, an individual might be in charge of a project yet, in another, be just one of the team members.

By removing some of the titles – thus status – that had set up artificial barriers, people previously in very separate parts of the organization can mesh together. SKF has removed titles from its chart and business cards expressly for this purpose. Some units within IBM have eliminated both titles and reporting lines from their organigram so that employees can move and connect freely. In many Japanese companies – like Matsushita, Canon and Honda – the organization chart does not show individual names, titles, or positions. Only units and projects are featured, reflecting the collective processes at work.[32]

- *Moving the fast track sideways* is consistent with new structures and work values. While service workers don't want to stand still today, moving forward doesn't necessarily mean upwards. It can mean sideways. Since there are fewer ladders and fewer rungs, a career is no longer an arduous groping and climbing process. Instead, it's a series of interesting lateral projects. The opportunity to move from one to the next is what motivates and rewards people. Whereas, before, only managers became executives and those with professional expertise got stuck, anyone can in theory move on today. The difference is that a good deal of the career development is headed for key customer facing positions. A comment by one IBM executive is a typical opinion:

Before, we promoted people away from customers. The better they did the further away from them they got. Now, the idea is to keep good people and teams with and as close to customers for as long as possible. The customer contact is where many of our better people now go.

But, with better people in the key customer positions, the question is how to keep them there. In the past, staying with one customer would have been a signal of failure. Today, it's a compliment. In the late 1980s, an account manager at Citibank typically spent three to five years with one customer. Today the goal is ten, or even as many as fifteen years, for key accounts. Which means that career planning has to be revised in order to motivate talented staff to stay with customers for long periods of time.

- *Creating flexible sales targets* gives firms more opportunity for teaming individuals. The sales targets which once figured so prominently as *the* standard against which people were tested has lost some of its attraction because they are too short term to produce customer value, too shortsighted to foster long-term relationships and too self-centred for any real partnering. A few years earlier, it didn't matter that sales targets were an end rather than a means, because they led to the high-volume that management and employees wanted.

Today high-value firms use sales targets as one of several tools, making them as flexible as possible. Take AT&T's Commercial Market Group, which comes as close to eliminating the rigidity as any company could.

Before, its sales people fought each other to see who could make or beat monthly quotas. So much energy was spent on this activity that the customer often got left behind, and profitability on accounts suffered. To get people to work together for and with customers, sales targets are now more flexible, set as they are by the individuals themselves and, in some areas, they have even been dropped.

With teaming so altered in service-intensive organizations the notion of leadership has had to change as well:[33]

Then: leaders were all powerful and at the top of the ladder. They possessed special skills, insights and charisma.

Now: leaders are everywhere, disseminated throughout the teams. They are found especially on the customer facing and interfacing jobs in order that decision-making will lead to long-lasting relationships with customers.

Then: the role of leader was bestowed upon people, often because of their status or length of service.

Now: leaders are customer and project champions who energize the group by virtue of their enthusiasm, interest and know-how.

Then: leaders were empire builders. They inspired, then created layers to protect themselves.

Now: they are social architects who deliberately design systems so that teams can operate without them. They are also relational navigators – sometimes called 'cybernetic' leaders (from the Greek *kubernetes* meaning helmsman or steersman); their role is to keep their team on course by resolving conflicts or dilemmas along the way.[34]

Then: leaders were in charge of resources, deciding who got what and why.

Now: they are resource arbitrators and moderators who move resources around as necessary, maintaining a constant dialogue and resolving conflicts.

Then: the leader was the boss, there to command control, monitor and dictate.

Now: they coach, counsel and facilitate the performance of others much like a captain of a team.

The words of an executive from Digital vividly describe some of these differences:

Leaders in today's terminology must lead without memos, inspire without actually getting on the playing field to play ball themselves. They can only succeed if the people around them do well. So instead of pushing themselves, they must help others to perform. Before, when we decided whether a person was a good leader or whether a leader had done a good job, we looked at the average result he had gotten from his people. Now, we don't look at averages. We insist that everyone does well in the leader's orbit and is consistently improving.

Becoming skilled at being multi-skilled

Firms never tried to recruit people with various skills and talent when all they wanted was to fill neat slots to perform certain pre-set tasks. Nor were they concerned about having multi-skills portfolios. Most industrial corporations were dominated by one or two functions and the know-how that was accumulated tended to be built around these areas. Danny Miller, organization professor, in his analysis about how exceptional companies bring about their downfall, says there's a lesson to be learned here. In his book, *The Icarus Paradox*, he makes the following observation about industrial type firms:

> Its employees and managers develop a very particular knowledge base that resides in knowing how to do various tasks, but not in knowing why things are done the way they are. The upshot is that most organizations unreflectively absorb a highly constrained set of skills and favor workers whose capacities centre on a single technology. . . . Organizations learn only certain skills; those required to implement their current strategies; those corresponding to the knowledge of the managers and departments most valued by the corporate culture. Unfortunately, firms do not retain many other skills since they fail to recruit people with different talents.[35]

But this is antithetical to modern firms' needs. And because these firms must be able to do more things well doesn't mean they need more people; more likely, they need different people and a different skills mix. For, only if employees have capacities that spill across conventional lines can they achieve the greater advantage of combining specialist know-how with generalist applications, operating as they are within ill-defined and ever-changing environments. Only through a multi-faceted workforce and skills portfolio can they provide customers with a seamless and integrated flow of value. This insight is increasingly reflected in corporate recruiting and training:

- British Telecom has added retail experts at its main outlets to complement the technical skills the company has always had. There are two reasons for this step: first, these customer interfacing experts can be taught telephony quite easily; and second, they become role models for the technical wizards who, experience has shown, are more difficult to convert.
- In a similar vein, when Digital started its European maintenance system in France, it was discovered that two-thirds of the time spent on service calls actually went into transit activities. Digital found that teaching a taxi driver

how to repair computers was easier than teaching a technician the intricacies of the Paris back streets! So, the company hired taxi drivers with an interest in electronics and trained them accordingly.

● When The Maryland opened its service support centres, the company decided to hire people with caring personalities instead of just exceptional technical skills and experience. The logic was identical to that of British Telecom and Digital; The Maryland would be able to train these exceptional personalities about insurance, whereas imbuing technical types to be sensitive to customers was more difficult. In France, Sprinks hires people today in line with what the company is trying to do for its customers. It looks for working experience in medical, property, construction and whatever other fields are necessary to provide its customers with solutions.

● Only a couple of years ago, BP prided itself on the fact that it paid its station employees less than others in the industry. But it also had a massive staff turnover rate, inheriting its competitors' rejects. Before, the employee being hired had to do two things: sell petrol and fill in administrative forms. Now, BP recruits business manager types who have broad-based people and coordination skills, and who can exercise these skills with customers and employees in the station environment.

● Typically, SKF recruited engineers or sales people with bearing experience. Most of the company's training went into the technicalities of bearings. Now, SKF also hires people who have experience in its key markets – like automotive engineering or factory maintenance, and training is devoted to understanding key customer groups and becoming experts in advising them on trouble-free operations.

● Today, ICI also needs executives who are capable of more than just selling paint in the refinishing division. They are required to have a broad managerial skills base as well as an intimate understanding of their customers' operations, so that they can provide the body shops with help on financial matters, computer systems, shop layouts, customer promotions, training and general management in order to increase efficiencies and throughput.

● In the past, American Express employees were either good at authorization or payment, either they were travel experts or claims people. Like so many other firms, the company now expects customer contact employees to cover the full gamut of business activities for customers. Which means that they must have people with broader skill capabilities, as well as those who have a wider skills portfolio within branches or regions.

● Specialists from Matsushita who go into people's homes to provide human electronic solutions have to be sensitive to the customer on various levels. They are trained, therefore, not only in the technical intricacies of setting up and maintaining the actual equipment – like stereo and audio-visual sets – but also on understanding the technological complexities and possibilities for creating one integrated intelligent home environment. They are also trained to cater to individual situations and people, providing know-how on such things as the right location for a stereo system, what furniture to use, add-on features, and how to do self-inspection and maintenance.

The fact of the matter is that it takes a different kind of person to deliver value added in the modern enterprise. They must know the customer's business as well, if not better, than their own. Rather than who they are – their position or qualification – it's what they do within the business process that is important. The language is beginning to reflect this change. Firms such as IBM talk about 'solution architects' who understand the hard and software, 'opportunity managers' who detect a market, analyze and develop it, 'segment managers' responsible for all activities to develop applications, and 'practice leaders' who lead inter-company teams.

In the high-value enterprise, value is derived not from the machines producing scale volumes according to the standards set by the all know(ing) corporation, but from people. This know(ing) can't be easily controlled, contained or replicated. If such people are indeed to be the new service masters, where will their skills be found? Is there a service type? Are they born or made? Is the new service worker – concerned more about outcome than output – in a better position to deal with the immaterial than previous generations? All these questions and more are being asked and answered currently by corporate leaders as they try to develop service hearts and skills from within, and capture the new service enthusiasts from without. A certain amount of unlearning must take place first before existing industrial minds within their firms can change, and sometimes new blood must be brought in. It's tough to find people who have the correct mix – deep know(ing) with the wider capabilities – that fully enrich customer relationships. Yet, here is where the key to customer satisfaction lies.

7 Managing the stepping-stones to customer satisfaction

No profit grows where is no pleasure ta'en.

William Shakespeare, *The Taming of the Shrew*, 1593

Robert Pirsig, in what may be one of the most interesting discussions ever on quality, uses a motorcycle as an analogy in his search for an adequate definition. Through the reflections and debates of his principle characters, the metaphysical philosopher and novelist demonstrates the multiple dimensions of quality, pointing especially to its multi-faceted character and the dangers of over-simplifying its meaning.

In his book, *Zen and the Art of Motorcycle Maintenance*, Pirsig concludes that it has both an objective and subjective side. In the case of a motorcycle, the objective refers to the mechanical device itself – the way the pieces are put together. Here it is straightforward enough to measure and agree on quality since the construction of the machine and the material used are tangible. Then, there is the subjective side, where the issue of how to define quality becomes much more complex. For, it can only be through the person who sees or uses the motorcycle that an opinion can be expressed fully. So much are assessments based on feelings, personal associations and the relationship of an individual to the offering that a common point of reference on which to base quality is almost impossible.[1]

This mind-matter dilemma has been an intellectual hang-up for centuries, Pirsig admits. As it turns out, it's not a question of either one or the other being more important in evaluating quality: they are inseparable. Without the objective the motorcycle wouldn't work. As magnificent as it may be, though, without the subjective it would mean nothing because no one would appreciate it. This is no philosphical debate – the analogy applies perfectly to the business world. Moreover, real quality is only achieved when the objective and subjective meet. For then, as Pirsig suggests, the whole becomes greater than the sum of the two parts.

By the end of World War II, quality had become an established school of thought in corporate circles. Once the overriding principle was accepted by manufacturers, they concentrated on embedding quality more solidly into their daily production activities. No effort was spared to get quality onto the assembly line. To make 'things' ever-more perfect became *the* priority in the post-war decades as, in their search for greater efficiency, high-volume firms strove to control the core inputs and outputs of their offerings more rigorously, and thereby maintain their competitiveness.

Although more slowly, the service sector also adopted quality as a major theme. Singled out for poor customer delivery, and with competitive pressure mounting, by the mid-1980s traditional service firms began to accept that being without a formal quality system was as absurd for them as for manufacturing concerns to be without process controls. In a scurry to counter potential customer losses, they turned to manufacturing quality tools in the hope that, by standardizing their intangible products – through engineering concepts – they could improve their market position.[2]

This was all very well then. Dealing as they were in tangible 'things', managers – particularly in products but in services as well – could treat quality fairly objectively, pre-setting hard and fast standards and measures. With sufficient controls – from bank loans to bulk feed and from phones to computers – they could continue to focus on reducing technical defects to the bare minimum in order to gain an edge on the competition. Flaws in 'things' not fully eliminated during production could be removed before reaching the customer. Their feedback was largely quantifiable, because what firms wanted to know related to the objective attributes of their offerings. And since assessments were based on hard evidence, any disagreement between buyers and sellers was not really a major concern.

However important quality may have become by the 1990s, much of the thinking and procedures in corporations continued to be designed for industrial settings. Superior products and services may have continued to come into the market through improved quality efficiencies but without the commensurate customer satisfaction which firms had expected. Productivity may have increased, due to the industrialization techniques which slashed away at costs and reduced human deviations, but unfortunately many times at the expense of high-quality delivery. Instead of improving quality standards, initiatives it seemed were antithetical to creating the value-adding capabilities that firms needed to compete profitably.[3]

Firms which profoundly understood what their customers valued, would have to change their approach to quality to increase their chances of success. There was certainly one lesson to be learned from the 1960s, 1970s and 1980s on this subject. In a world that requires close relationships, measuring pre-determined standards was hopelessly inadequate. For sure, any worthwhile quality system needed objective measures and methods. But, first and foremost, managers had to understand what was important. When they had judged quality solely on objective and hard criteria, they had lost instead of gained this insight. Veering out into the market now, they found that the subjective factors – though uncertain, vague and difficult to identify, express and appraise – played a more serious role in customer satisfaction. The behavioural factors, so critical to forming relationships, would be the key to influencing customers' quality assessments.

Constructs in quality had become very different from industrial precepts:

Then: the expectations of employees and customers were sometimes at odds.

Now: the vital link between how employees feel and what customers want is acknowledged.

Then: quality was concerned with input and output – the substance of the offering.

Now: how services are being performed – i.e. the process – is most essential.

Then: products and services were completely standardized, making measures of efficiency easy to set, monitor and compare.

Now: with mass custom-alized offerings moulded to suit 'markets within markets' and 'segments of one', each encounter between the firm and its customers is totally different, so as to make traditional quality approaches outmoded.

Then: quality was seen as discrete and measurable, fixed at a moment in time inside the firm's space.

Now: quality is a series of high value-added events, part of an ongoing flow of activities stretching over time inside the customer's space.

Then: quality was related to attributes that were visible and concrete.

Now: making things work for customers determines how well a firm's performance is perceived.

Then: quality was interpreted by formal specifications, contracts and agreements.

Now: quality is part of the informal social contract that characterizes new partnering concepts.

Making the subject the object

The Japanese, we are told, were the first actually to implement quality programmes inside corporations. They combined Western precision and cost-based tools with their own thoroughly cultivated human perspective on business, transforming Japan from a low-status, low-quality economy to one of the most successful in the world. This accomplishment was made largely by their dedication to quality.[4] W. Edwards Deming, the American statistician, not only succeeded in formalizing quality methods and techniques in Japanese business, but he also made quality accepted on a corporate-wide basis as a creed – almost a religion – that was practised by everyone in a firm. While he insisted on hard quality standards, he is credited with also having pushed beyond the numbers, insisting that it was only the customer who ultimately could decide whether or not an offering had quality.

Deming fashioned a new quality culture which spread across the world. By the mid-1980s, firms realized that without this quality culture, they were vulnerable. By the 1990s, they had also learned that, even with these quality techniques, they were still at risk unless they used tools based on value added for their customers. The fact that customers claimed to be satisfied on a survey sheet didn't mean a thing in and of itself. What, firms began to ask, was missing from their carefully worked out formulas for quality?

Andrea Gabor, a business journalist, attempts to answer this rather complex question in her book, *The Man Who Discovered Quality*, which specifically examines the life and work of Deming. She refers to Ford's experience to demonstrate how far off firms were from understanding customer motivation. Ford executives found that if customers didn't have any concrete problems with their car, that didn't mean they were necessarily happy with it. They may have been satisfied with certain attributes but, at the same time, equally dissatisfied with other – perhaps even more important – aspects. And, in this particular case, customer satisfaction had been based on attributes that weren't even being measured.[5]

Given that their full needs weren't being met, many customers were quick to migrate to other suppliers during the latter part of the industrial era. By the 1990s, firms were finally aware that trying to do the same things better was not leading to an improvement in quality as perceived by their customers. It seemed that internal metrics did not mean a great deal to firms unless managers were first able to determine what it was they should really be measuring to get results customers wanted. Some examples follow:

● Of course, customers expected packages to arrive on time. But, Federal Express discovered that they also wanted to know how their packages were doing at any given moment. Previously, as far as the firm was concerned, so long as there was 100 per cent on-time delivery, service standards had been met.

● AT&T was renowned for telephone services that were technically good by any standards, and customer surveys repeatedly showed the same pattern: customers were satisfied. After digging more deeply, however, the company found, that although the score given was high on the services being provided, it was what customers were *not* getting that lured them to competitors.

● When Nokia-Maillefer was selling cable machinery, product features and delivery deadlines were all important, and this is how its quality levels were expressed. But, in moving to productive capacity, the company soon discovered that customers judged quality by how quickly the production lines were operative, and whether or not more and cheaper cable could be produced relative to the past.

● Matsushita came to realize that what makes customers really unhappy is not just a delay in installation time, it's that during installation no one was advising them about the broader ramifications of their electronic systems, such as where in the home to put the audio set, or that certain carpets should be used and others avoided. Because of this customers were receiving inferior performance from superior machines.

● When Zurich Insurance Canada began to really delve into customer expectations, what did it find? Not what had been assumed, that customers wanted to move into a fancy hotel in the event of a burglary or fire. In fact, they preferred to stay in their homes or, at least get back to them as quickly as possible. So the company's thinking had to be adjusted and processes rebuilt to speed up renovation and rehabilitation.

● Hendrix Voeders could easily sell more if it raised the quality of its feed thereby getting pigs to eat more. But fatter pigs don't necessarily mean higher quality meat, nor do they automatically lead to better prices for farmers. What end users want – and retailers now demand – is meat from farmers whose animals are also healthy, nutritious and well cared for, having lived in the best possible conditions.

● Citibank's computers were up and running 99 per cent of the time, available to customers for their electronic financial management transactions. But due to congested lines and inadequate capacity, customers had trouble getting to the service. And by the time they were able to get into the system, a large chunk of their day had been wasted.

● For SKF, the real value of a bearing is when no one knows it's there. The best maintenance a customer can receive from Digital or IBM is probably no need for maintenance at all, they say. Insurance firms like Zurich Insurance and Kansa believe that preventing the loss for a customer is as important as paying the claim. Real quality lies in having a non-event rather than in rectifying something that has happened.

Viewing quality through customers' eyes is thus not just a matter of adjusting input or output. It requires updating and designing continuously different processes and activities that do something for and with customers. Ascertaining expectations is often a complex task. Neither firms nor customers can anticipate exactly what will be needed or when. Unlike the purchase of a product, customers do not always know what is involved in reaching a solution and so tend to change their minds along the way. To complicate this still further, in services, customer expectations depend on too many unknown factors. There is nothing really tangible that customers can see before they buy, so they largely rely on previous experience and word of mouth. And, as to whether or not expectations were met, responses can be as diverse as the human psyche itself, influenced by factors ranging from the time of day to the psychological state of the person at that moment.

Typically, solutions will involve more than one customer. All the various and diverse expectations thus have to be uncovered and satisfied. The buyer that Citibank encounters – a treasurer handling international finance for a large multinational corporation – may have a set of priorities that are very different from those of business managers who actually use an electronic cash management system. Procedures must be simple and easy for sales people to use in American Express merchant outlets, whereas accountants want forms and systems that can be well controlled.

Any discrepancy between what customers expect and perceive they get can negatively impact relationships.[6] Especially if it happens often or the cost of error to the client is high. So over and above having to understand the nature of customer expectations, high-value firms ask whether they are in a position to shape them. Rather than just create demand, they also make an effort to match what customers want and what the company is able to do. At the same time, modern managers look for ways to extend what they can do to a level exceeding competitors to be always one step ahead. It's always better for both parties to understand what's expected and what's possible. If managing quality in services is indeed 'keeping promises' to deliver results, as one executive from Nokia-Maillefer suggests, then one way or another the expectations of both the firm and the customer must be synchronized. And this, he adds, depends on a sense of reciprocity and trust that cannot always be captured in a formal document. He develops this idea further:

> Not so long ago, what customers expected and what we thought we had promised were not the same thing. Now, we try to make sure that doesn't happen. They want something done and we want to do the doing. We can put some of what they expect down in writing, and we do that in order to avoid misunderstanding. But, most of it we can't. Somehow we both have to understand what is possible and what's necessary, and then make it work.

For present-day firms, understanding and meeting customers' expectations and those of employees is inextricably bound up. The simple fact is: in services, the offering and the employee are inseparable. This has always been the case, but now with reliance on know-how, it's no marginal issue. Increasingly, the behavioural dimension – or how people interact – impacts on the potential of long-term customer relationships. And, needless to say, the state of a relationship affects a customer's perception of service quality.

Regardless of individual employees' level within the firm, their morale influences the quality of performance at that critical moment of truth where company and customer meet. This theme has been picked up by several writers recently. Leonard Schlesinger and James Heskett, who have carefully researched the area together, conclude that there is a cycle of failure in services directly related to poor employee morale and motivation. Several of their articles explain how service firms have found that dissatisfied employees create a syndrome which culminates in unhappy customers and, eventually, makes a dent in the company's profits. Not only do motivated people provide better quality services, they say, but also the expensive supervision so characteristic of industrial models becomes redundant.[7]

There are two dimensions of employee behaviour that are important in this context. The first is how well an employee performs technically, something that is usually easy to do and copy. The second, is how well the employee relates to the customer, which can be an entirely different story. It is both the most significant part of the relationship and the most difficult to accomplish. Firms like Matsushita now focus more energy on this latter aspect, having discovered that this is where the potential for quality lies. It is only by developing and harnessing correct attitudes and behaviour among staff, the company believes, that it can maintain its edge. Its approach is to have all the relationships between the company and its employees of the same high standard that is demanded between it and its customers on the front line. Just as employees are expected to empathize with customers, so the company tries to empathize with staff. Matsushita wants its employees to identify opportunities for customers; also, similar efforts are made by the company for its staff. The company demands that its employees be responsive to customers, so it makes sure that it too is correspondingly responsive.

Motivated service workers are apt to stay longer with a firm and thus keep the institutional learning within. Customers like to deal with familiar faces; and when this happens they will remain loyal for longer and give the firm a larger slice of their business. This fact shouldn't be underestimated, say firms like Price Waterhouse. Two partners can deliver the identical service and get a different quality response from the customer. It has nothing to do with substance of the delivery, which is exactly the same; it comes from the strength of the relationship. Customers want to keep these associations longer than in previous times. Earnings per customer are directly linked to the length of the relationship between the account executive and its corporate customers, Citibank has found.

But, if customers are to receive entire working solutions, quality must encompass the whole service-providing chain. For modern service enterprises, this means enlarging their quality horizons and initiatives beyond traditional boundaries:

Then: quality was confined to a corporation's own operations.
Now: quality initiatives extend throughout the whole distribution channel.
Then: quality was a local issue, to be managed on a geographic basis.
Now: customers increasingly view quality either regionally or globally – a bad experience in one country or area affects their overall assessment of the firm's performance.
Then: quality levels were left to individual corporations to implement.
Now: the solution providers coordinate standards and efforts so as to provide one, ongoing value-adding flow for customers.
Then: firms competed head on for quality.
Now: in their combined efforts to serve customers, they collaborate as well in their quality programmes.

To demonstrate, here are some examples:

- Through questionnaires and one-on-one discussions with fleet owners, Volvo Trucks solicits direct customer feedback from the market about the performance of its dealers. The results are then discussed with the dealers and, jointly, ways are found to adapt existing practices so as to increase the customers' satisfaction.

- Similarly, Honda surveys end users several times a year and shares the responses with its dealers to help them keep track of customer usage patterns and feelings. The company has also developed several training programmes for the dealers' staff – including examinations for engineers and technicians so that they can advance in their chosen professions. Service quality specialists, each dedicated to twelve to fifteen dealer clients, advise on how to improve quality performance and offer help with implementation.

- There's no point in giving pigs special care throughout their growth if, en route to the slaughterhouse, they become stressed, ill or hurt. Hendrix Voeders can't drive every truck that carries these animals, but it can select carefully those who do. The company does not try to deal with every minute detail involved in getting pigs from farmyards to consumers' tables, but it does set standards and early warning systems to monitor for effective outcomes.

- What IBM customers now want is consistent quality worldwide. As an example, Lufthansa Germany, which once left quality to the various countries to handle, expects service delivery to be identical at the 148 airports in which they operate around the globe. Under the auspices of the global account manager, quality standards – both technical and relational – now have to be coordinated and enforced extra-territorially.

- The only way to ensure that quality is consistent throughout Japan, Canon believes, is by assembling key people on the front line from the 1,600 dealerships so that data and experiences can be shared. Members of the network meet three times a year, to look for commonalities in complaints and customer feedback. They debate alternatives for improvement and set quality priorities, all of which is coordinated by Canon on an ongoing basis.

- On shared routes, Singapore Airlines merges its quality standards with those of its partners. Swissair, for instance, is typically better at some activities – such as serving drinks, because it has superior trolley services. Whereas Singapore is better at, say, serving meals which is done course by course. Rather than change their respective quality imperatives, these airlines jointly try to come up with new quality concepts on their shared routes.

A new alchemy for quality

When the Greeks first had debates about 'quality', about 700 years BC, they placed it in the same league as aesthetics – and, consequently, its definition was as complex as that of beauty.[8] These Hellenic philosophers played with the idea that it was easier to define what quality wasn't than what it was. Thus, the meaning of quality was not so much in its presence as in its absence. They also defined quality in terms of harmony – the perfect balance between opposing forces. The beauty of a face was not in the individual features, they said, it was all the features combined. To achieve a high-quality sound on a lyre, it was necessary to find the exact balance between the tension of the string and the distance it should be pulled. Architecture was built on the idea of quality as harmony: the dimensions of width, breadth, height and depth must be arranged in such a way that the angles create a sense of balance, perspective, stability and uniqueness.

Philosophically, these ideas were perhaps closer to the ones expressed today than those of previous decades. The Greeks looked at how things fit together and related to the whole instead of what each part represented in isolation. Quality was difficult to define, they said, but when it was missing, it was easily noticed. The forces brought to bear on managers during the era of mass production dictated that quality had to be visible, measurable and discrete. It was logical that quality initiatives were designed to improve product, people and process attributes. Any deviation from their set norm – whether physical or behavioural – was regarded as a defect that was undesirable and dysfunctional. For all intents and purposes, quality was conformance.

Much of this conformance was achieved by restraining employees. This way, firms reasoned, quality – whether in products, services or processes – could be controlled. Locked in, employees on the front line in classic service settings stuck to job descriptions, procedures, rules and regulations which, rather than producing better quality services, all too often compounded rather than solved service quality problems. As Leonard Berry and A.Parasuraman, two leaders in service quality, say, employees became good at regimented by-the-book services, when flexible by-the-customer services was what was really needed. In their book, *Marketing Services: Competing Through Quality*, they reiterate:

> Human beings were not meant to be robots. Yet managers treat them this way when they use their thick policy and procedure manuals to severely limit employees' freedom of action in delivering services. Rule book management undermines employee confidence in managers, stifles employee personal growth and creativity, and chases the most able employees out the door in search of more interesting work.[9]

Taken to an extreme, as it often was, this approach flew in the face of customer satisfaction initiatives. Particularly solutions, where quality unfolds over time. This doesn't suggest that rules and measures be completely dispensed with. However, as each encounter is unique, rules should serve merely as guides rather than as dictates, and measures must be linked to the output as received and perceived by customers rather than just the input. Citibank in New York rewards its frontliners on their ability to bend the rules if circumstances demand it in the interest of customer satisfaction. Questionnaires ask customers specifically whether or not this has occurred and, if so, employees are positively rated. The objective is to develop a flexible frame of mind ensuring that from the customer's point of view the outcome is always successful.

In a sense, it is the characteristics of quality itself which have changed. Classic product-based linear and mechanistic type ideas on quality are being replaced by those more fitting to modern customer satisfying settings. Perhaps it's more accurate to say that these new ideas on quality are not so much substitutes for the old as they are complementary – both being crucial for high-value performance. (Figure 7.1 compares industrial and service quality concepts.)

There can be no improvement if there are no standards. And variations on these standards are being constantly made narrower as firms try to keep their

Industrial	Service
Minimal variation lack deviation	**Maximum adaptation** capacity to respond
Right first time don't get it wrong	**Relevant through time** make it work
Attribute properties physical composition	**Experience properties** functioning performance
Zero defects no physical faults	**No vacuum** no interruption in flow
Fitness for use put value in	**Ability customer to use** get value out
Rigidity standards stick to rules	**Resilience system** ability to return to equilibrium self renew
Uniformity everything same	**Consistency** able to repeat
Durability it lasts	**Reliability** it is dependable
Cause and effect direct correlation	**Reactions and interactions** find solution

Figure 7.1 Industrial and service models for quality

core good as economic as possible for the 'generic within markets'. Federal Express, along with many other firms, places an enormous premium on these standards. It gives employees 120 seconds to complete an order and itemizes daily, in minute detail, the number of abandoned calls, and missing or damaged parcels. But beyond that, quality in services demands a capacity to respond to 'the markets within markets' and 'customers within customers'. This can only happen if the system allows maximum adaptation of both measures and methodology, so that employees can respond freely and adjust their behaviour to specific people and circumstances – in real time. The fact that the firm focuses on the numbers doesn't stop the 25,000 couriers from handling a problem as they see fit, including giving advice on alternative services if necessary.

Equally it is important to get it right the first time – no one wants mistakes, neither firms nor customers. Doing it right is also vital for spreading benefits internally. But accuracy doesn't necessarily mean efficacy. The trap into which industrial minds fell was that they believed avoiding mistakes was good. Avoiding mistakes was indeed good – but not good enough. In a learning environment, two things quickly become apparent: the first is that services which are done with minimum variation – right first time – are invariably routine: anyone can do them just as well: and customers take them pretty much for granted. Second, if employees are to learn while doing, engaged in a dynamic process of continuous and joint development with customers, well-worn tenets like 'getting it right' are somewhat simplistic. It's more appropriate to make the offering relevant throughout time. These questions have to be asked: Is the service what customers really need? Has this need changed? Can we talk through the options? Are we able to adapt to circumstances?

Electronic cash management services for corporate clients was accurate at Citibank. The problem was that customers wanted systems made simple and effective so as to minimize time taken. Which raises the next point – the difference between attribute and experience quality properties. In the former, quality is defined as the physical composition of the offering. For bearings or computers, this represents the material constituents of the product. In services like banking, they are such 'things' as interest rates, monthly investment sheets, cheque books, running statements and so on. Functioning perform-ance, involves a lot more: how well the whole system works for customers. New performance criteria have had to be set based on the experiences of users with the system. Quality was seen as achieving zero defects by industrial firms – no physical faults in a product at a moment in time – usually when something tangible was handed over to customers. Service-based concepts, on the other hand, work towards processes which have been set up to facilitate smooth operations, avoiding vacuums or any potential interruptions in the delivery flow. Now Citibank customers get all the information they need through one technological door on their PCs whereas just a couple of years ago customers would have had to spend an inordinate amount of time moving in and out of systems. Time is the one thing its large multinational customers can't afford: so now Citibank provides enough capacity for round-the-clock utilization.

Fitness for use rested upon product-based assumptions about quality – did an offering have the basic ingredients to make it work? But what goes into the offering is just the starting point. Quality includes what needs to be done so that customers can get the value out. Security passwords have to change regularly for the bank's customers. Before, clients were expected to know the new password and, if they didn't, it was their bad luck. Today, with results based on speed and quality based on results, customers receive warning signs and reminders that eliminate undue congestion.

If bank employees expect a blockage, their customers are told, and an alternative way is found for them to proceed with the transaction. The system – both the technological and human side – is built with sufficient redundancy so that it can absorb failure and blows, and spring back again. Rigid standards, no matter how high, are recognized as a vehicle, a means to a desired end rather than the end in itself. Which leads to consistency. In high-volume days, everything had to *be* the same because everybody *was* the same. Consistency has a very different nuance. Customers get the same high-quality services whenever or wherever because their activities are coordinated throughout the network globally. For routine services, this may mean that the substance of the offering has to be identical. But, more importantly, it's the process that must be consistent to ensure that customers receive the same high quality treatment repeatedly.

Quality meant durability of products – they were made to last – and, if broken, could be repaired. But, what if such a product was used badly, as in the case of SKF? Or in circumstances other than what was anticipated, as the Citibank example demonstrates? Reliability in services has to do with making the system work for customers, notwithstanding these complications. It means that through employee behaviour, customers know that something will take place at a future point in time.

Cause and effect relationships were the hallmark of engineering quality techniques. And, if two tellers out of five are missing during peak hours, there's no doubt that it will lead to dissatisfaction among customers. But does having five tellers ensure that there will be high-quality services? Obviously not. Experience and research show that quality as defined by modern firms can only be achieved through reactions and interactions on the front line. Which also means that if customers are given an explanation of why there are not enough tellers on duty, the level of dissatisfaction can be considerably diminished.

Why do cause and effect scenarios have limited application these days? Because they tend to look at an unchanging set of conditions in the short term. Apart from relationships spanning longer periods, services processes just don't always proceed with predictable regularity. Cause and effect may be useful in simple transactions but how complex relationships will finally unfold is much more uncertain. An executive from Citibank explains his company's experiences in an interesting way:

> Cause and effect is useful for common cases and routine services because a mishap or gap can be traced back to a particular source. We have a whole host of statistical tools to measure cause and effect, but for special cases – where we touch the customer or they touch us – which is the majority of cases now, they don't work. Faults can't be localized to one event or individual. It's a combination of things that cause the problem and, when this happens, the process needs to be understood as a whole.

He goes on to say that the only way to rectify these service failures is to get everyone who is active in the process together. Until recently, there were mounds of data on what went wrong and which standards had not been met, but no one really knew why or took responsibility to improve matters. What the bank does now is to bring these people together into problem-solving workshops. Rather than make anyone feel responsible for the problem, the effort concentrates in giving everyone a powerful sense of involvement, so that they own the resolution. Rather than being told what to do based on a rigid scheme, they redesign the process together and implement the changes.

Carrying the genetic code

Dennis Gabor won the Nobel Prize in the 1950s for inventing the theoretical principle of holography, which he later constructed using a laser. His optical system was a special sort of photography where a slide recorded a pattern of light coming from two sources after an initial beam was split up. What he found was that each individual part of the picture he had captured contained the whole in a condensed form.[10]

Before Gabor, it was thought that parts made up the whole. His work revealed that each part is both a part of the whole and a smaller version of the whole. He demonstrated in a very concrete way, says Gareth Morgan in *Images of Organization*, that it is indeed possible to create processes which reveal that within the entire system all the parts are encoded with each and every bit representing it and each other. Another interesting feature of a hologram, as it is called, is that if it is broken, any piece can reconstruct it, so there is ongoing recovery and renewal.[11]

Several disciplines had, each in its own way, shown that a holographic concept holds. In biology, Watson and Crick had proved that each cell throughout the body – skin, bone, hair, blood, nerves – of every creature carries the same genetic code. Each cell has the same mark, brand and identification despite having different life cycles and *raison d'être*. Stephen Gould, known for his work in biology and natural history, describes how a given trait is carried over many generations. In his book, *The Flamingo's Smile*, he illustrates how even though a breed may go through changes over time, these traits are locked into a genetic code which preserves whatever it is that lives on.[12] And in mathematics, Mandelbrot proved in both algebraic and computational terms that, no matter how many times an image is broken up, the same pattern will always appear. So in theory, if, using the correct equipment, a picture the size of a pin-prick were taken of the tip of someone's nose, the face of that individual could be discerned in it.[13]

If it's true that the whole can be interspersed in all of the parts, how does this relate to the modern service enterprise? In many ways, writers maintain who have tried to tackle this question. This phenomenon need not be limited to science – there are some equally valid implications for business, they say. One of the advocates is British academic Ronnie Lessem who, in the book *Total Quality Learning*, discusses his work on quality and learning within corporations:

> Within a holographic organizational universe, then, the whole, albeit in condensed form, is contained within each part. The appreciation and manifestation of such a whole, within whatever part, is the essence of quality. Moreover, the more intense the awareness of the whole, within each part, the more total the quality.[14]

Evert Gummesson, a Swedish professor focusing his research on service firms, agrees that this idea becomes all the more significant for these operations. People quite literally represent the company on the interface when they meet customers, he says in his essay, 'Organizing for Marketing and the Marketing Organization'.[15] The organization is expressed through its employees and, indeed, they *are* the organization. Unless all employees understand what the firm stands for, they cannot handle customer contact effectively nor provide the unbroken flow of services necessary for customer satisfaction. In a manner of speaking, the employees carry the genetic quality code, which is what ultimately delivers the ongoing consistency. This capability comes from applying some basic yet vital principles:

- *Employees are proxies for the corporation when they have to perform –* they become the company at that moment. Folklore at Singapore Airlines includes a tale about a supervisor who, late one night, was confronted by an angry customer who had just been told that his baggage was lost. By midnight, a tailor had been found and hired and, by morning, a new suit was ready for the customer who had to be at an important meeting by 8 a.m.
- *Employees must be able to substitute for each other –* the image of a company's service as ever present and seamless can never work unless

people are able to represent both the firm and their colleagues. When a customer calls into Federal Express, the person answering the phone is obliged to handle the query. If it is not possible, then that individual is responsible for making the correct connection. Each employee at a Kansa branch is primed to handle all customers. Settling a claim can be done by anyone, including sales or administrative people. When customers phone the service centre at The Maryland, the call is automatically routed to the person the client usually deals with – someone who is familiar. If that individual is unavailable, someone else gets the details of the account electronically and takes over.

Meshing the hard and the soft measures

Developing contemporary frameworks for service quality certainly does not reduce the need for managers to judge performance. On the contrary, as competition toughens, and *what* to look for changes, managers must decide *how* to measure appropriately. For measure quality they must, even though the methods they apply are becoming less rigid and precise. Behavioural dimensions feature strongly in new quality measuring systems.

For example, the Royal Bank of Canada finds that over a third of its customers value friendly, courteous, helpful staff above any technical consideration. With the competence of the people making repairs taken for granted, Matsushita customers now ask: were they sensitive to my home setup? Did they identify with my sense of urgency? How did they make me feel? For firms like Federal Express and British Telecom – which rely on the telephone for a lot of their customer contact – having clarity in communication, easy-to-understand accents, empathy and sensitivity in voice transfer are special quality considerations. Then, of course, when it comes to a company like Digital, the deep know-how which is now so all-important to customer relationships requires a completely different measuring approach than the hardware did.

Firms talk about getting a 'proxy' on customer satisfaction rather than just the hard facts when they sell solutions modules which are more about know(ing) and doing than making and moving 'things'. Dealing with customers over long periods of time means that quality perceptions can be subject to many interferences and influences. On this score, managers say, the best they can hope for is to make sure that they are on the right wavelength with customers and that their relationships are strong enough to be alerted to and rectify any mishaps in good time. That's not to say that the hard measuring methods no longer exist. They still do, and they include a variety of process control systems, logical tools, figures and indices, all of which serve their purpose. Not least of which is the fact that these methods enable managers to communicate to their employees some of the fruits and flaws of

Hard	Soft
Calculate	Assess
Quantify	Observe
Mass/average	Individual/customer specific
Figures	Language
Single-level	Multiple level
Static	Directional
Inspect	Reflect
Change	Improve
Schedule	Prioritize
Replicate	Originate
Set routine	Improvise

Figure 7.2   Hard and soft quality measures

their activities. Hendrix Voeders, for instance, works in three decimal points when it comes to measuring the pigs' weight. A 0.2 per cent difference in this weight – between one herd and another – can mean the difference between breaking even and really doing well for farmers.

Working in an immaterial world brings added challenges as managers have to measure both the hard and soft aspects of their firms' service delivery (see Figure 7.2). This means somehow combining soft methodology with hard appraisal methods, to reflect more of the know-how and relational dimensions of quality. Estimations, which were previously based on strict statistical calculations, now include assessment in general as well as more emphasis on self-assessment. Quantified data collected as feedback is matched by observations to get a better interpretation of the real reactions and interactions between service workers and customers.[16]

More and more, the figures are being replaced or supplemented by language and metaphor. Industrial instruments left little room for nuance. Any language being used was usually reduced to a simple 'yes/no', which was exactly the object of the exercise, when technical logic and rigorous survey techniques reigned supreme. Sheets were designed for standardization, with data easily transferrable into numbers. But what firms got were averages. What percentage of the time did planes leave on schedule? How many complaints came in for audio systems that week? How long did employees take to answer the phone? Without undermining this part of the quality assessment exercise, high-value firms see the need for a fuller picture than just the straight data to capture the customer's experiences. And sometimes they get this best through the use of language, says Matsushita, where firms can get much closer to understanding customer responses. Here's how one executive from that company expressed it:

> You cannot calculate the way customers 'feel' about a service through the numbers. It's in the language that you get a proper feeling about customers' impressions. You have to translate that back into some assessment instrument the company can use.

The point that Matsushita and several other firms make is that measures of how well firms are doing, say on a scale of 1–10, are sterile without the enrichment of the softer measures. Statistics are also not very useful for telling an employee what to do to next, whereas interpretation of the language and feedback from observation can be very helpful here. Like Matsushita, Citibank often has a coach present at customer encounters to get feedback on providers' skills and look for ways to improve their performance. It also investigates what happens when customers phone in. In the past, the company simply checked to see how quickly phones were being picked up and queries answered. Now, trying to ascertain the level of rapport between its employees and clients, it spends resources increasingly on monitoring and assessing the softer behavioural attributes.

For high-value firms, the reactions of individuals is what matters. Industrial-based techniques were mass tools designed for the 'mass within markets'. Acknowledging this, managers today are revising feedback mechanisms so that they reflect the feelings and reactions of 'markets within markets' and, more importantly, the individuals within those target groups. Assessments are likely to be more similar for tangible 'things', making averages more useful than in services, where perceptions are individualistic. Pushing still further, some firms not only want feedback from customers but they also want a better understanding of the one-on-one contact between the individuals providing services and those receiving them. For example:

● Before, statistics would inform Matsushita how its installation technicians were doing and, if 80 per cent got good ratings from customers, that was okay. Now, when an individual goes into a customer's home to repair or install electronic equipment, the company measures how well that individual did with that particular customer and why. By getting rid of averages, Matsushita believes it can improve the quality of each encounter.

● Citibank, in measuring its ability to make the bank work for corporate customers, categorizes them into five 'zones' so reflecting the strength of its relationship with each client. At one extreme, the relationship is sporadic; at the other, it's a real partnership, involving total immersion and a first call on business. Questions such as these are asked: What have we talked about with this customer and how often do we talk? What's the level of the discussion? How available is their information and how accessible are their key people to us? At what level in the firm are we dealing? What ideas have we given them during this period?

Assessments are made by account management and regional coordinators within the network. Rather than stick to single-level assessments, they get feedback on multiple levels, wherever the bank and customers connect. It is in both the details of this data and its synthesis that service quality lies ultimately. Interestingly, though, when Citibank comes to do the grading, it is the direction of the relationship rather than only earnings from the account *per se* that concerns management. The principle it works on is that investment in high-quality customer relationships will, by definition, bring profits. Thus, what Citibank is striving to achieve is upward movement in desired client relationships.

For most lead corporations, inspection of quality continues but with one key difference: the firm as a whole, as well as individual employees, will reflect on their experiences and assessments rather than merely accept static data, as either black or white. Of all the challenges in quality, the constant enhancement of delivery – both technical and behavioural – is at the crux. Formerly, managers strove to find flaws and correct them, usually having to make huge changes in the process. Once done, they assumed the problem was solved: today, quality is regarded as an ongoing exercise. This notion underlies '*Kaizen*', a philosophic base made popular by the successes of the Japanese in achieving quality. Kaizen, literally meaning ongoing improvement, starts from the premise that real quality can never be attained – it is a never-ending commitment to constantly improve quality, making adjustments incrementally as the firm learns.[17] Measuring is therefore no longer a set routine which replicates exactly what has been done before. People improvise, get and give feedback when appropriate, and extract from the plethora of information what they need to make useful assessments to enhance customer satisfaction.

Managing expectations through the customer's activity cycle

High-value relationships depend on each and every encounter received and perceived by customers to differing degrees, depending on how they are weighted in importance by them. A vacuum, or gap, in the seamless flow of value adding diminishes the customer's experience and overall quality of the offering. It also can jeopardize getting the desired result. As the solution is the actual process – from making the bank work for customers to trouble-free operations – it means that each critical point in the customer's activity cycle is an opportunity to satisfy or dissatisfy.

As Federal Express says, fulfilling customer expectations any one day is as important as the day before or the day after. Each facet of a bank customer's operation – from the currency desk at peak trading time to the switchboard operator – is a vital part of the quality link in Digital's delivery of networking systems. It's no good converting 1 kg of food into 2.5 kg of pig weight, Hendrix Voeders acknowledges, if that added weight is not evenly distributed so as to ensure that animals are both fat and healthy. After putting some of the company's best people at the receiving end of the telephone wire, American Express was amazed that customers were still unhappy and migrating. They subsequently realized that the process had been blocked because it took too long for employees to answer the phone – customers simply gave up.

So, to produce the results that customers seek, quality criteria – both objective and subjective, technical and behavioural – must be aligned to the customer's activity cycle over the entire re-occurring process. Take Honda, for instance. Intent on providing individual mobility for customers in keeping with their lifestyles and working patterns, the company set standards of performance for dealers during each critical value point in these auto owners' activity cycles – from the moment the first contact is made. One growing market for Honda are Japanese who frequently use their own car when doing business in China. Included in the quality criteria during their pre-purchase stage are numerous requirements such as: the ability of the dealer to decipher and translate travelling and usage patterns into a custom-made solution, with such special features as warranties and insurance; the depth of the dealer's knowledge about how to facilitate a good decision; and willingness to share information on options, going beyond normal working arrangements to accommodate customers with heavy work schedules. During the purchase stage, the company is concerned with the details of whether or not the customer received what was expected. Were the warranties correct, the insurance complete, the features as agreed? The post-purchase stage includes performance and speediness of repairs and servicing, particularly whether or not technicians explained why things had gone wrong, how to avoid future problems and reoccurrences, as well as any other relevant information even if not specifically requested. Also important to this particular customer segment is how quickly they can find assistance while away from home.

At each of these phases, Honda sends a questionnaire to its users. Additionally, for a three-year period, a comprehensive survey is done annually to determine how well the customers and the car are living together, and to what extent the advice given originally has added value to their travelling experience. The survey tries to ascertain: Has the usage pattern been too high or low? Was the correct decision made at the beginning? Did everything that was expected and promised happen during the process? In this way, dealers can judge retrospectively their original advice and overall delivery capability with a view to improving performance once the cycle restarts.

Major criteria for performance jointly make up an overall quality rating, but high-value firms recognize that this overall score means very little in isolation. Therefore, they analyse service performance at each and every critical value

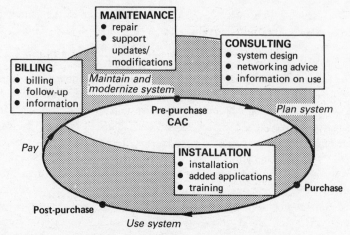

Figure 7.3   Critical value points in customers' activity cycle: AT & T

point in the customer's activity cycle. Here are some examples to demonstrate:

The process begins for AT&T General Business Systems customers with the design of the interpersonal communication system. The system is installed and, once operative, services are billed; then, the scheme is kept going through maintenance and modification services, until the technology is updated and the cycle repeats itself (see Figure 7.3). No aspect of what determines quality within the process is left to chance by AT&T. The criteria along each step of the way is intended to emphasize – both in effort and measures – those factors more heavily weighted by customers (see Figure 7.4 for a summary with weightings).

From the breeding of the pigs through their maturity and processing to the distribution and sale of the meat, Hendrix Voeders are involved in quality criteria to obtain the results farmers are after (see Figure 7.5 together with Figure 4.5). During the pre-purchase stage, it is the connection between the farmers, and the consultants and account team that is the key quality ingredient. These relationships can dramatically influence the outcome – both what farmers get and their perception of how the process was handled. During the fattening up period, several standards are set for food, medication and other conditions, and each pig is fed and tracked individually. The state of the animals – both psychological and physical – as they are being transported and handled is considered vital. Within 24 hours after processing, the final product – the meat, which is judged on various criteria including colour, weight, water content, and freshness – should be in the retail stores.

The next example looks in more detail at one critical activity, electronic transactions, which Citibank offers to its corporate clients for their day to day financial management. For users, getting into the system, getting through the

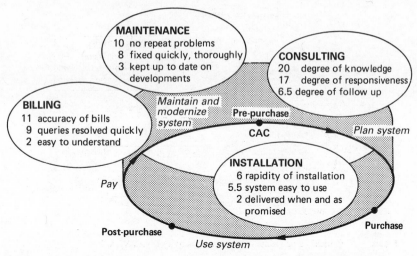

Figure 7.4   Performance criteria (weighted) during customers' activity cycle: AT & T

transactions and getting the job completed is a daily exercise. The bank's quality depends on a bevy of services so that clients get access 99 per cent of the time, and experience swift, easy and accurate cash transactions and reporting (see Figure 7.6). Quality criteria on the performance of products, people and processes at each point in the activity cycle are translated into a series of questions: Can customers using their PCs get through to us 24 hours a day and, if not, are we being alerted in time? Are we responding quickly enough to avoid a stoppage in their transactions? Have we sped up their

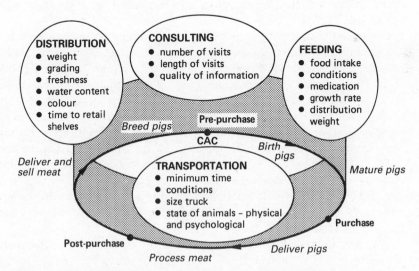

Figure 7.5   Critical value points and performance criteria: Hendrix Voeders

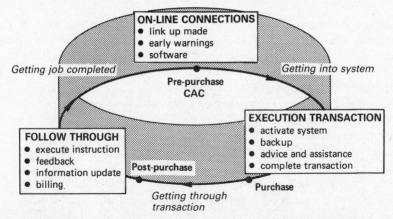

Figure 7.6 Critical value points in customers' activity cycle: Citibank (corporate cash transaction)

operations? Are people there when needed, able to resolve problems? Have we obviated all congestion at the customer's end so that the post-transaction paperwork can be completed rapidly and effectively? (see Figure 7.7.)

Standards for benchmarking standards

So saturated did industrial firms become with their own data that many forgot to look outside. With static, rigid comparative measures like 'market share',

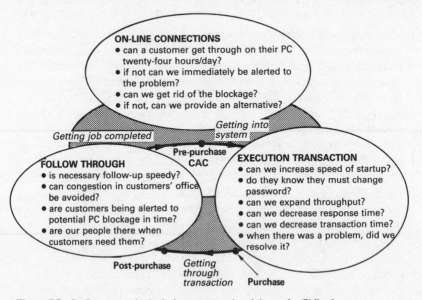

Figure 7.7 Performance criteria during customers' activity cycle: Citibank

'return on investment', 'profitability' and 'productivity' as their goalposts, many managers were blinded to the importance of the process behind the figures. Given industrial sentiments and setups, it was not really feasible to do otherwise, either within their companies or without. But ultimately, industrial firms found that the conventional ways of looking at quality and measures were not particularly useful for developing the value-creating capabilities they needed for achieving superior performance in the marketplace. In their quest for continuous improvement – now *the* quality imperative – managers go out actively in search of best practices in order to improve their way of doing things.[18]

The assumption behind benchmarking is really quite simple. The Japanese call it *'dantotsu'* or striving to be the 'best of the best'. If someone is doing better, there must be a reason which, if analyzed, adapted and transferred to their situation, can lead to significant improvements in service delivery. Rather than examining the core itself – input and output – each activity in the value-adding process is constantly examined to ascertain why something or someone is successful and achieves a better outcome.

To be truly effective, benchmarking can only be done on site. It's just not possible to obtain the information needed without observing and interpreting. Neither financial statements nor annual reports, customer surveys nor commissioned market research can provide companies with what they need to know – what steps they must go through in their service processes. While individuals may take some initiative in benchmarking, it is essentially an institution-wide effort that is ongoing, one that must be practised by contemporary firms on three levels:

1 *'Best practices'* (internal benchmarking): Here, firms look throughout their organization and try to determine why some divisions, units, groups or individuals are better able to produce value-adding capabilities for customers than others. Citibank takes great pains to compare branches and understand why some rate higher in customer satisfaction. Why is it that enquiries are handled so much more efficiently by one local outlet than by another? Is it the computer system or the calibre of the people? As it turns out, it has a lot to do with the quality of the learning environment – in other words, how often and how profoundly people talk to each other.

2 *'Best in breed'* (competitive benchmarking): Within industries, some firms are better at certain activities than others. Determining why this is so involves companies in comparing standards and methodologies against those of their toughest competitors. For instance, Digital compares itself to IBM, BP to Exxon, Canon to Rank Xerox, and Honda to Toyota. When it comes to convenience operations, BP doesn't limit itself to other gas stations, but it also uses as a benchmark the 711 chain in Japan, considered one of the best in the world despite the fact that most of BP's customers in Europe have probably never seen one. For the same reason, when looking

for a benchmark in restaurant operations, BP looks at Domino Pizzas and McDonald's.

To illustrate the point further, Honda sends its salespeople routinely to Toyota or Nissan to observe competition in action first hand. The company wants its personnel to know what it feels like to be a real customer, without preferential treatment. How were they handled by the salesperson? How were their repair problems dealt with? Honda also has formal arrangements whereby teams go to counterparts in competing firms to see how specific processes work. Why are they better at the customer information giving procedures? Do they spend more time in the factories? Have they shortened the line of communication between the technology experts at the plants and people serving customers? Is the training better?

Having broken through traditional boundaries by competing while collaborating, getting detailed answers to these questions – a phenomenon once practically unheard of – is becoming increasingly common everywhere today. It again requires a sense of win/win and reciprocity between firms, based on the principle of superiority in selective markets instead of domination en masse across the board. Accepting that no one can be on top indefinitely, many firms now believe that, unless learning is transferred industry-wide, the entire sector may lose. Their thinking is that all firms can gain potentially by this kind of collaboration, that they will maintain their competitive strength in markets and units of one by virtue of the way they translate these practices personally into their own unique operations.

3 *'Best in class'* (cross-competitor benchmarking): In fact, the best services practices may come from outside the industry. This is something that firms are discovering as they try to assess and emulate world class performance in the specific activities where they have been weak but have identified as being important to customers. Such activities may involve going even further afield – into sports teams, theatre groups, aircraft carriers or orchestras. Pushing beyond industry norms, firms actively seek and find the best company in a specific and vital activity, absorb and analyse their methods, practices and processes, and modify them to suit their own situation. AT&T uses Federal Express as a benchmark for its bill handling; Federal Express and Rank Xerox use American Express for their account processing; AT&T compares itself to Federal Express for on-time delivery, and to Benetton and Caterpillar for on-demand logistics. And, because Rank Xerox was not getting goods to distributors and users quickly enough, the company searched outside its own industry for a prime candidate involved in similar activities. After researching trade journals and consulting the professionals, L.L.Bean, the sports equipment and clothing mail order house, was chosen. This company, using one warehouse located in Maine, USA, ships goods to customers all over the world within 24 hours after receiving an order. Uncovering both similarities and differences in practice and performance, Rank Xerox incorporated L. L. Bean's

superiority into its own warehousing and distribution services, with the result being an overall significant improvement for the firm.[19]

Getting leverage from complaints

Consciously or unconsciously, tin soldiers avoided complaints, viewing them as nothing but trouble. Complaints were seen as flaws exposed, rather than what high-value firms call opportunities for improvement. Even if they are not able to fix each and every customer complaint, these firms believe that they can take the information, learn from it, and use the insights to improve generally performance within the organization.

In services, the problem was even worse because complaints often ended up as individual accusations, since the 'culprits' were easy to identify. All too often, afraid to report complaints up the line and ill-equipped to handle them head on, employees ignored them. In any event, complaints interrupted daily routines and interfered with internal priorities. Equally problematic, the people left to handle them were usually at the bottom of the hierarchy, badly trained and poorly esteemed.[20]

Something had to change. Research revealed that the vast majority of unhappy customers in a service setting – around 70 per cent – say nothing, they simply walk away. Dissatisfied customers are twice as likely to tell about a bad encounter as people who have had a positive experience, and those who have complained but get no response talk even more.[21] Firms such as the Royal Bank of Canada have found that one unhappy client will share its grievances with about ten people, whereas a customer will share a good experience with only two or three people.

Not only did firms begin to give complaints more attention in the 1990s, but also they proactively sought ways to use them for satisfying customers. Instead of using questionnaires merely as instruments for general feedback, they have become tools – vehicles for customer discussion – and a deeper understanding of what is dissatisfying. The service centres that were formed to fix 'things', and more recently to produce services, have become tangible ways to funnel complaints into organizations. But at all levels, high-value corporations are endeavouring to make employees feel more comfortable about complaints, to act on them and try to turn them into an advantage. And, specifically to handle complaints, many firms are recruiting a different cadre of service worker – people who are more educated, motivated and better trained, especially in problem-solving and conflict resolution. For instance:

● Recognizing that there is no substitute for first-hand customer contact, Matsushita has set up 215 'customer consultant centres' which handle 700,000 complaints on electronic systems a year. Seventy per cent are dealt with directly by the firm; the other 30 per cent must involve dealers, because there is a recurring problem to be sorted out. When customers are given questionnaires, they are reminded about the complaint system and have a toll-free number to use.

- The Royal Bank of Canada produces and distributes a brochure to all customers informing them about the company's complaint handling procedure. Included is information about to whom to write or call, when they can expect to receive a response and have the matter resolved. Advice is also given about complaint procedures for other types of goods and services.

- ICI's refinishing and decorative paint division has customer service and technical advice centres where – in addition to calling in for advice or support – end users, homeowners, distributors or body shops can register and discuss their complaints. The company has upgraded these employees by hiring better educated people and providing them with special training in complaint handling techniques – including telephone interviewing, listening skills and letter writing.

- For account management at firms like Digital, interaction with customers is so intense that complaint handling becomes part of the daily routine and discussion rather than being an extraordinary event. Today, it is the ongoing responsibility of an account manager to take on the role of arbitrator/moderator, working out complaints with customers whenever and wherever they arise.

- Since it is the teller who typically has to bear the brunt of most customer complaints, Citibank is trying to place more mature individuals in this kind of position, people accustomed to handling difficult situations. In the past, it was usually the younger, more junior, personnel who held such posts. Experts on human behaviour have also been brought in to counsel frontliners on better ways to deal with hostility, anger and confrontation, and to resolve problems.

The complaints process is also being made more visible to customers who are not often aware of what is involved in a resolution. Instead of simply producing an end result, firms are frequently taking the customer along through the process, either by word, phone or wire. It has been proved that if a complaint is uncovered and customers believe it was well handled, they will not only continue to do business with the firm but also will even spread the word. No matter how diligently services – even the high-value ones – are delivered, corporations are bound to have some poor encounters. No customer can be entirely happy all the time. But complaints are no longer mere statistics. To attain quality, the service delivery network's ability to respond and recoup is as important, therefore, as having no failure at all.

8 *Making services pay their way*

Time that devours all things.

Ovid, *Metamorphoses,* c. AD8

A quandary exists, as compelling and irresolvable for physicists and mathematicians as it is for social observers and historians. Is time finite or infinite? Is it reversible or irreversible? Man has always taken time for granted: it was simply there. For Plato – one of the first philosophers actually to write about it – as long as there was a universe, there would also be time. They were both immutable, unending and inseparable.[1]

Among the classical scientists, the infinite nature of time has been an established principle since Newton. While it is true that some of this century's great scientific discoveries – namely relativity and quantum mechanics – jostled long-held traditional assumptions and gave rise to an entirely new physics, there is one exception: the reversibility of time. It has never affected this school's theories. Whether time goes backward or forward, their equations continue to hold.

But, according to the new thinkers, the wrong things are being measured. What needs to be examined, they urge, is the irregularity and uncertainty so much more in line with real life than the regularity and predictabilty of laboratory situations. These scientists have come up with yet another set of equations based on conditions of uncertainty and chaos – for a world they say long past mechanistic precepts, which operate only when sheltered from the natural state. Ilya Prigogine, principal architect of new systems theory, and his colleague Isabelle Stengers, are experts on this subject. In their book, *Order Out of Chaos,* they elaborate on this theme:

> We have discovered that far from being an illusion, irreversibility plays an essential role in nature and lies at the origin of most processes of self-organization. We find ourselves in a world in which reversibility and determinism apply only to limiting, simple cases, while irreversibility and randomness are the rules ... (They were) considered to be exceptions. (But) today we see everywhere the role of irreversible processes, of fluctuations. The models considered by classical physics seem to us to occur only in limiting situations such as we can create artificially by putting matter into a box and then waiting till it reaches equilibrium.[2]

What these two writers are saying is that time is deterministic and reversible only in artificial situations. In the everyday life of open rather than closed systems, events are far from being in equilibrium; indeed, they happen over time. Once they begin to unfold, the outcomes are probabalistic not deterministic, unpredictable rather than certain. With time factored in, in short, the equation is completely changed. Nothing can ever be brought back to its original state, and the time spent is irrevocably gone.

Whatever the scientists may say, in reality the progression of time is central to all aspects of life. It is unwaveringly finite and goes only one way: forward. It can neither be stretched nor retrieved. Which is an important issue for organizations engaged in high value-adding intangibles. For, in services, the time that is available and the time that is spent are directly related to costs, and these costs to profits. Machines can be switched on and off, or left running as long as necessary. To programme people, decreeing how much time they spend on value-adding activities or customer interactions, is a different story. When products are unsold, they can be kept for another day, discounted and sold off. Stocks are said to be as good, or even better, than money in the bank, as they can appreciate in value. In the immaterial world, time expended can never be regained. Once lost, services cannot be brought back. If the plane from Stockholm to Tokyo takes off half full, that's that. Similarly, know-how which is neither used nor transferred is a waste. Just as with machines, lost capacity is a sunk cost. But when people – be they high-powered application engineers or check-in clerks – stand idle, a double cost is incurred: both the wasted time and the opportunity to interact with customers.

This paradox represents an important challenge for the modern manager who is trying to make intangible offerings pay. While time is a major resource, it is also a severe constraint. To be sure, doing a greater number of things in less time equally well is more productive – and customers demand this. But, the simple truth is that it takes time both to achieve the kind of results customers now want and to sustain relationships. So, the real issue becomes: how to boost profitability without reducing the quality of the service delivery process? How to get around some of the restraints of time? And how to avoid the industrial trap of setting prices that are based solely on hours spent for intangible items?

How services can pay their way

In an organization whose basic tenet is the service ethos, profitability comes from the capability to either add value to the customer's activity cycle, or to take the non-value added out. Bureaucratic preoccupations to get large volumes and internal efficiencies – and so reduce the cost for an ubiquitous market – are overshadowed by outward concerns for the value perceived by customers. Margin-based buyer–seller relationships, in which prices were squeezed and service gradually deteriorated, are replaced by a sense of mutuality in which, through the value-adding process, everyone eventually gains. This requires doing more, for more select 'markets within markets' and 'units of one', over longer periods of time. The value-added services may pay in several ways:

- *A greater portion of revenue may come from these services.*[3] For firms like IBM and Digital, this represents 40-50 per cent of their profits and they aim to increase this figure even more. Typical of many high-value firms, Mandelli gained over 90 per cent of its earnings from its machines and only 10 per cent from services contracts. Now, services account for more than half of the company's revenues. And from the classic service sector, firms like InterForward Germany, have seen a rapid growth in revenues since moving into selling solutions – in this case 50 per cent – with services earning the company 10–15 per cent more than traditional freight and forwarding.
- *Firms increase their know-how capability by providing services, thereby increasing their assets.* When Mandelli first sent a team to Caterpillar in the United States to provide engineering consulting for a new tractor model, its management knew that the company had a chance of being selected to build the entire factory system. Even if, at worst, the order didn't materialize, Mandelli would still be able to acquire a huge amount of expertise, however, which could be embodied in the company's know-how base and ultimately increase profitability. As one executive from Mandelli commented:

  We don't always do a job because we are going to make money then and there. Many times we will do consulting for a customer without charging, and we know it may require many people over long periods of time. But, we get a lot of experience that way which enables us to compete more vigorously.

- *Performing services for customers creates a valuable bonding.* Being involved with customers, present during their planning and decision-making, has many advantages, even if they don't show up initially on the quarterly financial statements. Working closely for and with customers deepens knowledge about them, increases the level of trust, and strengthens the relationship over time. The fact that Mandelli did the consulting for Caterpillar and was present throughout the design process gave the company a huge advantage when it came to making a successful bid for Caterpillar's automated factory.
- *Services also lead to a high degree of repeat business, thus reducing overall costs.* Firms that revert from high-volume to high-value strategies use services to increase customer loyalty. In the 1990s, SAS changed its focus: the company began to concentrate on increasing customer retention – trying to make sure that customers keep returning to use SAS, rather than just be satisfied on a single trip. Likewise, Zurich Insurance and Kansa, both in preventative insurance, try to achieve exactly the same thing – reach a higher retention factor so as to substantially improve bottom line performance.

- *Through value-added services, customer spending increases.* Nestlé had this experience when it introduced a category management system to French retailers. Because Nestlé as a brand name, and as coffee category, performed better for these retailers, they allotted it more shelf space. After ICI provided productive management and marketing services to assist body shop clients in their operations, the weekly throughput of damaged cars went up, with the result that it now sells these customers more paint.
- *Services permit higher prices to be set on core offerings.* Because the services offered by Hendrix Voeders have led to huge improvements in feeding efficiencies – directly translated into increased farm revenues for customers – the company enjoys 25 per cent extra on its feed products, which more than offsets its costs. BP has found that customers will pay more per gallon of petrol for a full service experience at a petrol station. The Maryland commands a premium because of the value added it provides to its customers. And, at DuPont, services result in a 20–25 per cent premium over commodity suppliers.
- *Value added from services increases the percentage of the market obtained.* Customers move their affiliation to firms able to provide the results they are after. Kao's annual 10 per cent growth is due to market gains stemming from its retail support services to the trade. Similarly, Canon now has 60 per cent of the independent dealers in Japan because of its logistic and distribution services. Market share for Hoechst paints in Europe went up remarkably after the company introduced risk-free dyeing; likewise, Rank Xerox gained in world markets after its move into documentation management.
- *The firm's percentage of its own customers' business goes up because of the services offered.* Firms are able to get a larger 'share of wallet' from existing customers by providing solutions. Profitability is increased, but this can happen only with stronger and longer-term relationships which result from activities through the customer's activity cycle. Take Citibank. Instead of asking 'What's our share of the pie?', the bank focuses on getting deeper penetration of customer spending over longer periods of time, as ultimately this is how both Citibank and its customers profit. Front-ended decisions on polymer moulding for Toyota's central console panels save the auto company money and lead to a better end product. So, Hoechst, after years of working closely with the auto manufacturer and its suppliers on this concept, now receives a much greater percentage of Toyota's business than when it had been involved only on a tender basis.

However firms assess the way that value-added services pay, making them economically feasible requires two things: keeping the costs of delivery as low as possible without sacrificing quality, and raising the perceived value as high as possible in order to justify commanding a premium from customers.

But, do firms really know the cost of these value-added services? What does it take in monetary terms to acquire, upgrade, and depreciate know-how, for instance? How far are firms from know(ing) exactly what these services are actually worth? How do they incorporate this value into their pricing? While the answers to these questions may not be altogether clear, they do raise some important managerial issues and priorities for the years ahead.

The cost of service and no service

That services are prohibitively costly is an old argument – the same one used a decade ago by people who resisted quality. 'Why do it?' they asked. 'Costs will soar and profits will plummet.' Now firms find that providing services not only adds value for customers, with all the concomitant advantages but also that they can bring down their own costs of doing business. Nestlé's joint forecasting scheme decreases expenses for both parties. Not only do retailers obviously benefit but also Nestlé can improve its own planning because it is in a better position to forecast. When a highly-trained expert at IBM answers a telephone service enquiry call, or when customers provide Matsushita's repairmen with the correct information about an appliance breakdown, the repair process is accelerated, thus significantly reducing the expense.

Although industrial minds were concerned with the cost of services, they never grasped fully the cost of losing business through poor or no service. Frederick Reicheld and W. Earl Sasser, after considerable research and analysis, discovered that, across a wide range of industries, customers who do not return due to poor quality services cost the firm an enormous amount of money. Although the amount is difficult to calculate precisely, if managers remember that unhappy customers turn others away, if they factor in the potential buying that satisfied customers might have done, as well as all the additional expenses required to attract new customers, they may be surprised at what they find.

The fact that managers avoided services was symptomatic of yet another problem. Having a short-term financial orientation blocked them from doing anything that didn't reflect positively, and rapidly, in their quarterly or annual bottom line profits. Unlike tangible assets – such as machines where returns were definable and predictable – value-added services often took longer to produce results and were also more difficult to quantify. Now, a customer's worth is no longer based on isolated sales during one discrete period, but rather on a continuous stream of revenue over time. With customers seen as investments, value-added services are not considered to be unnecessary costs – they are essential levers to profitability. But, unfortunately, today's accounting systems still do not reflect this concept, as Reichheld and Sasser explain in their article, 'Zero Defections: Quality Comes to Services':

Most systems focus on current period costs and revenues and ignore expected cash flows over a customer's lifetime. Served correctly, customers generate increasingly more profits each year they stay with a company. Across a wide range of businesses, the pattern is the same: the longer a company keeps a customer, the more money it stands to make.[4]

Having profits linked to the volume achieved in the short term meant that the reward system, instead of motivating employees to retain the firm's customers, encouraged them to pursue new ones. Now we know that there is more profit to be gained from existing customers. [5] Which means that firms are having to adjust their reward systems. Canon, whose incentives used to reflect the number of copiers sold, now bases a third of its rewards on customers retained. But, previously, how could firms know which customers were profitable, dealing as they were with them en masse? Today, firms can do it because they have systems in place that specifically measure the profitability of each customer, and employees are rewarded accordingly. Whereas the number of 'boxes' sold used to determine success, now the rewards accorded to Digital account management employees are largely based on the profitability of an account, where applicable, worldwide.

As firms move from industrial to service-based models, the economics change:

Then: services were a cost, and had to be squeezed into short time spans and offset rapidly.

Now: they are offset over several years, depending on expected future returns.

Then: with markets either mass or specialized, it was assumed that only some select customers would pay for differentiated goods and value-added services.

Now: all mass custom-alized offerings require increased value, differentiation and decreased costs simultaneously, though to differing degrees.

Then: those transactions which were most repetitive were also the most economical.

Now: there is potential for the learning or experience curve for the mass, customized *and* personalized aspect of the offering. For, as firms become good at doing things – even the most specialized of tasks – the learning becomes institutionalized and a part of more general applications.

For instance:

● Each and every consulting service Digital offered to customers used to be highly specialized. Now, 70 per cent of these services have some sort of economies from the common denominators among markets and customers associated with them.

- SAS has had to try and find ways to improve both the quality of its services and the range of offerings, while at the same time radically reducing costs. Although part of the company's effort is going into processes to improve productivity, more attention is concurrently being channelled into personalizing services.
- InterForward does indeed supply the mundane and basic services associated with forwarding. But, the company also uses this know-how to open up new markets. For example, InterForward in Germany has become so good at understanding the legal and commercial intricacies of distributing motorcycles throughout Europe that the company has applied this knowledge to stereo equipment, computers and appliances. The considerable expertise it has acquired with individual customers it is now able to apply on a wider scale thus benefitting from lower costs.
- InterForward regards some of its upfront expenses in value-added services like any other capital investment – since the benefits accrue at some future date, the costs are absorbed over a period of time. The same is true at Nestlé. The company takes a longer-term view of its food services, discounting them over extended periods of time. Its managers make the upfront investments in solutions which they know will take time to translate into increased sales.

Managing the capacity to serve

In services, a major factor determining success is how effectively capacity is managed. Being essentially an economic concept, capacity was driven largely by cost considerations in conventional industrial settings.[6] The point of equilibrium between demand and supply was predictable and critical to achieving profitability for corporations. Having no inventory and being very time dependent, the 'feast or famine' syndrome so typical in services tended to be sorted out in one of two ways – by manipulating the demand or the supply. So, from telephone companies to airlines, resorts to couriers, cleaners to auditors, firms encouraged customers to use their services at favourable rates in off-peak times, or they changed the supply by augmenting physical facilities – such as planes, outlets, warehouses – and the people needed to operate them.

While not negating the importance of making these adjustments in capacity management, high-value corporations add another dimension. Depending so crucially on having spontaneity between themselves and their customers, they concentrate on developing the 'capacity to serve'. In addition to managing demand and supply patterns carefully, they create a system which is flexible and resilient enough to navigate through peaks and valleys. Since their inventory is largely the availability of people – their skills and know-how – and their quest is to maintain a long-term relationship, they cannot predict demand easily nor simply obtain more supply.

Similarly, these firms cannot be constrained by traditional approaches to time. Intent on customer satisfaction, modern service networks build a certain amount of redundancy into their systems to allow for flexibility. Their excess capacity comes not only from the numbers of people and the time they have available – which would be much too costly – but also from the kind of people employed, how they are trained and how well they work together. Individuals have multi-faceted capabilities and are able to adapt their skills to cater to different situations. When there is an upsurge in demand or a special problem, service employees are grouped or combined, and reallocated according to the need. When there is a lull, they can be used elsewhere because they can move to other specializations and general assignments. When everyone plays a part in keeping the system functioning, jobs can take shape according to the problems at hand rather than merely following formal descriptions.

The one important challenge managers have to face in the 1990s is how to build sufficient, even excess capacity, without increasing their costs. Here are some techniques:

Creating permanent-temporary capacity

This is one way to convert some of the fixed overheads into variable costs. A certain number of people may be needed to achieve a critical mass and cover the base demand, but 'outsiders' should be brought in when additional assistance is essential. The reason this approach works so well is that increasingly today it's the highly-skilled and specialized people who are looking for these permanent-temporary liaisons.[7] They are paid either on a part-time or project basis and don't have the constraints imposed by full-time employment. Nonetheless, they are part of the culture, which is important, because at the point of customer interface they too represent the company. To illustrate the point:

- IBM uses its own software experts on a regular basis for specific customer application needs. But, they are bolstered by outside specialists in peak times. In some cases only outsiders are used, because they have competences that the firm does not want or need on a full-time basis. To work successfully together in this way, both IBM and the 'outsider' have a keen sense of reciprocity and understanding about the quantity and quality of their mutual commitment.
- DuPont's carpet fibre division bring in outside interior decorators who help account teams provide the state-of-the-art expertise needed to make total floor covering and design solutions for such customers as hotels and hospitals. The company's services gain credibility, yet this expertise is

made available without having to incur the full expenses. These 'outsiders' come to know the company's account teams and customers, so they can fit smoothly into their way of doing business.

- Ciba-Geigy's Information Agency has a 10 per cent buffer of outside and inside information specialists, used on a retainer payment basis, who can be called upon to serve customers at peak times but are not fully employed by the company. The difference between this arrangement and part-time work is that they are part of the culture. They are regarded as Ciba-Geigy employees, and the company assumes their fiscal and social contributions, paying them a fee when their services are used.

- Nestlé uses world-famous chefs when the company needs to give gastronomical advice to the teams who handle its hospital and hotel clients. This talent, which no firm could either attract or afford on a full-time basis, increases the quality of its offering, and gives the company the flexibility and versatility needed to serve a wide array of customers in a highly specialized field. Like DuPont, Nestlé also gains credibility from using an independent resource.

Subcontracting service capacity

Because firms may have to venture far afield to provide solutions, they are increasingly subcontracting services. While the principle of having access to skills without overhead is the same as maintaining a permanent-temporary workforce, the relationship is different. This arrangement is usually a formal contract between two companies, or between a company and an independent person. The subcontractor's skills, although essential, are substantially different from specialists employed and are usually not that sophisticated.

When working together in this way to serve customers, some agreement must be reached on what is and isn't a competitive infringement. Since the corporation providing the solution obviously owns the customer relationship, it's essential that all activities done by the subcontractor be funnelled through the account management system, and be delivered with the self-same standards demanded from the company's own employees. Some firms subcontract to their own customers, thus enlarging their service capacity without the concomitant costs; rather, they share the costs and benefits. Examples of some cases in point:

- Digital uses several building subcontractors in each local area to help with demolition and reconstruction. Both it and Zurich Insurance Canada work on the principle that, if the number of subcontractors is limited, more partnering type relationships form, the job will be done better and so, ultimately, the customer gains. Not only do these subcontractors become an extension of the firm but they also keep quality levels up as they are not forced to compete on price.

- DuPont subcontracts to a group of cleaners in the UK for all the maintenance of the carpets installed in its key projects. Together with DuPont's consulting team, the cleaning service draws up a plan and, once the carpet has been fitted, takes over the cleaning function on a contract basis. DuPont is nonetheless involved in the training of the cleaning staff and overseeing the quality control of the entire service delivery process.
- In a large project for the Swiss PTT, IBM subcontracted some of the activities to be performed – like programming – to the customer. While IBM remained responsible for the overall results, the PTT was part of the delivery team. Once the job was completed, IBM billed the PTT as a customer, and received a bill from it as subcontractor.

Using people's multi-skills capacity

One of the great differentiating traits of know-how workers is that their education and experience enables them to be both specialists and generalists. They enjoy having this versatility, say many of the experts.[8] Provided that individuals derive greater satisfaction, and the overall enterprise capacity is increased instead of fragmented, it's a way of extracting reserve capacity for the firm when it is needed, unions aside. For instance:

- SAS has fine-tuned the design of its service processes at check-in counters. The baggage ticketing procedure, which used to take employees twelve seconds to do, now takes seven seconds. Time is thus freed up on routine activities so that frontliners can spend more of it talking to customers and handling their individual problems, thereby adding extra value.
- What makes it feasible for Digital to play to the peak demands is that employees, even high-calibre application engineers, are allowed to float from one consulting and field project to another when they are not needed by their particular centre. Because they are 'accountable' to the firm for a certain amount of revenue, they are free when unoccupied – and even obliged – to look for other work, either inside the organization, or outside.

Buying out competitive capacity

Managing capacity has become as much an art as a science for modern firms as they search for ways to creatively handle the tradeoffs associated with providing high-quality services at low costs. Drawing together capacity within and across industries, they capitalize on common skills and complement each other's shortfalls. This kind of collaboration, a foreign idea to industrial mindsets, is becoming increasingly familiar. It can be application specific, seasonal or periodic and, once again, it works on the principle of reciprocity:

at one moment in time, a firm has a surplus of a given resource while another has a need.[9] Some examples illustrate:

- In Sweden, 40 companies have joined capacity in this way. SKF uses skilled personnel from its industrial competitors in the mechanical field, but not specifically in bearings so as to avoid head-on competition. These firms – say in hydraulics or electric motors – have people whose skill in mechanical engineering can be teamed up with SKF employees when necessary at a discounted market price.
- Nokia-Maillefer competes with three different kinds of firms: those in consulting which are specialists in cable manufacturing, large traditional cable manufacturers which are Nokia's customers but also sell their expertise to smaller firms, and other cable machinery suppliers. Each have spare capacity at times which Nokia draws upon. The challenge is to know whom to call for what and how to combine skills across several firms.
- InterForward is hiring the excess capacity from competing forwarding companies which had acquired assets in boom times. Many have ships or lorries, for instance, which they can only amortize by keeping them full. SAS and other airlines do the same with their partners. Using each other's aircraft, pilots and ground crews when additional capacity is needed, these companies are able to draw on what's available among them, thereby avoiding waste and saving on cost.

Growing capacity for doing

Firms may literally have to grow the 'capacity for doing' from within so that they can offer customers more services without increasing costs. By growing their capacity consciously in areas where they have traditionally been weak, they avoid having to bring in more people. For example:

- InterForward, having switched from a culture of moving things to sophisticated logistics, is continually on the lookout for experts inside the firm who have critical solution skills. These people can then be moved around into other geographic areas and divisions where demand for this expertise is high but supply is low.
- Canon now is distributing Apple computers in Japan in order to offer its customers a complete documentation system. The company is training existing staff to do the servicing, since they already know how to take machines apart, analyse circuitry, detect problems and fix them – core skills that can easily be adapted.
- Like some leading law firms in the UK, Price Waterhouse has moved to a 24-hour day to increase its capacity to serve. Partners can work a full day or into the night when necessary, and then return in the morning to find the typing and paperwork already prepared by the administrative services which operate around the clock.

● Hoechst is gaining more capacity worldwide by taking some of its best know-how from one country and using those people to increase the expertise wherever it is needed locally. For instance, a division in Europe may need certain expertise from Japan. Instead of expanding in the traditional sense of the word, the company brings people in from the East, and plants them in the European facility to develop a centre of expertise there with existing employees.

Shifting the in-house capacity

By shifting existing capacity creatively, firms are also able to increase their potential without incurring additional expenses. Having capacity that isn't what customers want, or is not available at critical moments, is of no value to anyone. The difference between 'service capacity' – the remnant of high-volume thinking – and the 'capacity to serve' found in high-value firms is that enough of the correct skills are available wherever and whenever needed so that the seamless flow of value-adding activities is ongoing. As a consequence, work schedules, routines and people are reshuffled. Examples follow:

● On paper, BP had plenty of people available to serve at its petrol stations and convenience stores, but they were not there early in the morning when commuters were on the roads or in the evening when people were going out. So capacity has had to be reshifted to these preferred buying times. By the same token, the business manager who used to work traditional hours is now around during these critical times when clients are being served.

● At ICI, personnel used to wait for orders to come in for CO_2, which was then expedited when capacity allowed. With the company's new stock-master plan – which ensures that no customer's stock of CO_2 ever dips below an acceptable level – 24-hour-a-day capacity is needed. Fewer people are on duty, but someone is there at all times, including weekends.

● Throughout the 1980s, SAS pilots flew 460 hours a year and wore their uniforms 8 hours a day. But, in fact, they spent only 4 hours a day actually flying. Similarly, because crews had to be flown from one destination to another to catch their flights, valuable time was lost. By having crews eat on board instead of on the ground and by changing work habits, SAS's capacity has been increased.

● The Royal Bank of Canada, which has to make sure that, despite a proliferation of ATMs – typically 1,500 machines – the company can give round-the-clock service. Why? Because a surprising number of the 250 million transactions a year are done after hours. The bank's staff take turns to be on call in their respective areas after hours to refill the machines with extra cash and paper for receipts, thereby augmenting capacity without extra expenses.

Learning to harness energy

Clearly, there is a correlation between the amount of energy and the capacity to serve. Whatever the number of people, the time available and the way employees are combined or allocated, a customer-serving network can only maximize profits when individuals and collective energy are harnessed and used in the most effective way.

Ever since the industrial revolution, managers have known that greater amounts of energy lead to higher levels of productivity.[10] It is not surprising then that all scientific and R&D efforts – both then and since – have been devoted to finding physical sources of energy. With one difference: the industrial concern with energy for machines is now being matched by a search to understand and improve human energy.

This is an irony of sorts. Humans could never compete with machines in industrial times, as they were completely overshadowed by them. Machines were more powerful, stronger, able to sustain energy for longer periods of time. No more. Mental energy – human thought, say the experts – is the most powerful energy of all.[11] Thoughts move faster than the speed of light. People are able to embrace a whole host of issues simultaneously, which to date no machine has perfected to the same extent. Unlike machines, the brain can adapt its mental and physical energy level effortlessly depending on circumstances, and it can draw on its reserve when needed.[12]

Using just the right amount of energy is characteristic of many living systems, where a way is found to maximize it over time despite differences in the amounts and patterns between individual units. There's a fascinating tale about ants, known to be super efficient. Within any one community, half of them will always work slowly while the other half operates at top speed. Yet, if the fast group is killed off, the same pattern will re-emerge amongst the slower group: half will work at maximum pace while the rest dally. Acting as one system, the entire community has learned how to maintain its overall level of energy.[13]

With people and their mental energy so important to the customer value-adding process, firms are endeavouring to try and understand how to mobilize and channel their energy more productively. Here are some techniques being used currently:

Making the workplace ergonomically sound

We now know that it's almost impossible to separate the cognitive from the emotional aspects of mental work. Increasingly, firms are therefore giving attention to the impact of the workplace on the energy of their service workers today, switching from understanding the physical potential of people – which so fascinated Taylor – to the effect of the environment on mental energy and capacity. Despite new technology improving employee productivity, if these ergonomic factors are ignored, they say, energy will be dissipated and the reverse of what was expected or desired will ensue.

Although the discipline has been around for ages, ergonomics has especially rich possibilities for designing more ideal environments for service workers. It looks at a variety of sciences – such as biology, chemistry, group psychology – and combines them with design engineering and systems thinking. How people work, value themselves and control their working lives is linked integrally with the environment around them. Ergonomics creates new workspaces and adjusts light, colour, temperature, decor and dimensions to optimize human energy levels. It examines how machine configurations influence people's work, the way individuals within groups interact in different situations, and the impact of the bodily and mental rhythms occurring in every person's 24-hour cycle on their productivity. It searches for reasons why the physical environment influences both the hard and soft – personal and relational, technical and behavioural – employee skills.[14]

Kansa, for instance, found that throughout Finland many of its employees were coming to work stressed, with low energy levels. As the day progressed and especially in the afternoon – the time when most calls from clients would come in – the situation deteriorated rather dramatically. Employees not only tried to reduce and even avoid customer contact but also the quality of their actions and reactions would become worse. The company redesigned offices and workspaces using ergonomic principles; the light and the decor were changed, and partitions rearranged. Break schedules and workloads were switched to suit each individual's own energy levels and needs. Productivity shot up but, more importantly, says the firm, employees were more willing to serve customers.

Indeed, this approach has become so successful that firms are making substantial investments throughout their service delivery network. Honda examined and analysed its dealer showrooms and repair shops in Tokyo to assess the impact of layout, aeration and lighting on its service workers' performance. The company began to change the size, angle and location of windows. The result was that employees were friendlier, the quality of their services was more long lasting, and customers had a more favourable impression. A recent discovery shows that service technicians who work in shops with shiny floors seem more energetic, are more precise and have a higher self image – associating the floors with clinical hospitals. Therefore, Honda is now working on installing new floors at all its major dealers throughout Japan.

Working concurrently and in parallel

The elimination of time delays has been an engineering goal for decades, accomplished step by step as decisions and actions are taken at each point of any given process. But as managers found, this led to rather than eliminated time delays. Today's problems require a different kind of approach where, like the brain, organizations are able to accomplish activities on a multiple and simultaneous basis.

High-value organizations are redesigning their own service delivery circuitry based on these principles in order to save on overall time and energy. Not only do they recognize the need for having multi-skilled staff within their firms but also that these skills be carried out concurrently. Take Ciba-Geigy. Previously, all information was passed through the company serially. It wasn't considered necessary for people to know something until it was their time to act. Today, information is disseminated simultaneously throughout the system to get instant feedback and comments from each person in a critical activity and get problems resolved. Citibank employees used to wait until it was their turn in the overall production process. Now, they decide for themselves when and what has to be done, to economize on time and distribute their energy levels more efficiently. The secret, managers say, is that everyone must understand the total picture, their role in it and, through information and good relationships, know exactly what is happening in the process at each critical point.

Letting customers do the work themselves

In service-based networks, the firm and the customer co-produce and share the workload to achieve the results they are jointly after. But, when costs are the sole motivation, letting customers produce part of the service can risk disrupting the seamless flow and damaging the ultimate solution. Providing customers get a better experience and a functioning system, everyone gains – including the company. The energy that is saved in certain areas can then be used more effectively elsewhere.

This distinction is understood very clearly by high-value firms. Matsushita's service engineers were exhausted from shuttling from one end of Japan to the other. And, at least half of what they were doing could have been handled just as easily by the customers themselves. By embedding self-inspection and self-help features into its electronic equipment, the company's service workers are now able to devote themselves to more complex problems, ones where they can add real value.

In Finland, Digital was providing breakdown services to some 1,000 customers with service contracts in record time. But, 65 per cent of the calls could have been solved by the customers themselves if only they had looked at the manuals. In another 25 per cent of the cases, the needed information could easily have been found inside their own firms, if they had been made aware of the fact. Which meant that only 10 per cent of the calls actually needed to be handled by Digital engineers. The company then developed an easy-to-use interactive database to replace the manuals; it takes customers through the process and enables them to fix problems themselves. This move reduced the number of incoming calls by close to 20 per cent during the first six months.

That customers have flexibility is essential. For those customers who prefer to have a service engineer from Matsushita or Digital, they are made available. When SAS introduced its various automatic electronic boarding systems, part of the strategy was to make sure that customers could choose whichever service suited them best. Merely having the service isn't enough though. An investment in training must also be made so that customers know how to perform these services themselves. Otherwise, the company could risk failure and additional expenses.

What we know we don't know about costing and valuing know-how

Services are becoming so successful that now new concerns are looming about traditional accounting metrics. The subject of costing and valuing know-how has recently been addressed in earnest by accountants, brokers, investors, bankers and lawyers, to say nothing of management commentators. It is one of the main challenges that managers face, given the extent to which know-how has become *the* value adder in industrial economies and modern business.

One might ask why it is that managers know so little about costing and pricing this know-how? Robert Reich offers some historical answers to this question which he describes eloquently in his book, *The Work of Nations*. The economy of the twentieth century, he says, was built upon those who owned and those who ran machines. These were the major sources of wealth and the major recipients. Accounting systems were thus designed to measure the costs of financial capital and labour, which in particular, made up a large chunk of expenditure. Today the percentage of the profits generated by this direct labour has been drastically decreased. Profits are now going to the people with know-how who, in his words, 'solve, identify and broker new problems'.[15]

While corporate profits have been declining, the earnings of the know-how worker have been rising. What has caused this gap, ask the experts? Could it be that firms have been underestimating what these service providers are worth? [16] Which raises the next question: what is the real cost of the 'white collar' – now 'gold collar' – service worker? And, how can the real value of what's in their heads be calculated?

But, as Peter Drucker says, the difficulty in coming to terms with these issues is that managers are still fixated on the wrong thing. Cost accounting that established the cost of production was fine when the inputs and outputs were hard and tangible. As a matter of fact, the strength of the system was that it confined itself to quantifiable items, which easily provided managers with objective answers. With intangibles entering the equation, however, and value given and taken over long periods of time, spread over several offerings, these tools have become outdated.[17]

Service managers inherited the same accounting methods used by manufacturers, which was not very useful to them. Using these systems, they have never really been able to know what an offering costs. Nor, in truth, have they ever known the relative contribution that each act in the overall service delivery process makes. Stephen Roach, the American economist and consultant, discusses this problem in his article, 'Services Under Siege'. One of the reasons that services are suffering is because the tools they inherited from manufacturing could never really provide an accurate reading of the costs and value of their activities, he says. Unlike manufacturers – which had more accurate figures and could, if they cut costs know exactly what would be eliminated – service firms can't be precise about what is being sacrificed. Like other commentators, Roach calls for a new accounting framework. Here is his view:

> Traditional accounting standards are oriented towards the needs of factories and are woefully inadequate in measuring white collar productivity. Since a service is more amorphous than a product, it would be a mistake to use the quantity-driven metrics of the factory. Services need an accounting framework which can identify which activities add the most value, enabling organizations to distinguish between routine and creative tasks. Only then can the costs of technology acquisition and white collar hiring be evaluated accurately in the context of an organization's strategic objectives and competitive realities.[18]

Another visible remnant of the industrial era was that balance sheets reflected the accumulation of hard assets only. These assets – exchangeable and replaceable – constituted the corporation's worth. Adding or subtracting from them was equivalent to improving or diminishing the company's standing. Any asset on a balance sheet was owned. The more a firm possessed, the more solid it was. And therein lies another irony. For people can neither be owned nor put on a balance sheet, even though they represent the main source of revenue generation for high-value corporations.[19]

Their know-how, talent and expertise has always been buried in the catchall term 'goodwill', together with the other intangible items such as contractual rights, relationships with customers, patents, brands, intellectual property, databases and trade secrets. An aggregate figure – invented ostensibly for the buying and selling of corporations – its usefulness is limited for today's managers in search of ways to make services pay. In any event, as an indicator of a service firm's worth it fails because a substantial portion of the amount can disappear when employees depart. Also, 'goodwill' cannot be used as a basis for pricing these intangibles since their value is not explicit and impossible to extract. [20]

With this in mind, a few Nordic companies are beginning to add human assets as an additional entry on their balance sheets. Still experimenting, they are trying to find some method for quantifying know-how. Two so-called 'Rhine-economy' states – Germany and Japan – are also using a value-added accounting system to show the results of this intangible contribution to total revenues. These attempts made by both service and manufacturing companies testify to the growing recognition that profits no longer rest on merely making and moving more goods; it is transferring know-how to customers which produces the results.

How know-how workers are valued by service enterprises is fundamental to how it is costed and priced in the marketplace. In trying to find a more appropriate way to estimate the cost and the value of this know-how, it's useful to compare some past and present assumptions (as presented in Figure 8.1). Previously, the people within the firm were seen as labour – a straight cost. Today, know-how is *the* asset which ensures a firm's capability to enjoy ongoing revenue streams into the future. Whereas, before, only the annual salary of these people was treated as a cost, managers today recognize that salary is just one small part of the calculation. Like machines, people have to be kept in working order, something which takes time and money.[21] They are different though from other resources which deteriorate over time. They gain value through their learning, association with the company, and the training and experience they receive. Replacement costs give a truer reflection of the cost of these assets therefore, for often it is when people leave that the full impact of this accumulation is felt.

The value of know-how workers to service enterprises cannot simply be determined by the supply and demand for specific skills in the marketplace at any moment in time. What customers ultimately want, and how that matches with employees' capabilities, now largely determines peoples' value. So, as

Industrial	Service
Labour seen as cost	Know-how seen as asset
Cost of hiring equals acquisition	Cost of hiring equals replacement
Costed at annual salary	Costed as total investment
Value determined by demand and supply in labour market	Value determined by demand and supply in customer market
Valued on individual skills	Valued on competency portfolio
Valued on present value of previous earnings	Valued at present value stream of future returns
Ability value	Application value

Figure 8.1   Costing and valuing know-how

know-how increasingly becomes the key consideration in market offerings, the real question is: What are peoples' value-adding capacities? Rather than valuing them in terms of their previous earnings or supposed cost to the firm, today it is the potential of their future revenue streams or contribution to the service delivery process producing these that matters. Whereas, before, it was peoples' skills or ability to be ever more proficient at their jobs which determined their value, now it's their portfolio of multi-skills which enable them to take complex problems and turn them into opportunities for customer satisfaction. An individual's application value, in other words, is what counts rather than just qualifications or technical ability.[22]

Contradictions and dilemmas in pricing services

Of course, there's more to services than deep know-how, despite its growing significance. And, the trouble with pricing any service is that, even if it were possible to determine the real cost – which it isn't – it probably would still be irrelevant in setting a price given that the customer's subjective perception of value is what is most relevant. Not only are value assessments very personal but also there is also a great deal of inconsistency in the way customers view price and services.[23]

Partly, this is because services and, indeed, solutions are bought sight unseen. Results come later – or so everyone hopes. Furthermore, since no delivery is ever identical, it's difficult to know what has to go into services beforehand and therefore cost and value them. Especially, as the computer and insurance firms are discovering, if the solution includes such non-events as no accidents or no maintenance. As far as 'things' are concerned, customers probably don't know, or care, how long it takes for them to be made. Whereas, with services being so transparent, they know, and care, and in fact often participate in the event.

There are several other complications related to how customers regard the value of services:

Fact: How much value a customer ascribes to a service is often linked to the relative value of the commodity within the overall cost. If paint is only 4 per cent of the cost of the whole car, for example, paint application services are likely to be considered marginal.

Yet: The cost of an error may be extraordinarily high, as the service may require sophisticated know-how and a great deal of the supplier's time.

Fact: Increasingly, customers want things done quickly and in real time.

Yet: Probably the longer an activity takes, the more value customers will associate with it.

Fact: A service is often consumed instantly, but its effects are long lasting, even indefinite – one only has to think of a doctor or lawyer.

Yet: Because products are visible and 'last longer', many customers still equate more value with them.

Fact: Customers don't want interruptions in the flow of activities.

Yet: If someone from the supplier – say a service repair person – is not visible often or long enough, customers begin to question the value they are receiving.

Fact: In solutions, a customer's perception of value is cumulative and evolves over time.

Yet: Customers tend to increasingly put a value on individual items and activities.

This last point raises a typical dilemma. Should services and pricing be bundled or unbundled?[24] In the past, most service firms bundled their services – banks being the prime example – and charged customers one lump sum. Manufacturers bundled many of their services into their products, and some still do so very successfully. There are various practicalities which favour bundling, not least of which is that costs of different services are usually difficult to separate out, trace and allocate. And, in many ways, bundling makes sense for one integrated offering, because it locks customers in and gives the company greater control of the outcome. For, once services are unbundled, customers may go 'cherry picking' – looking for the cheapest pieces – and thereby jeopardize the solution.

On the other hand, many customers prefer the unbundled approach. It gives them flexibility. It also provides the firm with infinite opportunities to distinguish activities and create separate profit units. Being mindful, though, of the 'cherry picking' problem, some firms that unbundle their offerings do not insist on exclusive inclusion of their goods in solution modules if there is another cheaper or preferred alternative. On the contrary, in a business where the money earned from services is beginning to exceed the profits on the goods – such as computers and copiers, or the interest on credit – that part of the solution may be incidental to the customer relationship and marginal in the total deal. Some firms like IBM go so far as to empower their account management to buy other suppliers' goods themselves if it's in the customer's interest. SKF has competitors' bearings in its automotive aftermarket kits, although only if the company doesn't make the bearing itself.

Firms are also able to provide more precise specifications of the various components in the overall solution when they are unbundled and priced separately. This obviates misunderstandings and the all-too-frequent hidden costs which can lead to complications later on. One Nokia-Maillefer executive put it this way:

> With one price, nothing was specific enough. None of us knew exactly what was expected. Worse still, neither did customers. How far we should go? We didn't know. Even if a formal agreement had been reached about the scope of a job,

things invariably cropped up and the inevitable question was: who's responsible, and who's got to pay?

Unbundling attempts to explain the benefits of what they are receiving more explicitly to customers. When Price Waterhouse bundled all its value added into the auditing function, it was not unusual to find partners literally giving away a service which may have taken an inordinate amount of time and money to develop. A software package, for instance, on 'takeover defence' might have been casually shown to a client at no extra charge in the course of a routine auditing consultation. With its value-added services now offered separately, Price Waterhouse – like other high-value firms – are better equipped to price these intangible offerings more realistically.

There's also the fact that unbundling facilitates having a choice for the 'individuals within markets'. Both the Royal Bank of Canada and Kansa have flexible offerings so that customers can decide which modules they want and are prepared to pay for. Working on the same principle, some airlines are contemplating a system whereby customers can choose their own 'menu' from the unbundled services offered on board and pay accordingly, instead of being constrained by a rigid first, business or economy class slot.

In selling solutions, the issue is not so much whether customers will pay, as when, and under what circumstances. Unbundling helps to control the pre-purchase activities for which customers have traditionally been reluctant to pay and firms have been hesitant to charge. Unbundling enables employees and customers to be clearer about when the selling ends and the consulting begins. They either pay for pre-purchase activities when they occur, or they negotiate some other formula. As an example, there may be up to an eight month period between the initial contact InterForward has with its customer and the logistics system becoming operative. If the logistics contract does not materialize for some reason or falls through the company can be paid a percentage of what the deal would have been worth. After the initial contact is made, Rank Xerox will charge for document analysis and solution design. If the customer proceeds with the entire documentation system, there is a reduction on the fee.

These are some other good reasons why it may be advantageous to price services separately:

- Customers have a sense of freedom if they pay for a service – especially consulting, and this independence leads to more confidence.
- The advice is likely to be seen as more objective, whereas it could be perceived as having built-in biases if it were bundled into the firm's offering.
- The quality of the service is likely to be higher as competencies are built up to meet standards of performance in the industry.
- Firms can more readily tell where their profits are coming from, thereby avoiding any misreading on what customers are really after.

- When customers have to pay for services, they are more likely to use them.
- When customers take their services more seriously, they expose their more senior people to them.
- Services can be sold into the wider market, thereby maximizing capacity utilization still further.

Notwithstanding the fact that high-value firms may unbundle pricing, they may still be trying to achieve one overall return from a customer. They may be prepared to take a low margin on some routine services – where competition is fierce and the ability to differentiate is difficult – so long as they can make a higher margin on others. This goes back to the need for a partnering spirit among firms and their clients so that both feel they have gained overall from the relationship.

Know(ing) the techniques of pricing services

The very survival of the high-volume company depended on knowing its costs and getting a premium on goods in sufficient quantities. High-value corporations, on the other hand, are concerned with the value-added customers get from their services during the entire activity cycle. They quantify the value for customers, know which costs contribute to this value and try to eliminate those that don't. Since so many expenses are fixed and difficult to distinguish, manoevrability comes not from cutting operating expenses, but by increasing their capacity to serve.[25]

Of course, time is a critical factor in the delivery of services. And will always be so. But, time spent is no longer *the* indicator of the value of resources expended or benefits received, or *the* focal point in the pricing strategy. High value firms base their pricing on value for the customer rather than the amount of time taken. These examples help to elucidate:

- In the past, Digital would ask: 'What does it cost to provide this customer with a new inventory management system?' and 'How quickly can it be done?' Now, the question is: 'What's it worth to this customer to reduce inventory by 20%?' Instead of 'I'll sell you a person for a week', Digital now tells its customer 'I'll sell you an analysis of your disk subsystem.'
- Rank Xerox no longer tries to extend the length of its training programmes as a way to entice customers. Now, the time is reduced so that clients' employees can get back to work quickly. For instance, the company has developed a one-day training module on how to formulate invoices, statements and other forms, a service that competitors take several months to accomplish. Because Rank Xerox is able to train more quickly, it commands a ninefold price premium on this service.

- Citibank knows that anyone can provide fast banking transactions. The problem is that many customers expect the savings gained through technological automation to be passed on. The real added benefit, therefore, must come from information that the bank can give its customers so that they can make a good transaction rather than just a speedy one. So, customers are not only able to do things faster but also they can also make better decisions.
- Most of the large accidents that happen in its clients' factories and retail stores have small beginnings, according to The Maryland. By analysing all the minor incidents unreported or uninsured the company demonstrates to its clients the process by which this occurs, how much money it costs them and what they can do about it. Through their value-added services it can proactively demonstrate value and command a premium rather than just react by responding in a reasonable time frame when things go wrong.

For routine services for the 'mass within markets' or even the 'markets within markets', cost efficiencies can be gained through time saving. But, when dealing with those parts geared for the 'individual within markets', time-based schemes really become a disadvantage. For, while customers want what they have come to expect, they also expect and value the exceptional. Also, there may be no set price that high-value firms can decide upon unilaterally, as well as across the board, for all customers. They may not even know how long a job will take. In fact, customers may participate in arriving at a figure. Setting a price or pricing formula jointly with customers – with room left for dialogue and negotiation if either party is not making adequate returns – is becoming increasingly popular. Modern concerns give their account managers as much freedom as possible to deal with ever more demanding customers, and do away with the fixed price lists so characteristic of the industrial era. The account managers at IBM for instance set a price when negotiating with customers based on the components needed in the solution. This flexible pricing method is aimed to encourage the building of modules for individual customers without the confines of pre-set formulas.

Some value-based pricing methods follow. They share several characteristics: all are based on results for customers; value is always directly related to customers' activities; and the value in all cases is quantified and communicated to them by the firm:

Quantified result pricing

This method is directly related to what the customer is promised and/or ultimately gets. Like many professional service firms, Price Waterhouse charges a 'success' fee for its corporate finance advice which rests on the tangible outcome its customers actually receive. There is no way of knowing these benefits before the event. If a price is pre-set by a firm, it can be adjusted along the way, depending on what transpires. For instance, Mandelli quantifies exactly what its customers can expect from its fully-automated factory lines, and at what point in the process. But, if the estimated goals are not achieved, the price may be changed. Volvo dealers also have a pricing method by which, at the end of a period, the cost-per-mile that customers actually got is compared with what was originally expected. Both Volvo dealers and the fleet owners open up their books, and prices are adjusted either way.

Relative gain pricing

The object of this method is to quantify what customers actually get or are expected to get against some previous result, making the value added transparent. This is done by comparing expected returns or outcome with previous experiences. A given percentage of the increase is paid to the firm at a given point or over a period of time as the results unfold. For instance, when Nokia-Maillefer sets up a new plant, the customer is told about the extra benefits to be gained both in terms of time saved and extra production of wire meterage. The company's forecast is based on the speed at which it can get the factory up and running, its know-how on machinery configuration, and its management of the production process. After calculating the relative gain for the customer, Nokia will negotiate a price.

Total cost pricing

SKF reaches a value-based price by looking at the total cost of the customer's operation and how much can be saved if SKF provides a solution rather than just the bearing. Customers may end up paying more to SKF than to competitors but they also save more, and this figure is quantified by the company. For instance, it will go into a paper mill and assess what it costs to stand idle rather than buy 'trouble-free operations'. Included in this figure will be the cost of disruption and other hidden expenses. SKF also looks at all the activities customers go through in the 'before' market in order to try and reduce the total cost of doing business. If the company supplies a solution to, say, an automobile firm for a total hub unit instead of just a wheel bearing, SKF tallies up all the activities the customer no longer has to do and bases its price on savings on the customer's total cost, rather than on just the cost to produce its bearing.

Opportunity cost pricing

With this method, the service provider uses a pricing technique related to opportunity cost. By showing customers what they would lose by not undergoing the service or doing business with it, it is able to assign a value to its offering. A portion of that potential loss is translated into an amount saved and becomes the basis for setting the price. For its potential customers, InterForward typically calculates the costs involved in materials handling, breaking down the customers' processes into minute details – like unloading the merchandise from the freighter and counting the parcels. The company then quantifies the activities which it is not handling for the customer, but should be – such as assessing damage and leakage, and quotes a price commensurate with the costs that would have occurred.

Some final points. Since these pricing techniques depend on the value received by customers, all minds and actions must focus on achieving results for products and services in use. High-value firms are beginning to think about providing the kinds of guarantees for their intangible offerings that goods manufacturers do. This guarantee is a promise that an outcome will occur at a future point. Making it happen may require that customers buy certain minimum solution modules however. It certainly presupposes a firm's involvement with customers throughout their activity cycle. And, even then, there will be risks. How long will it take to train a particular customer's employees? What extraneous factors will occur in dealing with that customer's specific circumstances? High on the agenda for the 1990s is to try and find ways to build new pricing formulas around these issues.

Market activity versus market share

The higher the market share, the greater the profits.[26] This was another variation on the cause and effect logic which held during industrial times. All very well, say George Stalk, Philip Evans, and Lawrence Shulman, three consultants who look at the ramifications of this in their article, 'Competing on Capabilities: the New Rules of Corporate Strategy'. But increasing market share, in the product/market sense of the word, is becoming simultaneously more difficult to do and less valuable:

> When the economy was relatively static, strategy could afford to be static. In a world characterized by durable products, stable customer needs, well-defined national and regional markets, and clearly identified competitors, competition was a 'war of position' in which companies occupied competitive space like squares on a chessboard, building and defending market share in clearly defined product or market segments.[27]

It seemed so clear during the 1960s, 1970s and 1980s that market share led to profitability. But, the experts now say it wasn't that certain then and it most definitely isn't that certain now. Examining past numbers more carefully, they assert that managers may not have really known what came first: a high return on investment (ROI) or market share. Gains in market share were associated with gains in ROI, but increased ROI also led to subsequent increases in market share. What else, they enquire, were firms doing to get these results?[28]

Having market share was one thing. Acquiring it was quite another. It meant biting into someone else's slice, which took inordinate amounts of time and energy, and inevitably led to price cutting. So intent were firms on increasing their share of the existing market that many continued to fight for larger chunks of a pie that was dwindling. They missed opportunities to satisfy unmet needs. In truth, customers were often sacrificed in this pursuit of having these ever bigger sales.

So obsessed were they with the figures that many firms didn't know whether they were gaining or losing individual customers and what the tradeoffs were, says Christian Grunroos in his work, *Services Management and Marketing*. He adds that, with market share, firms can't tell whether a given and perhaps even stable market share is due to a customer base that brings repeat business, or whether it is large numbers of customers just coming and going. And, bearing in mind that it's always more expensive to acquire a new customer than sell more to a satisfied one, corporations that chased market share may have damaged themselves in the long run.[29]

The trap with market share, commentators and modern managers warn, is aiming for that instead of focusing on the activities and capabilities that lead to it. Canon is a good example. The company no longer looks at increasing its market share as a guidepost to profit. Management now accepts that it's probably impossible to continue increasing the company's share of the copier market without cutting prices and forfeiting service quality. So they look at what else can be done to increase revenues to existing distributors and end users. The result may indeed be an increase in the share of copiers, but Canon doesn't rely on it. It is more realistic that profits will come from activities related to the distribution and use of the copier systems – including paper and office supply equipment – which it doesn't even make.

It's the knowledge bases and multi-skilled capacity to serve within the network enterprise which create competitive position today, rather than a large share of the core item market. As James Brian Quinn, Thomas L. Doorley and Penny Paquette write in their article, 'Technology in Services: Rethinking Strategic Focus':

> High market share and high profitability together come from having the highest relevant activity share in the marketplace – in other words, having the most effective presence in a service activity the market desires and thus gaining the experience curve and other benefits accruing to that high activity share. In service-dominated marketplaces – and most are – competitive analysis must focus on the relative potency of the activities or service power that undergird product positions. Too few strategists and companies realize this.[30]

None of this negates market share. As it stands, though, it is an artificial goal for contemporary settings. If profits are not derived from scale but from

Industrial (*Market share*)	Service (*Market activity*)
Static	Dynamic
Easy to measure	Difficult to measure
Relates to size of product or service market	Relates to sum of all competences in solutions activities
Sells as much as possible	Does as much as necessary
Current business focus	Customer business focus
Compares industry competitors	Compares all potential providers

Figure 8.2   Principles of market share and market activity

value-adding capabilities, and a combination of products and ever increasing services, the question is: 'market share of what?' Since many firms cannot perform all the customer satisfying activities alone, the other question is 'whose market share?' In sum (as Figure 8.2 shows), market share and market activity come from a different mindset, offering an alternative way of looking at the same problem: how to be successful and make profits.

Indeed, the very term share assumes something fixed and static – a given slice of a given market within confined competitive and national boundaries. Market activity is a dynamic concept and refers to what has to be done and how. Easy to measure, market share deals in precise equations over fixed periods whereas this is not as simple with market activity. Firms don't always know what parts of the mass custom-alized solution to compare and with whom. As aware as they may be of their own figures, it's also not sure they can be as specific about others. How large is the market? how much did we get? is the conventional market share approach. Now these 'lag indicators' seem so sterile compared to the 'lead indicators' used by high value firms which help them determine whether they have the potential capacity they need to serve customers in the long term compared to other providers. And so the classic *troika* formula – volume, economies, and market share – becomes more distant, it seems, with every passing year as firms increasingly concentrate on developing the customer satisfying activities upon which their profits now rest.

9 Linking, liaising and leveraging services through technology

Technology makes possible what good management knew but was formerly unable to achieve.

Walter Wriston, CEO, Citicorp, *The Listener,* 28 August 1986

A note in isolation means nothing – it's just a sound. Music, on the other hand, is made up of different notes which, when intricately combined, produce a distinctive melody. More than anything else, it's these connections that matter in music. The art lies in how the notes are joined, how the chords – or combinations of notes – are forged, and how the bars are linked. Without these connections, the work becomes disjointed, the tune breaks down and the flow is lost. That's what makes music into 'music', as opposed to just a cacophony of sounds.

To make a simple piece of music more profound, a composer may add more instruments – or voices – and themes. Strung together, these melodies give the composition more depth and texture. While they may harmonize and merge in a pleasing way, they are deliberately varied in order to add versatility. If the arrangement is taken apart, the individual parts are likely to have no resemblance or even little to do with each other. Except in counterpoint.

Here, the technique creates a very different kind of music. By replicating the original melody, several versions of one theme run concurrently throughout the piece. Each critical note in the main score is matched by the composer to its respective counterpoint note. Great resonance and depth are achieved because the accompanying melodies are not only based on the underlying theme but also are an extension of it. Each stage of the music leads into the next and eventually reverts back to the beginning, which results in ongoing continuity.

For centuries, the music world has been fascinated by the composer, Johann Sebastian Bach, *the* counterpoint master. While the exercise may seem to be relatively straightforward, no one to date has succeeded in using counterpart as proficiently. His music generates itself perpetually. Cohesion comes not from contrasting beats – as most composers have done – but by constantly reproducing the underlying theme, using it to propel the melody forward. Overlapping layers lead to an almost infinite number of variations of the same theme, with complementary melodies creating many complex refrains. The beauty is found not merely in the separate lines of the score, but in the intricate development of themes that are connected and interconnected in an endless flow.[1]

Interestingly, the counterpoint image can be compared to information technology (IT), as it relates – metaphorically speaking – to the way that high-value organizations today are using it. To be effective, IT is being designed with users in mind – beginning with customers' activity cycles. This goal is no longer achieved by creating more and different forms of IT, it is by making the existing technology more relevant to them. So as to ensure an ongoing process of adding value, links between the customer and the network enterprise have to be established. Just as counterpoint brings the underlying and overlapping themes together, so IT brings the customer and the firm together by connecting each critical activity and information point.

IT is unique in that it is the one technology which, like counterpoint, breeds on itself. The more information produced by IT, the more the knowledge base grows, feeding the technology which in turn produces more information – with the procedure continuing ad infinitum. Once connected to the customer's activities and aims, this self-generating feature of IT enables it not only to create information but also to enhance itself. IT thus becomes more and more powerful and fulfilling, giving and getting the value enhancing leverage firms need to have customer satisfying market potential.

Technology as it was and as it is

One thing which distinguishes human beings from other species is the ability to put knowledge to work. And this is done through tools. Technologies are in effect these tools – applications of what man knows and uses to facilitate life and work. It's obvious then that technology has been constant throughout human development, as Ferdinand Braudel, the well-known French historian tells us. In trying to account for the rise of civilization, especially in the Mediterranean region, he concludes that the progress of a society can, in fact, be tracked through the technology man has created. And, the pace at which such a society can grow and prosper depends on its ability to take scientific inventions and apply them in a practical manner.[2]

Technology has therefore always been an intentional extension of natural capabilities. In fact, many writers define technology in this way, although they are quick to point out that no one definition exists. Technology is the starting point of what can and can't be done, and it tries to make up the difference. James Beninger, an expert in information technology, offers an interesting illustration in his essay, 'The Evolution of Control'. The ability of a person to breathe under water, he explains, is an extension of man's natural capability: since respiration is a wholly natural function, it is not a technology, whereas the human ability to breathe under water implies that some technology has been put to work.[3]

Information technology has had the most profound impact on services. It is a set of technologies related to the processing and communication of information, embracing computing and electronic databases, linked through advanced telecommunications, found everywhere and anywhere today – from desks to sidewalks, jets to cars, malls to shop floors, in homes and briefcases. Expanding at a faster pace than any other technology in the history of mankind, IT is to the high-value company what iron ore was to industrial concerns.[4]

More than anything else, IT's recent progression has changed the way that technology is viewed by contemporary corporations:

Then: technology was designed for use internally to facilitate the firm's operation.

Now: it's externally focused with the market in mind, the objective being to add value for customers.

Then: technology was used by firms in pursuit of their own objectives.

Now: access is provided to the entire channel as organizations use technology to extend themselves up-, down-, and 'in-stream'.

Then: the idea was to use technology to replace people.

Now: the technology is placed squarely in people's hands to give them the tools for superior performance.

Then: technology locked customers out, with information guarded in a fortress-like environment.

Now: technologies lock customers in, because they get better value, relationships are closer, and the cost of switching simply becomes too high.

The contrasts between the traditional industrial and contemporary approaches to technology are significant and have influenced the way in which firms fundamentally think and compete (see Figure 9.1). Until now, technology's one overriding objective has been to supplement man's physical limitations. Industrial technology was involved essentially in creating greater amounts of physical goods and moving them more quickly. Ostensibly, through technology, physical mass could be handled in ways that compensated for human shortcomings. American professor, Shoshana Zuboff, looks at the impact of IT on the workplace. In her work, *In the Age of the Smart Machine*, she reminds us that technology was systematically related to the capabilities of the body. Originally, it redefined the production limits that had formerly been imposed by the physical weaknesses of a firm's employees. That the process of automation brought about a decline in the amount of punishment to which employees were subjected was one thing, she says; but, at the same time, it steadily diminished the level of know-how required of them.[5]

Information technology, on the other hand, creates and moves information and, in the process, reduces physical mass. For the first time, managers are

Industrial	Contemporary
Compensate man's physical ability	Complement man's ingenuity
Do better what do	Do what never done before
Electro mechanical power generation based	Information and know-how based
Limited and finite use	Organic and infinite application
Restricted to firm and buffered	Shared with outside and open
Produces output tangible	Produces value through intangible
People controlling	People controlled

Figure 9.1   Industrial and contemporary approaches to technology

dealing with a technology that produces the immaterial. Of course, automating and making things more accurate is still a valid function of IT but, additionally, it now accumulates and interprets information. By augmenting and spreading the firm's know-how, it complements man's ingenuity. Unlike electro-mechanical power generation, which has been directed at physical productivity ever since the steam engine, the new technologies improve people's problem-solving and customer serving skills. The information, together with employee experience and know-how, are able jointly to produce what neither could ever have done alone, thereby improving the firm's capacity to serve.

But, the amount of value added that can be gained from IT today depends very much on the participation of people. As Vincent Barabba and Gerald Zaltman note in *Hearing the Voice of the Market*, IT is no longer confined to a select few, which was the industrial approach. Now, high-value corporations try to find out who can use the technology most effectively and how to get it to these people. They go on to say:

> In contrast (to earlier times) the process of using information is a judgmental matter. Moreover, it is not desirable to depersonalize information use even if we could, since the effective use of information relies on the non-research frames that reference decision makers bring to a problem. As we move from data collection, processing, and storage to information use, we move from science to art or craft. Thus technologies for improving research use must be 'people involving'. The conversion of data into knowledge is necessarily a human (behavioral) process; no computer can do it alone.[6]

Attention has moved, then, from developing 'artificial intelligence' (AI) to what the experts call 'intelligence augmentation' (IA).[7] What they mean is that managers are using IT to amplify intelligence, making employees more powerful and competent rather than replacing the human mind with ever more powerful machines. Machines no longer control people; rather, it is the machines that are controlled – by employees who now have to supply the value added to the market instead of simply doing jobs focusing on set tasks and procedures.

Rather than just boosting productivity, as technology did in the industrial age – helping managers do better, more quickly and accurately what they already could do – today's technology has entered new frontiers, enabling high-value corporations to do different things. For one thing, IT – which was previously isolated – now holds the greatest promise, of all the technologies, for partnering in the 1990s. As a matter of fact, the word 'communicate' comes from the Latin verb *communicare* meaning 'to share'. Through telecommunications, information is now accessible to all, both inside a network enterprise and outside, binding people, disregarding boundaries. Since information is the only resource which increases in value when shared, having it available potentially to all now means its full worth can truly be realized. Whereas this possibility was absent when information was limited and finite in use, now, through IT, it's able to self-multiply, growing organically, creating rich and infinite opportunities to add value for customers through exchange and applications.[8]

From building to using information technology

Firms continued to invest in IT right into the 1990s at an unprecedented rate. How else, they reasoned, could they compete? They had no choice. But, just because they were making huge investments in IT didn't mean they were getting the best possible results. Several observers have tried to explain why, including Kenneth and Edward Primozic of IBM, and Joe Leben, an independent consultant. What they say in *Strategic Choices*, a book which looks at the long term – as opposed to just operational – importance of IT is that, until now, the great potential of IT has been seriously curtailed by its almost exclusively internal focus.[9]

Actually, the role of technology has shifted over the years as the relationship between the producer and consumer has gone through its various stages (see Figures 9.2 and 4.1). In the 1960s, when producers and consumers dealt with each other on a transactional basis, managers persistently regarded IT as a cost-cutting, efficiency-improving tool. Automation through technology led to significant reductions in costs and increased production in several industries. This continued into the 1970s but, by then, the price of IT was going down, and many firms got the economies and enhanced productivity

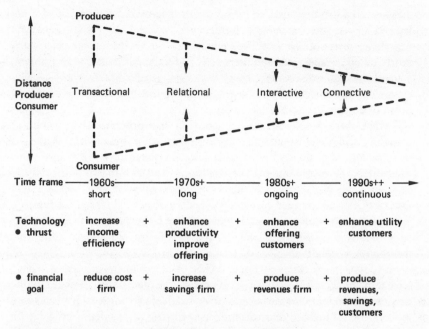

Figure 9.2 Stages in customer relationships and role of technology

from improved data processing.[10] Marketing had moved into the spotlight as well, so technology began to be applied to market research, customer survey and feedback instruments in order to improve offerings. Nonetheless firms still used IT more to increase their productivity and savings than to serve customers.

By the 1980s, despite the developments in IT, firms began to experience problems. There was a deluge of information – so much so that, ultimately, it did not always have an outlet or application.[11] Much of the accelerating corporate investment went under-utilized. Firms simply didn't have the people, expertise or facilities to cope with it. And so much time went into disseminating and digesting data, that many of them ended up with diminishing returns.

Service companies had made especially large investments in IT systems, which began to bloat costs and be a burden on overhead.[12] To aggravate matters, many managers had forced IT into their existing organizations instead of adapting their organizations to accommodate IT. And employees in traditional service firms often saw IT as a threat and in many instances didn't take to it readily. Frequently, they had not been trained to use it well enough, missing the benefits. At Federal Express, for example, couriers objected to the early tests of hand-held shipment tracking devices because they were being asked to input information that hadn't been required of them previously, a task that slowed down their pick-up and delivery process. Customers had also not learned to use the technology proficiently. Years later, some banks still experience resistance to automated teller machines (ATMs), a concept which nearly failed because potential users were not trained adequately. In addition, as the banks later discovered, many customers resented having to deal with technology rather than human beings, believing that their concerns could not possibly be taken seriously by machines.[13]

Despite these problems and resistance, IT had become a key feature in market offerings and a potential revenue generator for firms. Yet, it seemed as if technology was always one step ahead of management's ability to reap its full benefits. It wasn't until the late 1980s or early 1990s that IT was available to really deal with the overabundance of information. And it was then that managers began to realize that they had been so engrossed in building information infrastructures that they had not used it sufficiently to extend their corporations to customers and to those who served them within the distribution channel.

Since what the technology could do had changed, managers had to change what they did with it. Instead of saving money and generating revenues for the firm, as in previous decades, now they would have to use IT to enhance utilities for customers, and to produce revenues and savings for them. In effect, what managers had learned was that, as far as data was concerned, more was not necessarily better. As the last decade of the twentieth century approached, they had the technology – and the need – to mould data increasingly into information and structured knowledge, in order to use it as a value-adding tool. It wasn't just lagging behind competitors which concerned managers now: it was getting and keeping the customer connections through IT that they knew were essential to compete. And so, there was a change in emphasis in the 1990s, as these examples demonstrate:

● DuPont now provides customers with on-line terminals and both can log into the other's system, exchange information and ideas, and pursue a continuous dialogue on day-to-day problems and projects. DuPont is electronically connected to carpet mills, key retailers, and even end users in their offices and homes – either via PCs or telephones.
● Federal Express took its sophisticated network system – which provided ongoing customer courier service and information to customers – and converted it into what the company calls a 'powership management system'. This service allows key customers to set up their own timetable; for all practical purposes, they operate the entire set of courier logistic activities from their own desks.
● On a minute-to-minute basis, through Kao's IT category management system, retailers are aware of the movement of all goods on their shelves. Without any administrative or procedural intervention, items can be

restocked. This doesn't necessarily translate into increased sales for Kao, since retailers may find that competitors' brands are moving more quickly. But, the IT does tend to lock in customers more solidly, and for the long term, than mere brand movement would do.

● The Maryland can now give customers an instant response to their insurance queries or requests when they call in to service centres. Employees have the details about every customer on the screen – when they last put in a claim, the specifics of their insurance policy, and how they like to be handled. Policies can be updated immediately, requests like special coverage implemented, and quotes and advice provided then and there.

● Canon's logistics system for dealers works well because the company can expedite any order for supplies, parts and components to end users immediately when it is received. Through its IT, Canon also can foresee when each customer is likely to reorder, thus reducing lag time and lowering customers' costs still further.

● AT&T is using sophisticated IT to provide better services to customers on the front line by giving its own staff more flexibility. So as not to have employees stuck in offices, the company has created satellite centres that allow people to work at home or go into the field with access to all the information and backup they need in order to provide ongoing tele-communication solutions.

● Corporate customers had to abide by the machine rules in the past at Citibank. The only way transfers could be made electronically was through on-line linkups. Now, the technology will accept instructions for payments and funds transfers from a telex or fax. The software interprets unstructured messages and immediately executes the transaction.

Putting intelligence into information

Confronted by the need to supply ongoing solutions in an environment charged with uncertainty, high-value firms must devise IT that can strengthen their value-creating process in the marketplace. To do this, they need to convert data to information, and information to intelligence – what some people prefer to call structured 'knowledge'. Each of these levels is necessary in any support or decision-making activity made either for, with, or by customers. Starting with the data, each succeeding level becomes part of the next, building on the previous. (Figure 9.3 illustrates this.)

Level 1 - data: are the facts, the numbers probably undigested by the firm or receiving customer. They are objective, simple, factual and free of context. There is no room, or need, for interpretation: 'data' simply exists. It is said that the amount of data will double nineteen times by the year 2000.[14] Firms

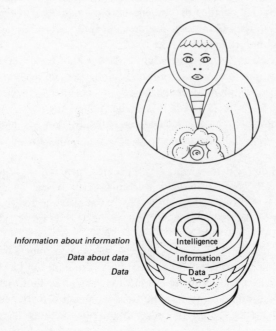

Information about information
Data about data
Data

Figure 9.3   'Levels' of information technology

have to have the infrastructure to store and retrieve that which is relevant to them.

Level 2 - information: is the aggregate of the facts, 'data about data'. The data is combined, organized and placed in context; its meaning is based on past events, experience, analysis and interpretation. Once data has become information, it becomes domain specific. It's no longer neutral, taking on relevance, applicable to a certain market or process. But, it has invariably been organized by others.

Level 3 - intelligence: is when the known information becomes synthesized, able to be applied beyond pre-set and normal conditions. This 'information about information' is essential when decisions have to be made which may or may not be routine but contain conditions outside the norm. The technology enables the system to 'think', understand why something is happening, make choices and anticipate the consequences of decisions. The technology is able to organize information any way it wants, and to internalize and integrate this information with everything else it knows. Being able to turn what's known into feasible alternatives and then choose the one most likely to work is what distinguishes knowledge-based systems from data or information systems.[15]

It's not a packaged solution – it's a process which tries to simulate the way that the human mind works. It uses what is known by others, thereby drawing on the expertise and experience of the whole company and customer network.

Arno Penzias, the current vice president of research at AT&T and a physicist who has written prolifically on IT, elaborates on the difference between information and intelligence. 'Intelligent' technologies are able to acquire and apply knowledge in a variety of circumstances, under changing real-world conditions, he says. Elucidating in *Ideas and Information*, he continues:

> As I see it, truly intelligent behaviour calls for the ability to use information acquired in one situation to solve problems in another. Without that ability, a system is little more than a programmable calculator – driven by an exhaustive set of explicit instructions. Thus the designer of an 'intelligent' system must devise a knowledge representation scheme organizing information storage in a way that permits the system to apply that information in unforeseen situations.[16]

The term 'wisdom' is used interchangeably with intelligence, although some people consider it to be yet another level. Others say wisdom is a uniquely human attribute which can never be replicated. Their argument is that wisdom is not even inherent in all human beings, let alone machines! Semantics aside, commentators seriously question whether computers can ever learn to emulate human thought and know(ing). Or the sort of fuzzy logic that man calls 'feelings'. On the other hand, what one might call wisdom in IT has probably already begun, since expert systems now capture, translate and transfer people's previous experiences and decisions. Some of their intuitive and interpretive powers have therefore already been incorporated into the system. What machines hoped to do – build on previous learning, and make judgements and inferences – is already largely being accomplished therefore.[17] These examples illustrate the various levels in practice:

- Hendrix Voeders had collected plenty of data on feed and animal statistics from farmers and others who worked in the agricultural field. It was, however, only a starting point as the company moved from bulk animal feeds to farming solutions. As soon as Hendrix Voeders began to aggregate the data and systematize it, it became relevant to the farmers who had to make decisions about which feed conditions and medications were appropriate for their particular kinds of animals. Next an 'expert' system was put in place to help farmers make real-time decisions when unusual conditions occurred – like an outbreak of disease or exceptional weather, and take advantage of all the experiences and knowledge about pig farming that had been accumulated.

● Instead of answering a customer's call for repair help, Rank Xerox now has sophisticated scheduled maintenance technology which enables the company to predict when the next breakdown in a document system will occur. When the artificial intelligence technology determines there is a need, Rank Xerox calls the customer to set up a service rendezvous. The technology contains not only the data and information about repair cases but also all the global use, breakdown and maintenance experiences from account teams and service technicians. It is looking constantly for the exceptions rather than the rule, using them to create patterns for improving the company's capabilities. It assesses if a customer's documentation system is working to standard, when it will go down, why, what the engineers should do to get the best results, special spare parts needed and where to get them. With luck, the client may not be involved in any of this activity, simply experiencing ongoing documentation operations.

● Data about individual card members comes in automatically to American Express as part of the company's normal business activities. How this data is used is extraordinary. It creates an information portrait of each customer, developing a credit approval system which, ideally, will speed up the process for all and avoid overloading the network. Because predictability is built in, the system accepts a purchase made by, say, a female customer who typically buys designer clothing in Paris. What causes delays, then, is the unpredictability of customer behaviour. So, embedded into American Express's current IT is the intelligence to make inferences when deviations from the usual occur. For instance, if the woman suddenly buys clothing in the Orient, the system will look at recent events and make a judgement as to whether or not it is indeed the same customer who is making the purchase. Has she bought a ticket to Tokyo? Has she bought travellers' cheques? Has she checked into a hotel in Japan? Has she phoned home from there?[18]

Creating mass custom-alized offerings with technology

Citibank was the champion of high-tech banking. Electronic banking, first introduced during the late 1970s, was for all the bank's customers. It was a giant step, a way to enable customers to bank more swiftly, conveniently, accurately, and cost effectively. Next, the bank began to identify separate markets: at the corporate level, an important one was the multinationals. Information – *the* value added to the transactions – was tied to specific industries so as to obtain the best possible returns. But, things were changing for these corporate customers. Dealing in so many currencies cross border, they now need a system which can encompass all the transactions being made to optimize each financial decision. Whether or not the treasury in the client's firm is centralized or decentralized determines what that customer can do for itself and where Citibank can fill the gap. IT has had to be designed to meet these individualized needs. Firms that operate centrally make the financial decisions for their subsidiaries and so want information on the particularities in each country at all times, as well as an infrastructure to implement these financial decisions. Since the decentralized operations make their own decisions, they need a global perspective and a network to coordinate information so that they can optimize decisions for themselves as well as for the company at large.

What Citibank is doing is mass custom-alizing its technology to provide customers with solutions. The data is still the bedrock, which is mass-produced to achieve economies of scale. From this source, the bank is able to customize the data into relevant information for specific industry require-ments. But, ultimately this information becomes an intelligent base, pertinent to the needs of individual decision-makers, based on their own special circumstances and their vast permutation of needs at any given moment.

Firms deliver mass-customalized solutions by means of technologies which can, for purposes of discussion, be called 'universal', 'applied' and 'sensitive' (see Figure 9.4). The 'universal technologies' are the mass technologies, those

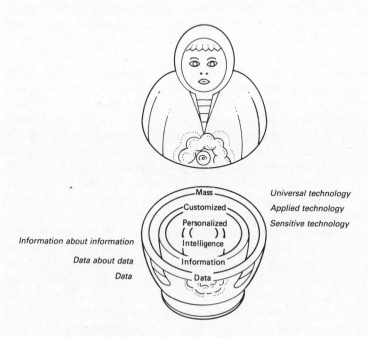

Figure 9.4 'Levels' of information technology

that are widespread and an accepted part of every offering today. They are non-differentiated, common to all, basically the plumbing – the cables, satellites, networks and digital highways through which data is gathered and transmitted. The 'applied technologies', geared for use by certain customers, are basically programmed software and on-line systems for specific uses. Without the universal level, this refined technology isn't possible. With only the universal technology, though, the benefits are marginal for users. Put differently, everyone can benefit from the universal technologies, but applied technologies are of value only to targeted users.

By using the 'sensitive technologies', high-value firms can personalize their offerings to customers, both in substance and through frontliners' responsiveness and behaviour. In this way, they can deliver products and services of unique value to corporate and individual customers. Sensitive technology goes beyond having the company merely feeding and gleaning relevant information to and from its markets. But, it does require an interdependent set of interactions between the firm and the customer in order to function successfully. Personalization often can only take place if it is designed as a two-way process, built for a high degree of customer input and participation.

Research on services by Johan Olaisen and Oivind Revang at the Norwegian School of Management highlights the impact of sensitive technologies on traditional service industries. It has, they say in their article, 'The Significance of Information Technology for Service Quality', brought about an entire change in the service concept.[19] Without this kind of technology, it was incredibly difficult to really personalize an offering – employees simply couldn't carry the necessary information in their heads. Today, the technology identifies the special traits and needs of customers. Unfettered by forms and chores, backed by sophisticated infrastructures, people in the customer-facing positions can focus exclusively on satisfying their clients' ever growing expectations. The IT system must not only be capable of capturing the data but also of translating and reacting to it. So, programmes must be built not only for accuracy but flexibility and resilience. There must be, in other words, a high tolerance level able to accept the unpredictable, respond to the inhabitual, while allowing customers the choice and the freedom to switch decisions without penalty.

Let's go back to Citibank. Despite having over 20 ATM terminals in some sites in the States, customers don't always want or have the time to go to one of them or to a branch. So, the bank has installed the same into their home phones. Using a 4×3-inch screen and menu-driven commands, customers can make all of their banking transactions – including paying 20–30 bills in ten minutes – get their balance, request loans, make transfers, and obtain a 'cash slip' for use in several, small retail stores to make purchases. When customers do go into their branch, they can use the electronic queueing device. By inserting a card into a specially designed terminal, they can make a request in advance and the account executive or teller should be prepared with all the relevant information to expedite their transactions quickly. And additionally, customers can be dealt with on a much more personal basis because of the knowledge accessed by employees through this customer activated procedure.

How can high-value corporations provide effective technology services in the most cost-efficient way? Only by finding the ideal combination of these three technologies. The first rule is to make the universal technologies accessible for the 'mass within markets', encouraging all customers to use them by making them affordable, user-friendly and reliable, and requiring no major adjustments in work or lifestyle. If a firm is going to be able to offer customized services for 'markets within markets', its technology must be designed with specific usage features, and that means having a close, ongoing knowledge of the customers being targeted. Next, for any market of one – whether corporate or personal – the firm has to open up its channels and allow a free flow of information to and from individual users.

Honda is able to trace the status of each individual buyer's car through its sensitive technology. It maintains an historical database on each customer for its dealers. Whenever a customer has a query or problem, the dealer can retrieve the relevant information at once. Every time the customer brings in a car to be repaired or serviced, the dealer in turn will update the information on the database. In this way, the vast quantity of knowledge accumulated about individual vehicles can be assimilated into a problem-solving IT package that dealers can access on their own workstation whenever they need it. The same universal and applied technologies are being used in sensitive IT, except that the technologies are being merged, and features that translate and respond to needs in a more individualistic way are being built in. The following examples illustrate:

● Federal Express uses satellite communications as the foundation for all value-added services. This technology gives the company the worldwide coverage needed to ensure efficient tracking of parcels and relevant information about them. This system is being linked up to workstations for the top 30 per cent of its large-volume customers, all of whom have access to the entire tracking IT system and each of whom have the same basic concerns. Where are their parcels? How are they doing en route? How quickly will they reach their destination? Have they arrived? Going further, the technology allows individual firms to pursue the activities that are most important to them – billing for direct shipments to customers, or printing custom labels, etc.

● The simple data gathering through communication networks at Hendrix Voeders first collects the basic facts about the animals – age, number in a herd, food intake, state of health, weight and other general conditions. Software is then developed for specific customer groups, depending on the size of the herds, the breeds, their locations, and climatic conditions. Farmers are also given laptops with a modem that can access the company's central database. Farmers can make specific decisions for themselves on a certain animal at a particular moment because of the sensitive technology lodged in the system which generates individualized resolutions.

● Using broad-based communication systems, InterForward knows the available capacity of each vehicle and warehouse in its transportation network. Since InterForward doesn't own any lorries or buildings, it is critical to know when and where capacity is available so that the company can match it with current needs. Through on-line systems, InterForward also permits other hauliers following established itineraries in certain geographic areas to use this capacity in order to keep their costs down. Individual hauliers out on the road are linked via mobile communications, thereby alerted to special requests as they come in.

● Airlines share reservation systems. The technology used is universal – an operating necessity rather than a value-adding tool; it is routine and well perfected, favours no one in particular and is essential to everyone. Using satellite pathways that allow easy and ongoing air-to-ground information and communications, Singapore Airlines has developed customized in-flight technology applications for business travellers which recreate an office environment in the sky. The IT now goes a step further, enabling the company to treat each customer as an individual. By the time passengers arrive at their seats, the frontliners not only know who they are and what they want, but also the system will have indicated all their special requests. Clients no longer have to follow a fixed schedule because individual facilities are located at each seat from which they can work, get Reuters information or watch one of several movies. As another example, SAS, rather than limiting its sleeper seats to first class passengers, allows anyone flying SAS to preorder the service at the check-in point for which they pay a fee.

● British Telecom considers the phone system today to be nothing but a sophisticated linkup of cables. This universal technology becomes more sophisticated almost daily through the use of optic fibres and satellite communications. Because the company's major customers use the phone so often, they don't want to be dependent on the public network. So, BT has isolated part of the public network and reserved it for these high-volume clients. Using these private networks, BT can offer industries many more customized services tailored to their particular location and special needs. The company has also created technology that is so sensitive it allows individuals within these corporations to adapt their calling services to what they are doing at different times. Phones can be programmed to follow them or to route calls to third parties. Phones can also be told when a call may interrupt the user and when it should be diverted elsewhere, as well as to whom and for how long. Display panels and voice recognition systems inform customers about the origin of a call, so *they* have the freedom and flexibility to decide what to do.

- Wireless communications and mobile telephony connected through IT networks make feasible the fleet monitoring system Volvo Trucks uses to ensure cost-per-mile for customers. Mobile PCs in cabs and trucks register requests, gauge distances, report on petrol prices and offer advice on the most efficient routes to take. Furthermore, taxis that are linked into train and aeronautical IT systems know when flights are arriving. Likewise, truck drivers can use the same technology to optimize the utilization of their vehicles to and from destinations. If a driver's vehicle breaks down, the terminal can be used to get diagnostic help from a service support centre and then call directly to the nearest dealer for help.

Using IT to link the customer's activity cycle

After Bach selected the notes that were critical to his composition, he created an overlay of melodies using these tones in order to make the music more meaningful. The technology boldly used by modern firms achieves an equally dramatic result. By aligning IT to the customer's critical value points, managers can create, facilitate and support superior service delivery. It is this point-counterpoint architecture which gives the firm much of the capability needed to offer cohesive, relevant and flexible solution offerings on a continuous basis.

It would be difficult to envisage uninterrupted performing systems for today's customers without the help of technology. The technological linkup is largely what makes it possible for high-value corporations to provide a seamless flow of services. No longer can firms do without IT. Nor can they necessarily satisfy customers merely by having it. Success will increasingly go to those that provide the value added needed through the customer' entire activity cycle. The examples which follow (and Figures 9.5–9.7) demonstrate how this works in particular instances:

- It's vital for Mandelli (Figure 9.5) that its technology can meet customers' changing requirements. The customer may design a car that needs a new engine, for which a factory must be built. Three years later, the model changes and so does the engine. Of course, these firms don't want to build a brand new factory or start from scratch with a whole new set of designs for each new model. So, Mandelli needs technology which can simply add or replace certain features, supply clients with the various options on their PCs, and recommend the best solution.

  At the pre-purchase point of an automated factory project – when a new or adapted model is being considered by a customer – Mandelli must either

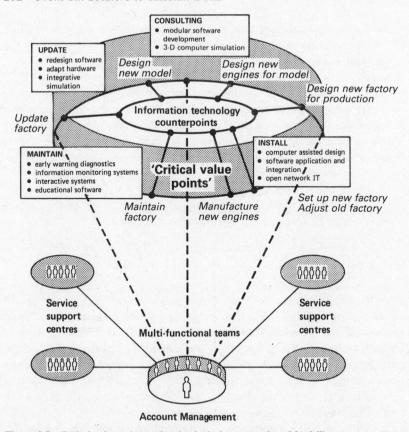

Figure 9.5 Critical value points and technological counterpoints: Mandelli

link into the customer's existing IT system or design one that is compatible. Working either remotely or on site, they consider design options jointly with all the financial and operational ramifications. Graphic, interactive technologies allow alternatives in machine design and factory layout to be set up three-dimensionally, then modified in real time as decisions are made.

Mandelli designs Computer Assisted Design and Computer Assisted Manufacturing (CAD/CAM) software that permits the manufacturing process to proceed without interruption once the production lines or intelligent factories are up and running. This includes software for education as well as monitoring production costs, flows and standards, with link ups directly to Mandelli. Maintenance of the system in the post-purchase phase is done using interactive technologies – including early warning systems, diagnostics and repair – provided by the company's expert sytems. Updates and adaptations begin almost immediately through

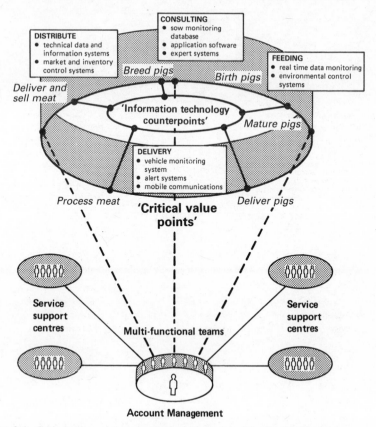

Figure 9.6   Critical value points and technological counterpoints: Hendrix Voeders

this software so that at the appropriate moment the client's activity cycle can be reactivated.

● The Hendrix Voeder's scheme uses an integrated IT system from the beginning until the end of the farmer's investment (Figure 9.6). Consultants are continually collecting technical and managerial information about the animals, expenses and revenues which is then fed into the firm's central expert system. So, when new breeding stock have to be bought, the ideal profile has already been worked out by the system. Thus, the consultants are able to give advice on the correct breeding conditions and medication for the sows. After the piglets are born and have reached maturity, they are fed and medicated based on recommendations from an interactive on-line system. The farmers rely on the intelligence available through this system for making their decisions. The IT linkup continues to assist them at each step, providing them with information on whether quality criteria have been met during slaughtering and processing – and if not why not, as well

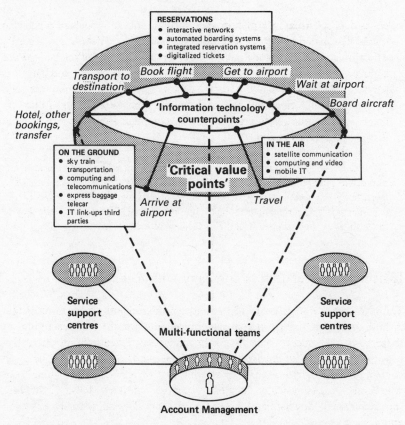

Figure 9.7   Critical value points and technological counterpoints: Singapore Airlines

as retail delivery and inventory schedules. Farmers can also find out how well their stock is moving at the retailer level and obtain all the information they need and want about their animals.

The idea behind Singapore Airlines' high-technology investments for business travellers 'on the ground' and 'in the air' – pre-voyage, during the journey and afterward – is to create one integrated solution (Figure 9.7). Singapore Airlines knows that customers want to get in and out of the airport as quickly as possible; therefore, interruptions and interventions between staff and customers on the ground are kept to a minimum. Better screens and improved menu-driven commands speed up the check-in process at Changi, and new user-friendly programs simplify rote tasks. An express telecar system moves baggage in record time from one terminal to another, while a skytrain transports passengers to and from flights so as to eliminate anxiety and congestion.

At the gate, passengers can insert their own boarding passes which contain all the usual information, plus special requests – such as vegetarian meals. Through a reader the software verifies check-in details and security. The aim is to transform the cabin of the aircraft into an 'office and leisure centre in the sky' which offers an array of entertainment and business services. Back at Changi Airport, customers proceed quickly through baggage, immigration, and can book hotels, transportation and follow-up travel reservations for future voyages. A comment from one executive at Singapore Airlines expands:

> The object is to give passengers as little distraction as possible on the ground and as much as possible during the flight. We use technology to make the best use of their time and ours. Once the technology becomes part of the traveller's experience, it's important to us to make sure they get the same quality while they are with us as they can get at home or in their offices.

Liaising across and cross company with technology

The most noticeable effect of technology on the modern organization is that it facilitates internal and external integration, aligning the firm's activities to those of its customers. Once IT got beyond being essentially an internally-based tool, it began to change the way people worked together. By being in contact electronically – regardless of what part of the firm they belong to or where they are physically located – people can now liaise 'instream', 'upstream' and 'downstream', operating as one all-encompassing extended entity.

What technology really does, though, is make possible the basic architecture for the close cooperation so necessary for success in services today. Importantly, it has strengthened relationships within firms. Because of IT's interconnective capability, multi-functional processes can be implemented cross-company. Working concurrently instead of step by step is now made possible, through IT platforms that provide everyone with the same information at the same time. Thereby they gain equal access to information, can choose what they need, add their own data and ideas, and take on tasks at the appropriate time – in sync with others rather than in sequence.[20]

Computers – mere dumb terminals in industrial days – are now live work centres. No centralized mainframe determines who gets what information any longer. Rather than simply receive the facts about passengers before take-off, flight attendants on a Singapore Airlines flight use portable PCs to access from and feed information about passengers into the system. Instead of filling in forms when a customer enters a branch to open an account, the contact person at Citibank can turn on a PC and together with the customer work out simulations of what various schemes and scenarios for buying and selling transactions might look like in years to come.

Unlike before, says George Gilder, political and social commentator on the impact of IT in the workplace, the power can really go the frontliners thanks to technology. Before, the brainpower was in the mainframe and went directly to the top of the hierarchy. Like their computers, users were considered dumb: they got the information they needed to get on with what they had to do. Only now, Gilder comments in his publication, *Life after Television*, is the power able to move to the bottom or fringes of the organization – into the heads and hands of the people who actually need it.[21]

But, many companies are still only putting the technology in, hoping that these people will talk to each other, and get the desired results. Michael Schrage, the American media specialist and journalist, warns in his book, *Shared Minds*:

> (They) invest in technology as the solution. They automate; they buy the latest equipment; they buy the whole concept of the information-driven organization. They're betting that they can plug technology into the organization as easily as a computer can be plugged into a wall socket. But the notion that connecting people up and managing information yields more effective and more productive people is flawed.[22]

Today, technology has to be viewed as a means for people to form close liaisons, to share ideas, information and experiences instead of simply passing on vast quantities of information. One problem until now has been that managers have used technology to 'wire the walls' instead of pulling them down. Whereas, before, technology was only directed at managing information, now it is also a medium for exchange and collaboration. To make the necessary leaps, above all else IT must encourage people to want to use it, must make them feel they are better off with IT than without it, be able to solve problems more quickly and work more easily by themselves and with others.[23]

In service intensive networks, it is difficult to distinguish who is in the company and who isn't. 'Insiders' and 'outsiders' see their destinies bound together, tied by reciprocal feelings and arrangements in modern networks. As Paul Leinberger and Bruce Tucker point out in *The New Individualists*, this change is largely due to the current technology. IT enables high-value firms to leave vertical integration and other conventional forms of control behind, and, instead, pool their resources and efforts in a mutual desire with other members of the distribution channel to serve and satisfy end users' needs. This doesn't mean that small firms will be shut out. On the contrary, technology has had quite the reverse effect. Small and large firms can now jointly produce value-creating services that neither could have successfully done alone. For the use of electronic communication has shifted the emphasis from the corporation to the individual who is participating in the service processes.[24] These examples help demonstrate what firms are doing in this regard:

- The only way that DuPont can work in tandem with carpet mills is by being in constant contact with them throughout the design, production and commercial process. What DuPont has done is not just use the technology to liaise on a corporate-wide basis, but also to link up each of the company's key people to the counterpart in the client's organization. Every proposal is therefore done jointly and, rather than having to go back and forth, projects can proceed simultaneously.[25]

- By using an integrated IT network, Kao's category management system begins by scanning as the cosmetics are being bought in the retail stores. The information is filtered through to Kao's factories, from where the needed goods are shipped to distributors. All interactions depend on electronic communication across the distribution channel. There are no warehouses and no finished goods inventories.

- Sprinks offers a 'lifeline' 24 hours a day to its customers through electronic linkups with other service providers – lawyers, doctors, garages and home security firms – in the company's network. When in trouble, customers call a special number to reach Sprinks directly; then the call is transmitted to the relevant parties. Frequently, any given mishap needs several services to be activated simultaneously, making inter-company linkups vital. The people involved maintain contact until the problem has been rectified.

- Handling the logistics for IBM's printer factory in Sweden means that InterForward must be linked into IBM's IT system as well as into that of its customers. When such a customer places an order with IBM, InterForward knows about it automatically, and can immediately start assembling the pieces, pack and label the printers, thus getting the logistics process underway. It's having a shared information architecture which all concerned can access that makes this arrangement operational. Because all information is shared, several procedural and administrative steps are eliminated, and everyone gains time and saves money.

- In Ciba-Geigy's agro-chemical division, speed is essential. With short product life cycles and substitutes quick to follow, all the professionals involved in producing a chemical compound – from its inception through to the formulation of the drug and its commercialization – have to work quickly and closely together. Intelligent PCs are used as a collective drawing board. Individuals can learn rapidly about the status of a project worldwide and can question each other directly for advice, making refinements en route which is saving as much as 50 per cent of the time previously taken.

Leveraging the value-added technology services

Man has always been a victim of time, space and distance. And probably always will be. But, it is less true today due to the technological advances in

services, where the effects have been especially dramatic. New meaning has
been given to time now that many more services can move instantaneously
around the globe. The IT advancements have been occurring so quickly that
the notion of space has altered from 'territorial' to 'shared', and from 'fixed'
to 'dynamic'. In other words, it's not always where people are physically
present that counts, but where they connect electronically. And, regardless of
the physical distance between the firm and its customer, there are certain
services which now transcend distance.[26]

It is because of this collapsing of time, space and distance that IT has gained
the ability to provide customers with superior solutions. Whereas when and
how services could be delivered used to be a restriction on managers, now
they represent great opportunities to attain value added. For instance:

Then: services were time dependent and could not be inventoried.
Now: because of technology, information is the one part of a solution which
can be stored, retrieved and transported.
Then: services always had to have local presence with providers physically
on the scene.
Now: many services can come from far away via remote linkups.
Then: services were culturally bound and were difficult to transplant from
one country to another.
Now: technology makes cultural differences less formidable.
Then: services were considered to be a domestic business.
Now: many services are global, customers neither know nor care where
they originate.
Then: most services were accessible only at certain times in clearly defined
places.
Now: it's possible to deliver a growing proportion of services anyplace and
anytime.

Satellites that send and receive information and images outside terrestrial
limits were one of the first major breakthroughs for value-added services.
Whereas, previously, only the big broadcasters – the PTTs and governments –
could use satellites, now they are increasingly being geared for individual
customer access and use. Much of this progress is due to the ever growing
sophistication of the microchip, which now enables single individuals to have
the electronic and computing power that was once reserved for large
institutions with the space and capital.

Fibre optics now permits huge volumes of information to be communicated
accurately and rapidly at the speed of light. Digitalization has revolutionized
imaging and computing, fostering a richly interactive and more open world for
the personal computer. Most importantly, technology has made it possible for
customers to use one receiver – like a TV, PC screen or telephone – for all
computing and communication transmissions. With the advent of tele-

computers, it has finally become possible to combine diverse signals like information, voice, video, data, film and photos. Service providers can design a tailor-made information component as they create solutions for 'markets within markets' and 'customers within customers', because of the limitless possibilities of these single workstations. And, with customers, firms can increasingly devise better solutions because of the interactive capability of the ascendant technology.[27]

'Teleconferencing', 'teleworking', 'telecommuting' and 'telemanaging' are all concepts which are evolving from the telecomputer. Through these technologies, information services will substitute for many of the more traditional and time-consuming ways of customer problem solving and communication. One of the key features of 'cyberspace' or 'virtual reality' – another technological breakthrough – is that it allows movement within a screen. A multi-dimensional representation of a product, a factory, a store or a component – as true to life as possible – can be created for users to 'see', 'hear' and 'touch'.[28] The following examples demonstrate how some of these advances are being translated into value-added services for customers:

- So that Matsushita could maintain the same consistent level of expertise with its 26,000 dealers and retailers throughout Japan, the company created Panasat – its own satellite broadcasting apparatus. Because the changes in electronic appliances are so rapid, the only way to keep these people up to date is through periodic two-way video communication. Apart from anything else, they have to be able to see the products in action in order to provide better installation, repair and maintenance.
- Mandelli's software is so sophisticated that it can create a virtual representation of a plant, including the production processes and how the various parts of the facility operate together. The customer can experience, for instance, the walking distance between one production line and another, can assess and modify options for the plant's layout on the screen, as well as see how the speed of production may be affected by changes to the setup. Prototypes that have all the dimensions and facets of the real thing can also be created on the screen, and may be adjusted using the keyboard.
- SKF has a piece of software called 'CADalog' which is available to customers through their PCs. Customers can watch a demonstration of a three-dimensional rotating bearing, observe the details of how it functions inside different kinds of products, how it can best be installed, cared for, and repaired. SKF has complemented this graphic aid with an on-line global communication system which links the company's engineers to customers, outside engineers and designers, in order to assist with the configuration and insertion of the bearings into various products during the design and manufacturing process.
- British Telecom has built technology for its credit card, hotel and airline clients which shuttles queries and reservations to wherever around the

globe offices are open and people available, thereby spanning time zones. In theory, therefore, BT's customers never experience any lag or gap in their on-line services to end users. The company has also added a computer translation service to its telephone system for certain hotel customers – such as the Marriott and Hilton – which receive a large percentage of calls from foreigners, so that language problems will not cause any delays.

● Citibank now offers customers several additional services on its 'enhanced telephone'. The instruments are able to pick up the Dow Jones stock reports, Reuters news service, sports programmes and weather broadcasts. The computer phone can also receive and transmit requests for airline and hotel bookings, as well as orders for retail stores. Individual users decide which services they want to have and how often, using this single terminal.

The human side to high-tech services

Individuals are shifting their attention from how IT works to how it is used. The value no longer lies in the hardware that processes or transmits IT, but in the people who interact with it. Companies now know how to acquire all the data and information they need to have at their disposal. How this is turned into knowledge that is transferable to the customer still depends however on the firm's employees. Increasingly, by using the technology, corporations are learning to capture and understand the finer points of individual needs. But, how they translate and act upon this knowledge rests largely on the skills and talents of those people who hold the positions facing and interfacing with customers.

What the technology is doing is making the firm and its employees more knowledgeable about customers; what it can't do, however, is do the job for them. Rather than offload tasks or diminish the importance of the service provider, the technology imposes a new kind of challenge. In fact, with IT unleashing so much opportunity, companies must take even greater care to avoid focusing on it rather than on their clients' business problems, and the applications and results they are after.

As customer needs become more complex and individualistic, as environments become more collaborative and interactive, the need for IT will, of course, increase. However, the great firms in the decades ahead will be those that can manage the human technology interface best. The experts say that the most desirable technologies will be ones that augment how people work and collaborate rather than radically changing behaviour. IT is more likely to succeed, they reiterate, when it extends to what users do in their professional and personal lives, rather than force them to acquire a completely new set of attitudes.[29]

In organizations based on a service ethos, there is no question of either using technology or using people to reach customers. These firms and their employees must be able to foster and operate in environments which simultaneously nurture relationships with customers on a long-term basis – using ongoing learning and experimentation – and operate with a level of high tech that requires speed, precision and rapid change. While some may have considered these two cultures antithetical until recently, they are now two sides of the same coin.[30]

Although Citibank previously relied on its technology almost exclusively, the idea today is to merge the bank's employees with the IT in order to provide customer satisfying solutions. Like the Royal Bank of Canada, Citibank can do almost anything electronically for customers. Yet, it recognizes that customers who want the added value that technology provides also want to have discussions and dialogue, which means contact with frontliners. Despite what Hendrix Voeders may have gained using technology, the company maintains that no expert system can achieve the same results without having a continuous interaction and trust between – in this case – the consultants and the farmers. The same applies to Singapore Airlines, which has put as much investment into the people who support its total travel experience as into the technology. And, while firms like IBM and Digital are the beacons for advances in IT, they too insist that it must be accompanied by steadfast customer relationships.

Life has grown too complex for the high-value organization to manage without technology. But, at the same time, it is becoming clearer that technology and the people who must provide the value adding and bonding are inseparable. There's incredible potential in technology for delivering services, but only if the rapport between the firm and its customers is solid. Ted Levitt puts this very well in his article, 'The Marketing Mode'. making the point that, although the world is increasingly driven by high technology, relationships continue to be influenced and managed by individuals. It's their high spirits, emotion, energy, drive and persistence that really matters, he reiterates. The relationship between people develops slowly over time. So, despite the high-tech level of today's world, it's the people who are integral to creating and sustaining a competitive market position.[31]

10 *Looking ahead and beyond*

And in today already walks tomorrow.

Schiller, *Wallenstein,* (translated by Samuel Taylor Coleridge), c. 1800

What do we know about the twenty-first century? Are the ideas which will influence it already discernible? If so, can we anticipate how they are going to unfold? What are the important developments which will have an impact on a firm's ability to generate returns? Will the trends already strongly evident in services continue, or are providers and consumers on the verge of something brand new? How are relationships with customers likely to alter in the coming decades, and what must firms do to prepare for dealing with these changes?

As we look ahead, there are no clearcut answers. What we do know is that solutions and the services within them will become more complex. Adding value for customers will be even more difficult – not easier. And more, not less, dependent on the intangible in offerings. Some compelling trends are already evident. First, there is the growing diversity among customers – both personal and corporate. Through their accelerating independence and affluence – plus the technology constantly being made available to them, they will have at their disposal the necessary means to make their individuality felt even more acutely. And from this will stem demands for an ever differentiated treatment.

Contemporary managers are already mass-custom-alizing their offerings to attract and retain these customers. Ten years down the line, the individualism within customers will become that much more pronounced, making relevance even more important for attaining a competitive position, and obtaining economies that much more difficult. The art will be knowing how to use tools and techniques more creatively so that they produce value – as perceived by these individuals – in a cost-effective way. Efforts will have to be harnessed throughout the network enterprise in order to get better still at combining efficiencies with refinements. As amorphous as they may become, this increasingly elaborate set of relationships – some tight, some loose – will have to learn to deliver the benefits, as well as spread the overheads, as one entity.

Second, there is the rate at which technology becomes obsolete.[1] Which means that value will have to come from learning how to use and apply the technology economically, while at the same time make it ever more pertinent for these 'markets of one'. The idea will be to continue to make services more immediate and indispensable to customers – ever present in their daily lives and activities. Increasingly the technology will be able to do for customers what was performed by employees. But, the critical factor in customer relationships will still have to come from the kinds of people able to supply the sense and sensibility, form and interpretation, to the multitude of requests and solution alternatives.

Another complication for the high-value corporation will be that know-how will age more rapidly in the years to come.[2] Where service workers may now be able to provide the same expertise to customers from one year to the next – provided it is constantly updated – it is not likely that this will continue in the future. There are several reasons for believing that things will change. First, know-how is being created by computers at such a clip that what's known at one moment quickly becomes outdated. Second, customers' needs and operations are changing so fast that what this know-how is being applied to is in a constant state of flux, again making it much more difficult for firms to keep up.

In addition, there is the growing ethical and environmental dimension to business which promises to change the balance in managers' pursuit of present and future objectives. On the one hand, high-value firms must manage for today's customer relationships, as challenging as that may seem. But, providing added value to the lifestyles and professions of present-day consumers is only part of a whole compendium of new imperatives. More and more, firms will find themselves in a more complex web of relationships, where they have to ask the question: provide solutions for whom? They will have to learn to deal not only with new customer values but also with new societal values, and to extend their thinking and activities to encompass managing for the world as a whole.

Solutions for whom?

Ironically, while firms find that individuals become more demanding and central to the customer satisfying process, their particular values will concurrently become much wider, encompassing more than their own immediate needs. Although still fiercely individualistic, people in the next millennium will be much more concerned with their surroundings. Seeing themselves as part of a total picture, they will share a common concern for the environment in which they live and work.

This pattern is already being observed by specialists in the sociological, political and business fields who are trying to fathom the new value constructs emerging in the industrialized world. What their research shows is that individuals are different today from their 'me-istic' predecessors in very particular ways. For one thing, rather than being 'for themselves and against others' they are much more involved – 'for and with others'. They consider themselves accountable to those in their circle and community. With the ability to make choices and exercise individuality now taken for granted, they are shifting to issues beyond themselves to which the previous generation tended to be oblivious.[3]

Some authorities, like Danish professor Peter Gundelach, explain how new values are making people both more heterogeneous and fragmented, yet at the same time more localized. While they feel more diversity within themselves, they identify strongly with the collective needs of their community. He explains in his article, 'Recent Value Changes in Western Europe', that these social values tend to emerge among the young and well educated in urban areas first, then later gradually diffuse into other groups in society. So, while these trends may seem marginal today in many countries, they will be firmly entrenched by the time the century turns.[4]

Another interesting facet of his work is that these people don't necessarily see a tradeoff between meeting their own needs and the collective good because, for them, the two are integrally dependent. The Club of Rome, which has been studying the impact of social and technological trends on the globe for decades, states the same observation in a recently published book, *Question De Survie*. While, previously, it was assumed that individual and collective needs were incompatible, research now shows that they can and do co-exist. In addition to individuals becoming more community and locally bound, there is also a heightened awareness for the global issues that run common to all peoples and local geographies. Robert Reich, in commenting on the predicaments of latter twentieth century America, contends that, unless a sense of global citizenship – in addition to national and regional – exists among people, none of the three can be exercised fully. Yoneji Masuda, Japanese economist and futurologist, sees this concept as highly probable due to advances in IT. His major point in *Managing in the Information Society* is that, while technology may have enabled individuals to have an even greater sense of autonomy, it has also forced them to depend even more on associations with others and to be aware of a joint global destiny.[5]

In the not too distant future, every solution provider will have to think about the implications of these trends on building close relationships with customers. Managers will need to have a firm grasp of these values and a greater insight into their ramifications on customers' buying and usage patterns. Their solutions will have to consider the universal 'values within all markets', the 'values of communities within markets' and the 'values of individuals within markets' (sketched in Figure 10:1). Their perspectives will have to span existing notions of time and space so that solutions include the needs of 'existing customers within markets', 'existing communal groups within markets', as well as the generations which follow – the 'future customers and groups within markets'.

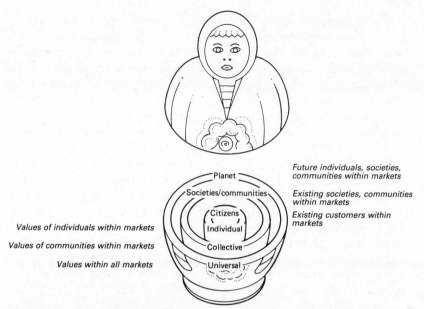

Future individuals, societies,
communities within markets

Existing societies, communities
within markets

Existing customers within
markets

Values of individuals within markets

Values of communities within markets

Values within all markets

Figure 10.1 Future customer solutions

Sustaining value for seven generations

Industrial mentality was based on the twin premises that man could control nature and that nature was abundant enough to serve all of man's needs. This was part of the clockwork view of the world described by Newton and Descartes, based on nature as inanimate and machine-like. From that point on, industrial man's official ideology became the conquest of nature. Technology was designed with that in mind. There was always *the* tradeoff to be made: progress or the environment. Man and nature were inevitably in opposition.

We know nowadays that the planet is a living organism rather than a machine. We also understand that, like all living organisms, it responds to interferences. Works now abound on the subject. Rupert Sheldrake, an English biologist, is one of those studying this field. His book, *The Rebirth of Nature*, examines the intricacies and interdependencies of man's relationship with the planet. The planet is a self-organizing and self-generating system, he reminds the reader. It has responded to man's invasions by holding back resources, producing those less than the ideal and ultimately in the process inhibiting man's so-called progress. While before, working with well-worn mechanistic assumptions, managers saw their organizations as being separated from the planet, now they have the tools and insights to understand and measure more systemically the limits of nature and the consequences of the plunder which has relentlessly ensued.[6]

It has thus become imperative that, whatever producers and consumers do, they must work with Mother Nature rather than against her. It seems that those living closest to nature have understood this better than urban man. According to Navajo Indian folklore, for instance, a chief cannot make a decision for his tribe alone. Each decision taken must consider the possible effects on seven generations down the line. The reason is simple. Dependent as they are on nature, they are more attune to the probable natural consequences of each decision, and how any action would affect the viability of following generations.

What Takeshi Umehara, playwright, philosopher and director at the International Research Centre for Japanese Studies in Kyoto, has to say is that present values have simply played themselves out. Post-modernism, as he refers to the world ahead, will make individuals' relationships with the 'other', whatever that may be – nature, other societies, communities or citizens – as or more important than self interest. His words elucidate:

> Modern ethics which make individualism the absolute value have now reached their limit – causing us to forget that our essential responsibility is not self expression or personal freedom but passing on life to posterity. Certainly what is needed today is an ethics in which the highest value is placed not on the absolute rights of the individual, but on the continuity of life, the continuation of civilization, of the species and the ecological system of the planet itself.[7]

It is axiomatic of our times that corporations are being judged for results which may or may not occur in the future. But, to reach that future, they have to come to terms with new values increasingly being expressed by customers today in their buying decisions. It's one thing, says Frances Cairncross, environmental editor for *The Economist*, to have governments and legislators demand more eco-friendly behaviour from corporations. It's quite another when consumers begin to make choices about what to buy, and from whom, based on a firm's environmental position. In her work, *Costing the Earth*, she reiterates how seriously consumers are beginning to take the environment, demonstrated amply by their spending habits.[8]

The new generation is not wrestling with whether or not protecting the environment is a good idea. They know it is. Granted, for the moment those most concerned tend to be younger, more educated people, but this group will be *the* market of the third millennium. Swedish consultant Bengt Wahlstrom describes them in greater detail in his book, *Management 2002*:

> New consumers are much more willing to take personal responsibility for the consequences of their actions so their buying habits and use patterns will be substantially different from those of previous generations. This is the generation of the 'children of ecology' for whom pollution and the environment are as important as world peace. They don't regard highly the values of their predecessors and refuse to make the same mistakes. They are still young, but by the end of the century will be the decision makers. [9]

They are part of a new world phenomenon, where individuals are not only more concerned with an 'ethics of responsibility' than with the 'ethics of success', but also with their role in upholding it. Hans Kung expands on this position in his work, *Global Responsibility*. The erudite Swiss-German theologian and philosopher suggests that, since people are becoming more ethics-conscious – of which concern for the environment is part – they are favouring companies which display this same attitude, either by virtue of doing something or abstaining from doing something. No longer is there a contradiction between profitability and the environment, or between the profitable and the ethical. And behaving in an ethical fashion is not unbusinesslike; the companies that will be most successful economically in the future will be the ones that include ethical, social, and environmental factors in their offerings.[10]

High-value corporations recognize that environmental awareness represents an enormous opportunity for them to differentiate and add value to their offerings. Far from creating a break with customers, it represents a way to make solutions that much more pertinent. While perhaps all the criteria needed for achieving results seven years hence may not be that clear, it's obvious that the most realistic way to resolve environmental problems is to create alternative technologies and new services within the economies that have the wherewithal to achieve it.[11]

The challenges facing corporations in the century ahead will be vastly different from those experienced by managers during the industrial era. And it will take them beyond paradigms aimed at satisfying present sets of

	Yesterday	**Today**	**Tomorrow**
Thrust	Productivity firm	Utility customer	+ Sustainability total system
Time frame	Immediate 'now'	Over long period 'continuous'	+ Long term 'through time'
Aim	Create value firm	Add value customer	+ Minimize disvalue
Market behaviour	Conspicuous consumption	Concern for relevance	+ Conserving and considered
Buying pattern	Replace for originality	Purchase for functionality	+ Renew for reusability
Offering	'Individual units'	'Functioning systems'	+ 'Durable systems'

Figure 10.2 Challenges: yesterday, today and tomorrow

consumers only, or providing value added for customers as we understand them today. (These differences are shown in Figure 10.2.)

Aiming at productivity in industrial times meant achieving economies of scale, readily accomplished by using whatever quantity of resources was required to produce as much as possible. Even though the attention may have turned to having utility for customers, it doesn't mean that firms have implicitly considered the environment. However, increasingly modern managers realize that the concept of ensuring the 'sustainability' of nature's resources is essential. In principle, these managers agree that they do not own resources: they merely hold them in trust. Economic activity should not just be efficient – even if this efficiency is destined for customers; it should also be socially and ecologically responsible.

Although there is no consensus on exactly what 'sustainability' means, what it does do is urge managers to think in the same way about what must be done differently. In other words, how they can continue to grow without using or providing products and services that could eventually jeopardize future generations becomes a major part of the business agenda.[12] Instead of excessive or heedless use of resources in the design, delivery and support of solutions, they rethink the plan with its potential impact on the environment. In their actions, they take into account the confluence of factors needed to preserve the natural system and keep it in working order. Through new, value-added services, they provide present utility for customers as well as future utility for those who are to follow.

Solutions stand the test of time even though the chronological frame may be uncertain. Breaking out of the short, immediate horizons of the industrial era, managers try to project costs and returns into the future. They get results for customers now, but they look beyond, too. In other words their solutions create value for customers but simultaneously minimize disvalue. On a basic level, such diminishing value would, one way or another, eventually become a real cost to customers. More complex to calculate is the cost to the community or the planet. The experts are trying hard to be more precise. For instance, they ask: what will be the future cost to the quality of life because of the present misuse of a resource? What is the net present value of future returns for resources that have been sacrificed? Though the answers are not yet clear, this new slant means that managers will have to find innovative ways of measuring the results they achieve for customers over multi-generations, an issue that most have not yet had to deal with. Additionally, the intangible value of natural assets will have to be calculated in more concrete monetary terms.[13]

Rather than the conspicuous consumption so typical of the 1960s, 1970s, 1980s and even the 1990s, the new consumer group can best be described as one which is ever more conserving and concerned. While functionality will remain crucial to them, it will take on a deeper meaning – with offerings having built-in capacities for renewal and reuseability. Products will not have just a single life cycle but several, and new services will make this feasible. So long as customers were replacing the original product, they were buying more of the same. Now, value-added services will be the way to keep the system functioning, which means sustaining its durability. This entails keeping it going through several tranformations – even when one or more parts are used up.

To prolong extended life and prevent disposal, maintenance services will have to maintain the various parts in sync so that the system as a whole is durable. This means that the life cycles of products and components will have to be coordinated. Mechanisms have to be set up to allow customers to return used items – which otherwise would have been discarded – for recycling, rejuvenating and reuse. Where, in the past, logistics systems delivered goods to customers and often returned empty, they will now have to pick up and return the used goods to reprocessing centres. And, since customers are more likely to return goods if they are leased rather than owned, leasing services will feature more prominently in offerings. Only by having these services and others delivered with the same high-calibre standards, accompanied by know-how on durability and reuseability, can firms follow through on their hopes to achieve sustainable development.[14]

The way 'things' may be

Already, high-value corporations are defining those aspects of business destined to distinguish one company from another. Their first task has and will continue to be to change ideas and ideologies, from 'things' to services – the material to the immaterial. The coming years will see an even further move into the world of the immaterial, which will lead to a de-materialization of values. What does this mean and what are some of the probable trends that can be expected? (Figure 10.3 summarizes and compares yesterday, today and tomorrow):

The value adding will be through the 'de-material'

First, it was the material that created the value; then the immaterial added to the value. Now, the immaterial *is* the value. Services have their own leverage and profit potential; no longer are they dependent upon – although they're still related to – the core items from which they emanated. Since services are the new raw material, it is only when they are transformed that they can continue to improve solutions for customers. As this happens, offerings will correspondingly continue to de-materialize.

We have also reached a stage where the material going into 'things' is diminishing every day. More and more intelligence is being embedded into

	Yesterday was/were	Today is/are		Tomorrow will be
Value adding . . .	material	immaterial	+	de-material
Services and service delivery . . .	static 'come to us'	dynamic 'or we'll come to you'	+	nomadic 'and we'll move around with you'
The service-intensive organization . . .	fixed	flexible	+	virtual
Knowledge . . .	internalized for firm	specialized for and from customers	+	massified for and from more customers
People skills . . .	mainly know(ing) what	mostly know(ing) how	+	also know(ing) why

Figure 10.3   Towards the year 2000

smaller and smaller bits. As mass goes down and services go up, the de-materialization process unfolds. But, although things are getting smaller, their value to users is potentially expanding. We don't need huge quantities of matter to have utility anymore. In fact, performance is coming from ever smaller units that create ever greater applications.

For managers primed to add to wealth by building on the material, the biggest challenge will be how to achieve the same ends with the immaterial. As French academic Thierry Breton, a researcher in the field of technology and business strategy, makes clear, what one can 'do' with existing services will become *the* value-adding process. His book entitled *La Dimension Invisible* goes into more detail on this concept, pointing out that the real gains in the future will be in combining, augmenting, refining and applying this immaterial. In other words, the future manager will be inventing more intangibles, thereby de-materializing value still further.[15]

Service delivery will be more nomadic

Man is becoming increasingly nomadic, and this characteristic is not going to go away. So, more and more service delivery is being designed to cater to this lifestyle. In so many instances in the past, customers had to go to the suppliers' sites for their services. More recently, technology lets these services enter into homes, work and public places, enabling recipients to receive such services anywhere, at any time, from anyone.

What's likely to be new is that services will increasingly move with people, literally becoming a part of their daily existence. Small single items are now capable of picking up, transmitting and receiving vast quantities of information. Not only will they make use of combined technologies but also they will become portable, lightweight, and comfortable to carry and use. We are not only talking about highly individualized services anymore, therefore, but also services that follow the highly individualized movement of customers.

With time being of the essence for both producer and consumer, he who is first to market will make the biggest sale. And, the company that is first to provide services will be the company which is always *with* the customer. Whether the customers' activities are routine or complex, any future technology will be construed as a natural extension of their lives rather than as an exceptional event in it. Nicholas Negroponte from MIT talks about this approach in his article, 'Products and Services for Computer Networks'. What he says is that today's IT makes it extraordinarily easy for customers to stay home. But, since this is not the most interesting consequence of better technology, the real value added must come from electronic services which help customers move around and still stay in touch with their home and workbase. In this way, consumers will ultimately be more or less independent of space and time.[16] What this all boils down to is expressed very well by Thierry Breton. He says that many services will cease to be a territorial affair, attracting potential buyers to a given site, and will increasingly become a time-based activity:

> The most powerful company will thus no longer be the one that can multiply its points of sale and get customers to come to it, but the one that will possess the networks that will permit it to quickly reach the largest number of customers within a very short time span over great distances without increasing its costs. It will no longer be a question of 'covering territory', but of running with, and against, time.[17]

Networks will become virtually 'virtual'

To get the most value from the de-material, firms or chunks of organizations will have to become more 'virtual'. Why? Because a chief objective will be to devise structures which facilitate the most rapid means of communication between people who have the know(ing) and those who need to apply it. Current models do not yet go far enough – as flexible as they may be – to facilitate the discourse, exchange and communication necessary between specialists scattered inside and outside corporations.

'Virtual' means 'on the verge of becoming' – not real. Virtual organizations are formed by teams that are brought together frequently to work on a project or in a process – short or long term – and then are disbanded. Although they don't appear on any organization chart – or have any formal identity – for the time they are together they behave like a mini- or quasi-organization. In their book, *Enterprise Networking*, Ray Grenier and George Metes, two Digital executives, describe a world in which such a virtual setup will be made ever more possible by modern electronics.[18] With networking applications, people who need to think and work together will do so as if they were in the same room, albeit a 'virtual' rather than a physical place. This linkup of people and wires will bring diverse skills together to solve problems with and for customers. In fact, what is envisaged are virtual organizations that include customers.

In no way intended to supplant the organization, these groupings will increasingly supplement what already exists. Pieces of the various organizations involved in the customer problem-solving process will be spun off for as long as it takes, and then spun back into their respective firms. As this virtual feature becomes more prominent in firms, coordination will be even more important. The more that splintering takes place, the greater the need will be to strengthen the account management mechanism. Virtual organizations, after all, only make sense if their efforts are channelled into the customer satisfying process. Like a great deal of business today, the details of how this process will work can only unfold over time.

Knowledge will become more 'massified'

Know-how will always differ from other assets, both in terms of how it is found and how it is applied. Other assets are relatively easy to find and, if not, can be fabricated – even information. And, most of these assets can be uniform: more of the same can be produced if desired. Knowledge can only really be acquired by individuals, accumulated incrementally. This is good and bad. On the positive side, it can never be depleted because, unlike 'things', even when it is given away it is still retained by the person from whose head it came. And, when the correct know-how is matched to customer needs, it's that much easier to provide personalized solutions.

On the other hand, knowledge tends to be highly specific and not always easy to use widely. Herein lies the twist: for unless it is made accessible and applicable to larger numbers of customers in the future, it may not be economic enough to justify its cost, despite its importance in solutions. The price of knowledge doesn't go down by acquiring more – it only happens by spreading it as widely as possible. And it is only by making it available to larger numbers of people that it really begins to self-generate and benefit communities and societies at large.

These concerns lead us to the growing need to 'massify' knowledge. Where now knowledge is largely the component which customizes and personalizes solutions for 'markets within markets' and 'customers within customers', in the future it will need to cater to the 'generic within markets' to make offerings economic as well as effective. As this trend gathers momentum, the knowledge obsolescence factor, fuelled by IT, will become exacerbated. It will therefore be crucial for managers to find ways to separate the 'massified' knowledge gathered for and from customers, from that which represents their unique value added.

The edge will come from know(ing) why

To tin soldiers, knowing *what* to do meant promoting speed and efficiency in making and moving things. Those who knew what to do were better off than those who didn't, because that's what the system expected from them and rewarded them for. In a world made of Russian dolls, interdependent and connected, the currency that matters is know-how. When people know *how* to do something, it means that knowledge and learning have taken the form of competence and, through education and experience, have become a capability. In today's terms, because service workers have know-how, they are able to solve problems thereby playing their part in the customer satisfying process through the activity cycle.

But, ironically, if this know-how is too expert, it runs the risk of becoming mechanistic. People who know how things work may sometimes end up losing sight of any broader perspective. Know(ing) why is another facet of know(ing) how. It isn't just applying a body of knowledge – it's having a talent that understands the reasons and implications of things, even when they are not always apparent. While know-how makes things happen, know(ing) *why* understands the reasons they may or may not have happened. It asks these questions: what are the possibilities? why can certain results be achieved or not achieved? why do some people think in a certain way? can it be replicated?[19]

The task will be different in the future. More – not less – responsibility will be carried by know(ing). Employees will have to know why first and then how – instead of vice versa. The ramifications will be as important as the acts themselves, especially as corporations work within the context of a much larger system. In matters great and small, high-value corporations will need employees who not only are presented with a problem and able to solve it, but who understand why a problem is there in the first place and how it is related to others. They will need to see the longer horizons and have the capability to perceive patterns that give them a better grasp of what may evolve.

Visions for a no-matter future

Though history is not particularly concerned about round numbers, man somehow expects to see a dramatic change at the turn of a century. It's a capstone and a culmination; a threshold suddenly reached. At this point, people take stock, begin to ask questions. Despite themselves, they try to fathom what has gone before and what lies ahead, and see if they can somehow discern connections.

But, as the new sciences have so amply taught us, we do not live in a deterministic system. And, as we now know, we cannot extrapolate from our present state what the future will bring. Yet, when we look around, it's obvious that high-value corporations already have an image of the future. They have begun to articulate an agenda for the new millennium, thereby already setting it into motion. So, the stage has been set for the next century – one in which the immaterial will, more than ever, affect what firms will do and how they make their money. Opportunities for wealth will come consistently from making and moving intangibles rather than 'things', regardless of time, space or distance. Value is being found where it never was sought before – in the natural world, and from a communal and global sense of individual responsibility.

The inroads made by services will continue into the next millennium. In fact, they are likely to be even more predominant, bringing success to those corporations which have made the transition from tin soldiers to Russian dolls – from an industrial to a service ethos. Ironically, services have become the contemporary manager's way of making the intangibles more tangible for customers. As the industrial age fades still further into history, so the criteria for success and failure become more apparent.

But, whereas the service ethos is now the competitive differentiator, it will become a condition for corporate survival in the future. As the year 2000 draws nearer, rather than having to make dramatic changes – from high volume to high value – managers will be looking for new and better ways to keep adapting to ever changing conditions and customer requirements. Having established the groundwork for the design, delivery and support of service-intensive solutions, they will be intent on avoiding the industrial trap of simply delivering more of the same uniform offerings more cheaply.

Will the value-added services continue to give business the astonishing opportunities for satisfying customers that we are witnessing now? There can be no doubt. Can firms develop these services in the next century at the same pace that they did for 'things' in the last? Well, they must. For how else will they compete?

Never again can the material matter as much as the immaterial, or matter be as important as no matter.

The only question is: who can be best at it? . . .

Notes and references

Chapter 1

1 Morgan, G. (1986) *Images of Organization*, Sage Publications, London, p.23. Another version of Frederick's talents and interests can be found in Hofstadter, D. (1979) *Godel, Escher, Bach: An Eternal Golden Braid*, Penguin, New York, p. 3.

2 See Russell, B. (1959) *Wisdom of the West*, Rathbone Books, London, pp. 44–46, 97–102. McKeon, R. (1941) *The Basic Works of Aristotle*, Random House Press, New York. See also Morgan, note 1 above.

3 Descartes, R. (1968) *Discourse on Method*, Penguin Books, London, pp. 73–74 (first published in 1637). For an analysis of the Cartesian, as well as other, approaches to reality, see Danto, A. (1989) *Connections to the World: The Basic Concepts of Philosophy*, Harper & Row, New York. The consequences of mechanistic thinking inherent in Cartesianism is addressed by Capra, F. (1989) *The Turning Point: Science, Society and the Rising Culture*, Simon & Schuster, New York. See also Ackoff, R. (1981) *Creating the Corporate Future: Plan or Be Planned For*, John Wiley and Sons, New York.

4 Halberstam, D. (1986) *The Reckoning*, William Morrow and Company, New York, pp. 79–81. Halberstam's book – almost 800 pages – gives a detailed account of the emergence of the car industry and the Ford family's role in creating it. As Halberstam notes, Ford's name 'was attached not just to cars, but to a way of life, and it became a verb – *to fordize* meant to standardize a product and manufacture it by mass means at a price so low that the common man could afford to buy it'. (p. 67).

5 Womack, J.P., Jones, D.T. and Roos, D. (1990) *The Machine That Changed The World*, Rawson, New York, pp. 21–25. Comparing the American and Japanese manufacturers, the authors suggest that the mass production which transformed the car and practically every other industry carried the seeds of its own destruction. Similar thoughts about the demise of mass production can be found in Piore, M. and Sabel, C. (1984) *The Second Industrial Divide: Possibilities for Prosperity*, Basic Books, New York.

6 Bell, D. (1974) *The Coming of the Post-Industrial Society*, Heinemann,

London. Among the first to deal with the new era which would herald massive socio-economic changes throughout the Western world.

7 Block, F. (1990) *Postindustrial Possibilities: A Critique of Economic Discourse*, University of California Press, Berkeley, p. 75.

8 See Morgan, note 1 above, pp. 23–24. Zuboff, S. (1988) *In the Age of the Smart Machine: The Future of Work and Power*, Heinemann, London, p.109.

9 Day, G.S. (1990) *Market Driven Strategy: Process for Creating Value*, The Free Press, New York, p. 19.

10 Several writers have commented on the consequences on productivity and efficiency of strict employee conformity to rule books: Albrecht, K. (1990) *Service Within: Solving the Middle Management Leadership Crisis*, Business One, Irwin, Homewood, IL; Pascale, R. (1990) *Managing on the Edge: How Successful Companies Use Conflict to Stay Ahead*, Penguin Books, New York; Reich, R. (1992) *The Work of Nations: Preparing Ourselves for 21st Century Capitalism*, Vintage Books, New York.

11 Porter, M.E. (1990) *Competitive Advantage of Nations*, Macmillan, London, and (1985) *Competitive Advantage: Creating and Sustaining Superior Performance*, Free Press, New York.

12 For an analysis of the evolution of the notion and the role of services: Riddle, D. (1986) *Service Led Growth: The Role of the Service Sector in World Development*, Praeger, New York, in particular pp. 67–70, and for Marx, see p. 151. Also Gershuny, note 6 above, pp. 20–25.

13 Benton, P. (1990) *Riding the Whirlwind: Benton on Managing Turbulence*, Basil Blackwell, London, p. 89. Benton's work examines the changes in attitudes, perspectives and objectives of companies, especially those once regulated, in adjusting to an entirely new set of values.

Chapter 2

1 Those who have observed these trends include: Etzioni, A. (1988) *The Moral Dimension: Toward a New Economics*, Free Press, New York; Glucksmann, A. (1990) *Le XIieme Commandement*, Flammarion, Paris; Kinsmann, F. (1991) *Millennium: Towards Tomorrow's Society*, Whallen, London; Kung, H. (1991) *Global Responsibility*, SCM Press, London; Levy, B-H. (1990) *Les Aventures de la Liberté*, Grasset, Paris; Masuda, Y. (1991) *Managing in the Information Society: Releasing Synergy Japanese Style*, Basil Blackwell, London; Toffler, A. (1990) *Powershift: Knowledge, Wealth and Violence at the Edge of the 21st Century*, Bantam, New York.

2 Naisbitt, J. and Aburdene, P. (1990) *Megatrends 2000: Ten New Directions for the 1990s*, William Morrow, New York, p. 298.

3 Clark, K. and Fujimoto, T. (1991) *Product Development Performance:*

Strategy, Organization and Performance, Harvard Business School Press, Cambridge, MA, p. 2.

4 Among others, see Ackoff, R. (1981) *Creating the Corporate Future: Plan or Be Planned For*, John Wiley & Sons; New York; Davis, S. (1988) *2001 Management: Managing the Future Now*, Simon & Schuster, New York; Davis,S. and Davidson, B. (1991) *2020 Vision*, Simon & Schuster, New York; Kanter, R.M. (1989) *When Giants Learn to Dance*, Simon & Schuster, New York; Naisbitt, J. and Aburdene, P. (1990) *Megatrends 2000: Ten New Directions for the 1990s*, William Morrow, New York; Pascale, R. (1990) *Managing on the Edge*, Penguin Books, New York; Peters, T. (1987) *Thriving on Chaos: Handbook for a Management Revolution*, Pan Books, London.

5 On globalization, see Bartlett, C. and Ghoshal, S. (1989) *Managing across Borders: The Transnational Solution*, Harvard Business School Press, Cambridge, MA; Levitt, T. (1983) *The Globalization of Markets*. Harvard Business Review, May/June; Ohmae, K. (1985) *Triad Power*, The Free Press, New York; Porter, M. (ed.) (1986) *Competition in Global Industries*, Harvard Business School Press, Cambridge, MA; Vandermerwe, S. and Chadwick, M. (1989) The Internationalisation of Services. *The Services Industries Journal*, Vol 9, No. 1, January. For more on globalization and deregulation, see Vandermerwe, S. and Rada, J. (1988) The Servitization of Business: Adding Value by Adding Services. *European Management Journal*, Vol. 6, No. 4; S. Vandermerwe (1987) Deregulation in Services and the Marketing Challenge, *The Services Industries Journal*, Vol. 7, No. 1, Jan.

6 For specific examples of how companies have tried to keep pace with the rapid technological change, see Roberts, E. (ed.) (1987) *Generating Technological Innovation*, Oxford University Press, New York; Henry, J. and Walker, D. (eds.) (1991) *Managing Innovation*, Sage Publications, London.

7 *Scientific American* (Sept. 1991) Special Issue on Communications, Computers and Networks. Includes several essays on technological convergence and its implications for business. See also Davis, note 4 above.

8 Keen, P. (1991) *Shaping the Future: Business Design through Information Technology*, Harvard Business School Press, Cambridge, MA. Rada, J. (1987) Information Technology and Service, in *The Emerging Service Economy* (ed. O. Giarini) Pergamon Press, Oxford.

9 Pascale, R. and Athos, A. (1981) *The Art of Japanese Management*, Simon & Schuster, New York, were among the first to underscore the difference between Western and Japanese management approaches. See also Abegglen, J. and Stalk, G. (1985) *Kaisha: The Japanese Corporation*, Harper & Row, New York. For a broader picture of Japanese life, social patterns and business ramifications: Van Wolferen, K. (1990) *The Enigma*

of Japanese Power, Papermac, London. For insights on the business potential of keiretsu: Ferguson, C. (1990) Computers and the Coming of the US Keiretsu, *Harvard Business Review*, July/Aug.

10 For more information on SKF, see Vandermerwe, S. and Taishoff, M. (1991) *SKF Bearings: Market Orientation Through Services (A,B,C)* IMD Cases M 383, 384, 385, Lausanne. (Available from the European Case Clearing House, Cranfield, England.)

11 Drucker, P. (1989) *The New Realities*, Harper & Row, New York, p. 230.

12 *Time Magazine* (2 Feb. 1987) America's Cry of Woe: Why is Service So Bad? (title story)

13 Quinn, J.B. and Gagnon, C. (1986) Will Services Follow Manufacturing into Decline? *Harvard Business Review*, Nov./Dec. Over the years, this critique of the service crisis has not abated: Davidow, W. and Uttal, B. (1989) *Total Customer Service*, Harper & Row, New York. Drucker, P. (1991) The New Productivity Challenge, *Harvard Business Review*, Nov./ Dec. Roach, S. (1991) Services Under Siege – The Restructuring Imperative. *Harvard Business Review*, Sept./Oct.

14 Many commentators have emphasized the importance of customer responsiveness on overall corporate performance. See Band, W. (1991) *Creating Value for Customers: Designing and Implementing a Total Corporate Strategy*, John Wiley & Sons, New York; Carothers, H., Sanders, R. and Kirby, K. (1989) Management Leadership in the New Economic Age, *Survey of Business*, Summer; Lele, M. and Sheth, J. (1987) *The Customer Is Key: Gaining an Unbeatable Advantage through Customer Satisfaction*, John Wiley & Sons, New York; Levitt, T. (1980) Differentiation of Anything. *Harvard Business Review*, Jan./Feb.; Levitt, T. (1960) Marketing Myopia, *Harvard Business Review*, July/Aug.; Schonberger, R. (1990) *Building a Chain of Customers: Linking Business Functions to Create a World Class Company*, The Free Press, New York; Simon, H. (1991) Kundennahe als Wettbewerbsstrategie und Fuhrungsher- ausforderung. Working Paper 01–91, *Lehrstuhl fur Betriebswirtschaft- slehre und Marketing, Universitat Mainz*; Walker, D. (1990) *Customer First: A Strategy for Customer Service*, Gower, London; Whiteley, R. (1991) *The Customer Driven Company: Moving from Talk to Action*, Business Books Ltd, London.

15 Ohmae, K. (1990) *The Borderless World: Power and Strategy in the Interlinked Economy*, Harper Collins, London, p. 41.

16 Reich, R. (1992) *The Work of Nations: Preparing Ourselves for 21st Century Capitalism*, Vintage Books, New York, p. 82.

17 On the importance of 'living with customers': Kosnik, T. (1991) Perennial Renaissance: The Marketing Challenge in High Tech Settings. In *Managing Complexity in High Technology Organizations* (eds M.A. von Glinow and S.A. Mohrman) Oxford University Press, New York; Peters,

T. (1990) *Drucker, Ohmae, Porter & Peters* (Economist Management Briefings, Report 1202), London, Economist Publications.

18 For more information on SAS, see Vandermerwe, S. (1989, 1990) *Scandinavian Airlines Systems (A,B)* and Vandermerwe, S. (1992) *Scandinavian Airlines Systems Revisited*, IMD Cases M 416, 417, Lausanne. For more details on Singapore Airlines, see Vandermerwe, S. & Lovelock, C. (1991) *Singapore Airlines: Service Quality Through Technology*, IMD Case M 408, Lausanne. (Available from the European Case Clearing House, Cranfield, England.)

19 See Peters, note 17 above.

20 Von Bertalanffy, L. (1950) The Theory of Open Systems in Physics and Biology, *Science Magazine*, Vol. 3. and (1968) *General Systems Theory: Foundations, Development, Applications*, Braziller Publishers, New York. These works were among the first exposes of systems thinking. An examination of broad systemic applications is in: Boulding, K. (1956) General Systems Theory – the Skeleton of Science. *Management Science*, Vol. 2; Boulding, K. (1978) *Ecodynamics: a New Theory of Societal Evolution*, Sage Publications, London. On a broad managerial level, see Capra, F. (1983) *The Turning Point*, Fontana, London; Flood, R. and Jackson, M. (1991) *Critical Systems Thinking*, John Wiley & Sons, New York.

21 Lovelock, J. (1988) *The Ages of Gaia: A Biography of Our Living Earth*, Bantam Press, New York. More on cell theory and how cells 'communicate' through DNA, in: Thomas, L. (1974) *The Lives of a Cell*, Bantam Press, New York. Thomas, L. (1983) *Late Night Thoughts on Listening to Mahler's Ninth Symphony*, Bantam Press, New York. For discussion on the works of Francis Crick and James Watson, see: Crick, F. (1989) *What Mad Pursuit*, Basic Books, New York; Hardison, O.B. (1989) *Disappearing Through the Skylight: Culture and Technology in the 20th Century*, Penguin, New York.

22 Prigogine, I. (1984) *Order Out of Chaos*, Random House, New York. A more recent view in the interview with Prigogine in Sorman, G. (1989) *Les Vrais Penseurs de notre Temps*, Fayard Press, Paris.

23 Heisenberg, W. (1975) *Across the Frontiers*, Harper & Row, New York, and (1971) *Physics and Beyond*, Harper & Row, New York. Less esoteric discussions of quantum theory and the uncertainty principle can be found in Stacey, R. (1991) *The Chaos Frontier: Creative Strategic Control for Business*, Butterworth-Heinemann, London; Gribbin, J. (1984) *In Search of Schrodinger's Cat*, Bantam Press, New York and (1986) *In Search of the Big Bang*, Bantam Press, New York; Zohar, D. (1991) *The Quantum Self*, Bloomsbury, London.

24 The development of the 'chaos' school is handled in the landmark work on the subject: Gleick, J. (1987) *Chaos: Making a New Science*, Cardinal, London.

25 Godel, K. (1962) *Formally Undecidable Propositions*, Basic Books, New York (Originally published in 1931). For further discussion of Godel's work: see Bolter, J.D. (1986) *Turing's Man: Western Culture in the Computer Age*, Pelican Books, London; Hofstadter, D.R. (1979) *Godel, Escher, Bach: An Eternal Golden Braid*, Penguin, New York; Mandelbrot, B. (1983) *The Fractal Geometry of Nature*, Freeman Press, New York. For a discussion of Mandelbrot's work, see Gleick, note 24 above, and Hardison, note 21 above. Refer also to Stacey, note 23 above, who links it to the managerial domain.

26 Bayer, F. (1981) *De Schonberg a Cage: Essai sur la Notion de l'Espace Sonore dans la Musique Contemporaine*, Dunod, Paris; Bosseur, D. and Bosseur, J-Y. (1986) *Revolutions Musicales: La Musique Contemporaine depuis 1945*, Minerve, Paris.

27 Examples of these two writers' works include: Pynchon, T. (1991) *Vineland*, Minever, London; Pynchon, T. (1991) *V: A Novel*, Burgo Press, London; Handke, P. (1991) *Absence*, Methuen, London.

28 Henderson, L. (1983) *The Fourth Dimension and Non-Euclidean Geometry in Modern Art*, Princeton University Press, Princeton. Some of these trends are analysed. See also Lucie-Smith, E. (1989) *L'Art d'Aujourd'hui*, Nathan, Paris.

29 Darwinism, and especially the Social Darwinism which followed in its wake, is addressed in the book by Schmookler, A. (1988) *Out of Weakness: Healing the Wounds that Lead Us to War*, Anchor, New York.

30 For more on the Japanese approach, see note 9 above. For an analysis of the different kinds of relationships between upstream and downstream players in the Japanese distribution chain, especially in the auto industry, see Womack, J., Jones, D. and Roos, D. (1990) *The Machine that Changed the World*, Rawson, New York.

31 Piore, M.J. and Sabel, C.F. (1984) *The Second Industrial Divide: Possibilities for Prosperity*, Basic Books, New York, pp. 23 and 25.

Chapter 3

1 Linguistic assessments of language differences can be found in, among others: Whorf, B.L. (1956) *Language, Thought and Reality*, John Wiley & Sons, New York. For a modern appraisal, see Chomsky, N. (1986) *The New Syntax*, and Chomsky, N. (1981) *Reflections on Language*. For an anthropological view: Hall, E.T. (1980) *The Silent Language*, The Greenwood Press, Westport. Also, for an anthropologist's general view of the differences in primitive versus modern cultures, including languages, see Levi-Strauss, C. (1955) *Tristes Tropiques*, Paris.

2 Among those who have commented on this move to functionality and use made possible through services: Gadrey, J. (1991) Le Service n'est pas un Produit: Quelques Implications pour l'Analyse Economique et pour la Gestion. *Revue Politique et Management Public*, March, who traces the changing nature of value from the user's standpoint. For the evolution of services overall, see Delaunay, J-C. and Gadrey, J. (1987) *Les Enjeux de la Société De Service*, Presses de la Fondation Nationale des Sciences Politiques, Paris. For the role of services in the economy, see Giarini, O. and Stahel, W. (1989) *The Limits to Certainty: Facing Risks in the New Service Economy*, Kluwer Academic Publishers, Dordrecht. See also Giarini, O. (1980) *Dialogue on Wealth and Welfare: An Alternative View of World Capital Formation*, Pergamon Press, London; Reich, R. (1992) *The Work of Nations: Preparing Ourselves for 21st Century Capitalism*, Vintage Books, New York.

3 Barcet, A. and Bonamy, J. (1988) Services et Transformations des Modes de la Production. *Revue d'Economie Industrielle: Numero Special – Le Dynamisme des Services aux Entreprises*, No.43. (Note that this quotation is a translation.)

4 Additional analysis of Mandelli can be found in Oliff, M. and Huycke, C. (1991) *Mandelli S.P.A. (A,B,C,D)* IMD Cases POM 140, 141, 142, 143, Lausanne. (Available from the European Case Clearing House, Cranfield, England.)

5 For a discussion of the move to a results-based strategy, see Vandermerwe, S. (1990) The Market Power is in the Services: Because the Value is in the Results, *European Management Journal*, Vol. 8, No. 4. See also Gadrey, note 2 above. Simon, H. (1991) Industrielle Dienstleistung und Wettbe-werbsstrategie. Working Paper 04–91, *Lehrstuhl fur Betriebswirtschaft-slehre und Marketing, Universitat Mainz.*

6 Drucker, P. (1989) *The New Realities: In Government and Politics/In Economics and Business/In Society and World View*, Harper & Row, New York, p.230.

7 Levitt, T. (1980) Differentiation – of Anything. *Harvard Business Review*, January/February. See also Levitt (1960) Marketing Myopia, *Harvard Business Review*, July/Aug.

8 Corey, E. R. (1976) *Industrial Marketing: Cases and Concepts*, Prentice Hall, Englewood Cliffs, NJ, pp. 40–45; Giarini, note 2 above. Grunroos, C. (1990) *Service Management and Marketing*, Lexington Books, Lexington, pp. 3–19; Heskett, J. (1987) Lessons in the Service Sector, *Harvard Business Review*, Mar./Apr.; Ohmae, K. (1991) *The Borderless World: Power and Strategy in the Interlinked Economy*, Harper, London, Chapter 3: 'Getting Back to Strategy'; Vandermerwe, S. and Rada, J. (1988) The Servitization of Business: Adding Value by Adding Services, *European Management Journal*, Vol. 6, No. 4; Vandermerwe, S., Matthews, W. and Rada, J. (1989) European Manufacturers Shape Up for

Services, *The Journal of Business Strategy*, Nov./Dec.; Vandermerwe, S. (1990) *Brave New Services for a Brave New World*. Presented at the Netherlands Institute of Marketing Conference, the Hague, and published in the yearbook of the Netherlands Institute.

9 For more on Nokia-Maillefer, refer to Vandermerwe, S. and Taishoff, M. (1991) *Nokia-Maillefer Cable Machinery: Pricing Know-how Services*, IMD Case M 402, Lausanne. (Available from the European Case Clearing House, Cranfield, England.)

10 Additional details on Hendrix Voeders in Cummings, T. Jenster, P. and Rada, J. (1992) *BP Nutrition/Hendrix Voeders B.V.: The Consultancy Support System*, IMD Case M 386, Lausanne. (Available from the European Case Clearing House, Cranfield, England.)

11 The need to extend beyond traditional boundaries is increasingly being discussed. For example: Hamel, G. and Prahalad, C.K. (1991) Corporate Imagination and Expeditionary Marketing, *Harvard Business Review*, July/Aug.; Prahalad, C.K. and Hamel, G. (1990) The Core Competence of the Corporation, *Harvard Business Review*, May/June. Stalk, G. Evans, P. and Shulman, L. (1992) Competing on Capabilities: The New Rules of Corporate Strategy, *Harvard Business Review*, Mar./Apr.

12 Peters, T.J. and Waterman, R.H., Jr. (1982) *In Search of Excellence: Lessons from America's Best Run Companies*, Harper & Row, New York. See in particular Chapter 10: 'Stick to the Knitting'.

13 Among the services specialists who talk about the augmenting or enhancing of core offerings through services are: Berry, L. and Parasuraman, A. (1991) *Marketing Services: Competing Through Quality*, The Free Press, New York, pp.147-149; Grunroos, C. (1990) *Service Management and Marketing: Managing the Moments of Truth in Service Competition*, Lexington Books, Lexington, pp. 71–91; the author presents an analysis of the core and augmented service offerings; Eiglier, P. and Langeard, E. (1987) *Servuction: Le Marketing des Services*, McGraw-Hill, Paris; Maister, D.H. and Lovelock, C. (1982) Managing Facilitator Services. *Sloan Management Review*, Summer. Levitt, T. (1983); After the Sale is Over, *Harvard Business Review*, Sept./Oct.; Normann, R. (1991) *Service Management*, 2nd edn, John Wiley & Sons, New York.

14 Bowen, D.E., Siehl, C. and Schneider, B. (1989) A Framework for Analyzing Customer Service Orientation in Manufacturing, *The Academy of Management Review*, Vol. 14, No. 1; Quinn, J.B., Doorley, T. and Paquette, P. (1990) Beyond Products: Services-Based Strategy, *Harvard Business Review*, Mar./Apr.

15 Harvey-Jones, J. (1989) *Making It Happen: Reflections on Leadership*, Collins, London, pp. 59–60.

16 Quinn, J.B., Doorley, T. and Paquette, P. (1990) Technology in Services: Rethinking Strategic Focus, *Sloan Management Review*, Winter. See also Giarini, note 2 above, and Simon, note 5 above.

17 For more background about Ciba-Geigy: Vandermerwe, S. and Taishoff, M. (1991) *Allcomm: Making Internal Services Market Driven*, IMD Case M 391, Lausanne. (Available from the European Case Clearing House, Cranfield, England.)

18 Mass customization has been discussed by: Bloch, P. and Hababou, R. (1991) *Dinosaures & Cameleons: Neuf Paradoxes pour Reussir dans un Monde Imprevisible*, J. C. Lattes, Paris, pp. 64–70; Bressand, A. (1989) *Strategic Trends in Services: An Inquiry into the Global Service Economy*, Harper & Row, New York, pp. 21–23; Davis, S. (1987) *Future Perfect*, Addison Wesley, Reading, MA, in particular the chapter entitled: 'Mass Customizing' (pp. 140–190); Drucker, P. (1990) The Emerging Theory of Manufacturing, *Harvard Business Review*, May/June; Piore, M. and Sabel, C. (1984) *The Second Industrial Divide: Possibilities for Prosperity*, Basic Books, New York, especially pp. 28–48; Schonberger, R. (1990) *Building a Chain of Customers*, Free Press, New York, Chapter 12: 'Success Formulas for Volume and Flexibility'.

19 Some additional insights on the inseparability of goods and services can be found in: Bowen, Siehl and Schneider, note 14 above and Breton, T. (1991) *La Dimension Invisible: Le Defi du Temps et de l'Information*, Editions Odile Jacob, Paris. See also Gummesson, E. (1988) *Marketing: A Long Term Interactive Relationship: Contributions to a New Marketing Theory*, Anderson, Sandburg, Dhein Publication on International Business Marketing and Communications, London. See also Reich, note 2 above, and Vandermerwe, notes 5 and 8 above.

20 The impact of technological advances on services has been addressed by: Davis, S. *Future Perfect*, Addison Wesley, Reading, MA; Davis, S. and Davidson, B. (1991) *2020 Vision*, Simon & Schuster, New York; Hackett, G. (1990) Investment in Technology – The Service Sector Sinkhole?, *Sloan Management Review*, Winter; Quinn, J.B. and Paquette, P, (1990) Technology in Services: Creating Organizational Revolutions, *McKinsey Quarterly*, No. 3; Shostack, L. (1987) Service Positioning through Structural Change, *Journal of Marketing*, Jan.

21 See Gadrey, J. note 2 above. (Note that this quotation is a translation).

22 Schlesinger, L. and Heskett, J. (1991) The Service Driven Service Company, *Harvard Business Review*, Sept./Oct.; Grunroos, note 13 above. Chase, R.B. (1978) Where Does the Customer Fit in a Service Operation?, *Harvard Business Review*, No. 56. See Bowen, Schneider, Siehl, note 14 above.

23 Vandermerwe, S. and Rada, J. (1988) Servitization of Business: Adding Value by Adding Services, *European Management Journal*, Vol. 6, No. 4, 1988. Vandermerwe, S., Matthews, W. and Rada, J. (1989) European Manufacturers Shape Up For Services, *Journal of Business Strategy*, Nov./ Dec.

24 Riddle, D. (1986) *Service Led Growth*, Praeger, New York, discusses the evolution of services terminology.

25 For recent managerial and economic literature on the impact of services both within the economy and within corporations, consult Giarini, O. (1991) Notes on the Concept of Service Quality and Economic Value. In *Quality in Services: Multi-disciplinary and Multinational Perspectives* (eds S. Brown *et al.*) Lexington Books, Lexington. Refer also to : Bowen, D. and Cummings, T. (1990) Suppose We Took Services Seriously? In *Service Management Effectiveness* (eds D. Bowen and R. Chase) Jossey Bass, San Francisco; Grunroos, C. note 13 above, who differentiates between the official and the 'hidden' service economy; Simon, note 5 above, in his analysis of the role that services play in traditional German manufacturing companies. For a specific look at the predominant role of services in the value chain, see Quinn, J.B., Doorley, T. and Paquette, P. (1990) Technology in Services: Rethinking Strategic Focus, *Sloan Management Review*, Winter; Barcet, A. and Bonamy, J. (1988) Services et Transformation des Modes de Production, *Revue d'Economie Industrielle, Numero Special: Le Dynamisme des Services aux Entreprises*, 1st trimester.

Chapter 4

1 Some of these features unique to services have been discussed by, among others: Bowen, D.E. and Cummings, T.G. (1990) Suppose We Took Services Seriously? *Service Management Effectiveness: Balancing Strategy, Organization and Human Resources, Operations and Marketing* (ed. D.E. Bowen, R.B. Chase and T.G. Cummings) Jossey-Bass, San Francisco, pp.1–14; Heskett, J. Sasser, W.E. and Hart, C.W.L. (1990) *Service Breakthroughs: Changing the Rules of the Game*, The Free Press, New York; Normann, R. (1991) *Service Management: Strategy and Leadership in Service Business*, 2nd edn, John Wiley & Sons, New York.

2 From a variety of different domains, writers have examined the implications of mass production on customer relationships. See Bowen, D., Siehl, C. and Schneider, B. (1989) A Framework for Analyzing Customer Service Orientation in Manufacturing, *Academy of Management Review*, Jan.; Piore, M. and Sabel, C. (1984) *The Second Industrial Divide: Possibilities for Prosperity*, Basic Books, New York; Shaw, J. (1990) *The Service Focus*, Dow Jones Irwin, Homewood, IL; Womack, J.P., Jones, D.T. and Roos, D. (1990) *The Machine that Changed the World*, Rawson, New York.

3 Certain writers have underscored some of the consequences of failing to see the customer as a long-term investment. See Day, G.S (1990) *Market*

Driven Strategy: Processes for Creating Value, The Free Press, New York; Gummesson, E. (1987) The New Marketing – Developing Long Term Interactive Relationships, *Long Range Planning*, No.4; Levitt, T. (1991) *Thinking about Management*, The Free Press, New York.

4 Senge, P. (1990) *The Fifth Discipline: The Art and Practice of the Learning Organization*, Doubleday, New York, expounds on the notion of 'shifting the burden' for the sake of short-term expediency.

5 Ashkenas, R.N. (1990) A New Paradigm for Customer and Supplier Relationships, *Human Resource Management*, Winter. See also Carlisle, J. and Parker, R. (1989) *Beyond Negotiations: Redeeming Customer – Supplier Relationships*, John Wiley & Sons, Chichester.

6 Peters, T. (1988) The Great Management Paradox, *Hyatt Magazine*. The author describes the relationship between firms and customers as having long been characterized as 'warlike'. See also Grunroos, C. (1990) *Service Management and Marketing*, Lexington Books, Lexington, pp.134–137; Womack, Jones and Roos, note 2 above, suggest that one of the major reasons for the success of the Japanese car industry has been its focus on creating amicable and even family-type relationships among suppliers, assemblers, distributors, dealers and customers.

7 Levitt, T. 'The Marketing Imagination'. The author was one of the first to single out the transactional approach as being insufficient by itself. See also Jackson, B. (1985) Build Customer Relationships that Last, *Harvard Business Review*, Nov./Dec.; Lessem, R. (1990) *Developmental Management: Principles of Holistic Business*, Basil Blackwell, London, analyses the different stages in marketing development.

8 The '4 Ps' of the marketing mix were first proposed as a tool by McCarthy, J. (1964) *Basic Marketing: A Managerial Approach*, Irwin, Homewood, IL, and Borden, N.H. (1965) The Concept of the Marketing Mix, *The Science of Marketing* (ed. G. Schwartz). Some academics, particularly members of the Nordic Services School, have begun to question an exclusive reliance on the marketing mix, seeing it as too short-term and transactional given changing customer requirements and competitive conditions. See Gummesson, E. (1988) *Marketing: A Long Term Interactive Relationship*. In, Contributions to a New Marketing Theory (Anderson, Sandberg, Dhein Series on International Business Marketing and Communications); Grunroos, C. (1989) Defining Marketing: A Market Oriented Approach, *European Journal of Marketing*, No.1; Simon, H. (1992) Marketing Science's Pilgrimage to the Ivory Tower. Working Paper 04–92, *Lehrstuhl fur Betriebswirtschaftslehre und Marketing, Universitat Mainz*.

9 Vandermerwe, S. (1974) The Influence of the Marketing Concept on Company Performance, Doctoral Thesis, University of Stellenbosch, Cape Town. The author examines the evolution of the marketing concept and shows a correlation between the marketing orientation of a company's

CEO and overall corporate performance. The marketing concept is presented as a philosophy to be embraced by the entire firm, beginning with the CEO. Also: Kotler, P. (1988) *Marketing Management*, 6th edn, Prentice Hall, Englewood Cliffs, NJ; and Day, note 3 above.

10 Edvinsson, L. and Richardson, J. (1989) Services and Thoughtware: New Dimensions in Service Business Development. In *Strategic Trends in Services: An Inquiry into the Global Service Economy* (eds A. Bressand and K. Nicolaidis) Harper & Row, New York, p.37.

11 For more on the 'moments of truth': Normann, R. note 1 above; Carlzon, J. (1987) *Moments of Truth*, Ballinger, Cambridge. Industrial marketing provided much of the impetus for the interactive approach. See Ford, D. and the Industrial Marketing and Purchasing Group (eds) *Understanding Business Markets: Interaction, Relationships and Networks*, Harcourt Brace, New York; Ford, D. Hakansson, H. and Johansson, H. (1986) How Do Companies Interact? *Industrial Marketing & Purchasing*, Vol.1, No.1.

12 Lessem, note 7 above. See also Band, W.A. (1991) *Creating Value for Customers: Designing and Implementing a Total Corporate Strategy*, John Wiley & Sons, New York; Kanter, R.M. (1989) *When Giants Learn to Dance: Managing the Challenges of Strategy, Management and Careers in the 1990s*, Simon & Schuster, New York; Peters, T. (1988) *Thriving on Chaos*, Alfred Knopf, New York; Rockart, J.E. and Short, J. (1991) The Networked Organization and the Management of Interdependence. In *The Corporation of the 1990s* (ed. M.S. Scott Morton) Oxford University Press, New York.

13 Kanter, note 12 above, p.143, examining primarily how power would shift in and across companies as partnering became more current.

14 Womack, Jones and Roos, note 2 above, p.186.

15 Davis, S. and Davidson, B. (1991) *2020 Vision: Transform Your Business Today to Succeed in Tomorrow's Economy*, Simon & Schuster, New York, examine the strategic importance of time. Also: Harvard Business Review (1991) *Revolution in Real Time*, Harvard Business Review. Cambridge, MA; Merrills, Roy (1989) How Northern Telecom Competes on Time, *Harvard Business Review*, July/Aug.; Simon, H. (1989) Die Zeit als Strategischer Erfolgsfaktor. *Zeitschrift fur Betriebswirtschaft*, 59, Heft 1; Stalk, G., Jr. (1988) Time – The Next Source of Competitive Advantage, *Harvard Business Review*, July/Aug.

16 Some of the strongest proponents of process came from the quality field. See Deming, W.E. (1982) *Quality, Productivity and Competitive Position*, MIT Press, Cambridge, MA. For more recent studies of process, see Hill, T. (1991) *Production/Operations Management*, Prentice Hall, New York. For a look at the different ways of mapping processes, from a manufacturing or services viewpoint: Schmenner, R.W. (1990) *Production/Operations Management: Concepts and Situations*, Macmillan, New

York.

17 For a discussion of some of the disadvantages of a narrow process approach, see Florida, R. and Kenney, M. (1990) *The Breakthrough Illusion: Corporate America's Failure to Move from Innovation to Mass Production*, Basic Books, New York; Sirkin, H. and Stalk, G., Jr. (1990) Fix the Process, Not the Problem, *Harvard Business Review*, July/Aug.

18 Some recent writers who have examined the corporation as a series of processes include: Davenport, T. and Short, J. (1990) The New Industrial Engineering: Information Technology and Business Process Redesign, *Sloan Management Review*, Summer; Hamel, G. and Prahalad, C.K. (1991) Corporate Imagination and Expeditionary Marketing, *Harvard Business Review*, July/Aug.; Hammer, M. (1990) Reengineering Work: Don't Automate, Obliterate, *Harvard Business Review*, July/Aug.; Kaplan, R. and Murdock, L. (1991) Core Process Redesign, *McKinsey Quarterly*, No.2; MacDonald, K.H. (1991) The Value Process Model. In *The Corporation of the 1990s* (ed. M.S. Scott Morton) Oxford University Press, New York. Quinn, J.B., Doorley, T.L. and Paquette, P.C. (1990) Beyond Products: Services-Based Strategies, *Harvard Business Review*, Mar./Apr.

19 Drucker, P.F. (1992) *Managing for the Future*, Butterworth-Heinemann, London, pp. 253-254.

20 Wycoff, D. (1984) New Tools for Achieving Service Quality. *Cornell Hotel and Restaurant Administration Quarterly*, Nov. The author's 'fishbone analysis' has become a classic flowcharting method in services to show the causes of poor service performance. See also Shostack, G.L. (1984). Designing Services That Deliver, *Harvard Business Review*, Jan./ Feb. Other services writers have also advocated the use of a process type tool: Albrecht, K. and Zemke, R. (1985) *Service America: Doing Business in the New Economy*, Dow Jones-Irwin, Homewood, IL; Eiglier, P. and Langeard, E. (1987) *Servuction: Le Marketing des Services*, McGraw Hill, Paris; Heskett, J. (1987) Lessons in the Service Sector, *Harvard Business Review*, Mar./Apr.; Lovelock, C.H. (1988) *Managing Services: Marketing, Operations and Human Resources*, Prentice Hall, Englewood Cliffs, NJ.

21 Albrecht, K. (1990) *Service Within: Solving the Middle Management Leadership Crisis*, Business One Irwin, Homewood, IL, pp.170–171. The author highlights these shortcomings from being too dependent on flowcharts in service operations. He repudiates some of the concepts that he and Zemke formulated five years earlier, in their *Service America*, note 20 above, which promoted the use of extensive flowcharting techniques in service operations.

22 For an introduction to the the idea of the 'customer's activity cycle', see Vandermerwe, S. (1990) The Market Power is in the Services: Because the Value is in the Results, *European Management Journal*, Vol.8, No.40, Dec.

23 Barabba, V. and Zaltman, G. (1991) *Hearing the Voice of the Market: Competitive Advantage through Creative Use of Market Information*, Harvard Business School Press, Cambridge, MA. The authors indicate some of the shortcomings of traditional market research and market surveys. See also Simon note 8 above, who finds similar inadequacies in many market research methods for current environments.

24 For more on the Toyota 'full ownership experience', see Womack, Jones and Roos, note 2 above, especially pp. 181–185.

25 See Davis, S. and Davidson, B. (1991) *2020 Vision: Transform Your Business Today to Succeed in Tomorrow's Economy*, Simon & Schuster, New York. For more on the relationships between Toyota, its suppliers, dealers and customers, see also Davis, S. and Davidson, B. (1990) Management and Organization Principles for the Information Economy. *Human Resource Management*, Winter.

Chapter 5

1 Penzias, A. (1989) *Ideas and Information: Managing in a High-Tech World*, W.W. Norton, New York, pp. 106–111.

2 The brain's built-in redundancy is illustrated in experiments on rats done by the American psychologist Karl Lashley. See Taylor, G.R. (1979) *The Natural History of the Mind*, Dutton, New York. For managerial implications, see Miller, D. (1990) *The Icarus Paradox: How Exceptional Companies Bring about Their Own Downfall*, Harper Business, New York, pp. 188–190. Morgan, G. (1986) *Images of Organization*, Sage Publications, London, pp. 77–78, as well as Chapter 4: 'Toward Self-Organization: Organizations as Brains' for more on how the brain distributes what it knows; Pagels, H. (1988) *The Dreams of Reason: The Computer and the Rise of the Sciences of Complexity*, Simon & Schuster, New York, especially pp.114-141 for an examination of the significance of the neural linkages and interactions within the brain and how these principles can be used in management.

3 See Pagels, in note 2 above, pp. 50–52, for a description of the dualistic nature of the brain, both hierarchical and networked. For a discussion of the computer developments modelled on the brain's neuron circuitry, see Hardison, O.B., Jr. (1989) *Disappearing through the Skylight: Culture and Technology in the Twentieth Century*, Penguin, New York, Chapter 35: 'The Right Connection'. Rheingold, H. (1991) *Virtual Reality*, Secker & Warburg, London, pp. 295–297, analyses some of the new computer systems whose features and functionings are based on the 'neural network of connections in the brain'.

4 Anthony, R. (1965) *Planning and Control Systems: A Framework for*

Analysis, Harvard Business School Press, Boston, MA, was the first to represent the hierarchy in what soon became its classic, pyramid form.

5 Ferguson, M. (1987) *The Aquarian Conspiracy*, St. Martin's Press, New York, p. 213.

6 More on the brain's lack of any known control panel: Pagels, H. note 2 above, p.50. Few organizational theorists or scientists today advocate an entirely hierarchical or an entirely networked structure. For a discussion by one proponent of the hierachical structure, see Jacques, E. (1990) In Praise of Hierarchy, *Harvard Business Review*, Jan./Feb.. Mills, D.Q. (1991) *Rebirth of the Corporation*, John Wiley & Sons, New York, describes the emergence of what he calls the 'cluster organization' – a team-based and networked type of structure. His view is that 'a residual or limited hierarchy is necessary and exists in all cluster organizations . . . ' See in particular pp. 68–69; Schoonhoven, C.B. and Jelinek, M. (1990) Dynamic Tension in Innovative, High Technology Firms: Managing Rapid Technological Change through Organizational Structure. In *Managing Complexity in High Technology Organizations* (eds. M.A. von Glinow and S.A. Mohrman) Oxford University Press, New York. The authors press for the need to have quasi-structures and dotted line organizations, which combine the best of networks and hierarchies.

7 Morgan, note 2 above, observes that although hierarchy certainly exists in Japan, it is more in the feudal 'samurai' tradition – which emphasizes protection of one's employees and working together – than it is of top/down control. See in particular pp.115–117. For more on the class structures which characterize Japanese society and permeate corporations, see Van Wolferen, K. (1989) *The Enigma of Japanese Power: People and Politics in a Stateless Nation*, Macmillan, London. Whitehill, A. (1991) *Japanese Management: Tradition and Transition*, Routledge, London. The author also discusses the influence of hierarchy in Japanese companies. Pascale, R. and Athos, A. (1981) *The Art of Japanese Management*, Simon & Schuster, New York. Although rigorous structures do exist in Japanese corporations (and society overall), the authors make the point that, in contrast to their Western counterparts, Japanese executives have been 'taught to become interdependent with others, integral parts of a larger human unit, exchanging dependencies with others'. See in particular p.118.

8 The problems with current organizational structures have been examined from a variety of angles. See Handy, C. (1991) *The Age of Unreason*, Business Books, London; Kanter, R.M. (1989) *When Giants Learn to Dance: Mastering the Challenges of Strategy, Management, and Careers in the 1990s*, Simon & Schuster, New York; Powell, W. (1990) Neither Market nor Hierarchy: Network Forms of Organization. *Research in Organizational Behavior*, Vol. 12; Sadler, P. (1991) *Designing Organisations: The Foundation for Excellence*, Mercury Books, London. Stewart,

T. (1992) The Search for the Organization of Tomorrow, *Fortune International*, 18 May. Schonberger, R. (1990) *Building a Chain of Customers: Linking Business Functions to Create the World Class Company*, The Free Press, New York.

9 Morgan, see note 2 above, p.78.

10 Devanna, M.A. and Tichy, N. (1992) Creating the Competitive Organization of the 21st Century: The Boundaryless Corporation, *Human Resource Management*, Vol. 29, No. 4.

11 Pascale, R. (1990) *Managing on the Edge*, Penguin, New York, p.109. Pascale's observations on the differences between a 'fail safe' world and a 'safe to fail' world are based on work done by Kenwyn Smith. See Smith, K. (1984) Rabbits, Lynxes and Organizational Transitions. In *Managing Organizational Transitions* (eds J. Kimberly and R. Quinn) Irwin, Homewood, IL.

12 Grunroos, C. (1990) *Service Management and Marketing*, Lexington Books, Lexington, p. 248. See also Bowen, D. and Schneider, B. (1988) Services Marketing and Management: Implications for Managerial Behavior. *Research in Organization Behavior*, Vol.10; Kanter, note 8 above; Normann, R. (1991) *Services Management*, 2nd edn, John Wiley & Sons, New York. For a businessman's view, see Carlzon, J. (1987) *Moments of Truth*, Harper & Row, New York.

13 Reich, R. (1992) *The Work of Nations: Preparing Ourselves for 21st Century Capitalism*, Vintage Press, New York, pp. 98–99.

14 Albrecht, K. (1990) *Service Within: Solving the Middle Management Leadership Crisis*, Business One Irwin, Homewood, IL, p. 7.

15 Service writers and professionals are calling for a valorization of the front line. Among the latter, see Carlzon, note 12 above. See also Chase, R. and Hayes, R. (1991) Beefing Up Operations in Service Firms. *Sloan Management Review*, Autumn; Schlesinger, L. and Heskett, J. (1991) The Service Driven Service Company, *Harvard Business Review*, Sept./Oct.; Schlesinger, L. and Heskett, J. (1991) Reversing the Cycle of Failure in Services, *Sloan Management Review*, spring. General management specialists have also recently been encouraging the promotion of the front line. See Peters, T. (1987) *Thriving on Chaos: Handbook for a Management Revolution*, Alfred Knopf, New York.

16 The more holistic approach in Japanese companies has been ascribed to a combination of social, religious and cultural traditions. See Pascale and Athos, note 7 above, in particular Chapter 5: 'Interdependence'. See also Morgan, notes 2 and 7 above; Lessem, R. (1991) *Developmental Management: Principles of Holistic Management*, Basil Blackwell, London; Umehara, T. (1992) Ancient Japan Shows Postmodernism the Way, *New Perspectives Quarterly*, Vol. 9, No. 2. spring. For a discussion of the problems specific to the West because of over-functionalization, see Albrecht, note 14 above; Peters, T. (1990) *Drucker, Ohmae, Porter and*

Peters: Management Briefings, The Economist, April.

17 Florida, R. and Kenney, M. (1990) *The Breakthrough Illusion: Corporate America's Failure to Move from Innovation to Mass Production*, Basic Books, New York, p.64.

18 The 'boundaryless' organization is a concept which has been popularized by Welch, J. (1990) General Electric Co., Annual Report, Chief Executive Officer of GE. In the Annual Report, he describes the 'boundaryless' company as one 'where we knock down the walls that separate us from each other on the inside and from our constituencies on the outside'. For discussion on a cross-functional approach to 'making walls membranes', see Vandermerwe, S. and Oliff, M. (1991) *The Convergence of Marketing and Manufacturing*, IMD, Lausanne, Working Paper. For some of the organizational and human resource implications of 'boundarylessness', see Tichy, N. and Ulrich, D. (1990) The Boundaryless Organization. Special Issue of *Human Resource Management*, Winter.

19 Devanna and Tichy, note 10 above, make this point about the importance of trust in new organizational structures.

20 Lawrence, P. and Lorsch, J. (1969) *Organization and Environment*. The authors have coined the term 'the loose/tight paradox' to describe the organizational dilemma of finding the right balance between internal cohesion on the one hand, and the ability to respond quickly and appropriately to changing marketplace conditions on the other. See also Pascale, note 11 above. In Chapter 2, the author examines the same dilemma in a different light, using the term 'fit/split paradox'.

21 Shapiro, B. (1977) *Sales Program Management: Formulation and Implementation*, McGraw Hill, New York. In particular Section Four: 'Account Management', where the author says that 'the truly astute firm is not interested in only making sales; it wants to build account relationships.' Shapiro's work was primarily directed at sales managers. More recent works are promoting account management at every level and across all professions. See Craig, S.R. (1990) How To Enhance Customer Connections. *The Journal of Business Strategy*, July/Aug. For the notion of 'accountable management', see Barabba, V.P. and Zaltman, G. (1991) *Hearing the Voice of the Market: Competitive Advantage through Creative Use of Market Information*, Harvard Business School Press, Cambridge, MA.

22 How to maintain the same degree of service delivery, regardless of location, to ever more international customers has been discussed by: Dahringer, L. (1991) Marketing Services Internationally: Barriers and Management Strategies, *The Journal of Services Marketing*, summer; Heskett, J. Sasser, E. and Hart, C. (1990) *Service Breakthroughs: Changing the Rules of the Game*, The Free Press, New York; Normann, note 12 above; Simon, H. (1992) Service Policies of German Manufacturers: Critical Factors in International Competition, *Lehrstuhl fur*

Betriebswirtschaftslehre und Marketing, Universitat Mainz, Working Paper 03–92; Vandermerwe, S. and Chadwick, M. (1989) The Internationalisation of Services, *Service Industries Journal*, vol. 9, No. 1, Jan. For an examination of the consequences on business in general of the internationalization of customers and their needs, see Bartlett, C. and Ghoshal, S. (1989) *Managing Across Borders: The Transnational Solution*, Harvard Business School Press, Cambridge, MA; Ohmae, K. (1990) *The Borderless World: Power and Strategy in the Interlinked Economy*, Harper Collins, London. See in particular Chapter 6: 'Getting Rid of the Headquarters Mentality', which proposes a different way of organizing for international business.

23 Chandler, A. (1977) *The Visible Hand*, Harvard Business School Press, Cambridge, MA. Refer also his earlier work: Chandler, A. (1962) *Strategy as Structure*, MIT Press, Cambridge, MA.

24 Drucker, P. (1992) The Emerging Theory of Manufacturing. In *Managing for the Future*, London, Butterworth-Heinemann, questions the validity and efficacy of the extensive vertical and horizontal integration, which firms such as Ford had once practiced for 'control'; Davis, S., and Davidson, W.H (1990) Management and Organization Principles for the Information Economy, *Human Resource Management*, Vol. 29, No. 4, identify an underlying sense of insecurity as one of the reasons for extensive upstream and downstream integration. .

25 Schumacher, E.F. (1973) *Small is Beautiful*, Harper & Row, New York. The author challenges the 'big is better' slogan which once dominated so many aspects of industrialized society. For further discussion of Schumacher's theories, see Capra, F. (1982) *The Turning Point: Science, Society and the Rising Culture*, Simon & Schuster, New York; Capra, F. (1988) *Uncommon Wisdom: Conversations with Remarkable People*, Simon & Schuster, New York. Although Schumacher's view was a macroeconomic appraisal, the difficulties inherent in managing large corporations has been observed as well. See: Drucker, P. (1968) *The Age of Discontinuity*, Harper & Row, New York, who points out the difficulties of maintaining large structures in turbulent times. For other reassessments of 'big is better', see Ginzberg, E. and Vojta, G. (1985) *Beyond Human Scale: The Large Corporation at Risk*, Basic Books, New York; Kanter, note 8 above, in particular the section: The Coming Demise of Bureaucracy and Hierarchy, pp. 351–355, singles out excessive organizational size as one of the reasons for corporate rigidity and sluggishness; Piore, M. and Sabel, C. (1984) *The Second Industrial Divide: Possibilities for Prosperity*, Basic Books, New York, note 8 above.

26 Rappaport, A. and Halevi, S. (1991) The Computerless Computer Company: Should the US Abandon Computer Manufacturing? *Harvard Business Review*, July/Aug., state that the most successful computer firms in the future will be those that outsource the manufacture of their products.

For a view of the debate provoked by this challenge, refer to *Harvard Business Review*, Sept./Oct. 1991. Other writers have indicated the benefits to be gained, both internally in terms of efficiencies and externally in terms of better customer relationships: Davis and Davidson, in note 24 above, in particular p.379. Hamel, G. and Prahalad, C.K. (1990) The Core Competence of the Corporation, *Harvard Business Review*, May/June; see also Hamel, G. and Prahalad, C.K. (1991) Corporate Imagination and Expeditionary Marketing, *Harvard Business Review*, July/Aug.

27 Hamel, G. Doz, Y. and Prahalad, C.K. (1989) Collaborate with Your Competitor-And Win, *Harvard Business Review*, Jan./Feb.; Badaracco, J.L., Jr. (1991) *The Knowledge Link*, Harvard Business School Press, Cambridge, MA, examines alliances with competitors in much the same way as alliances with partners in general; Lewis, J.D. (1990) *Partnerships for Profit*, The Free Press, New York, looks at working with competitors.

Chapter 6

1 Hawking, S.W. (1988) *A Brief History of Time: From the Big Bang to Black Holes*, Bantam Books, New York. See in particular pp. 125–127.
2 Peters, T. (1991) The Boundaries of Business: Partners – The Rhetoric and the Reality, *Harvard Business Review*, Sept./Oct. The author makes the point about a 'Copernican revolution' in business. See also Drucker, P. (1992) *Managing for the Future*, Butterworth-Heinemann, London, notably Part II: 'People'; Peterson, D. (1991) *Teamwork: New Management Ideas for the 90s*, Victor Gollancz, London. The author, the former CEO of Ford Motor Company, also places people at the centre of the corporation.
3 Handy, C. (1991) *The Age of Unreason*, Business Books, London, p.71. Also on the subject of accomodating new individual needs and aspirations: Garratt, B. (1990) *Creating a Learning Organisation: A Guide to Leadership, Learning and Development*, Director Books, London; Nyhan, B. (1991) *Developing People's Ability to Learn: A European Perspective on Self-Learning, Competency and Technological Change*, European Interuniversity Press, Brussels; Sadler, P. (1991) *Designing Organisations: The Foundation for Excellence*, Mercury Business Guides, London; Stewart, R. (1991) *Managing Today & Tomorrow*, Macmillan, London.
4 See Mayo, E. (1933) *The Human Problems of Industrial Civilization*, Macmillan, New York; and Mayo, E. (1945) *The Social Problems of an Industrial Civilization*, Harvard University Press, Boston. Drucker, P. (1991) The New Productivity Challenge, *Harvard Business Review*, Nov./Dec., examines some of the implications of Taylor's and Mayo's theories

on service worker productivity; Pascale, R. (1990) *Managing on the Edge: How Successful Companies Use Conflict to Stay Ahead*, Penguin Books, New York, views the Hawthorne experiments as having contributed to controlling cultures; Zuboff, S. (1988) *In the Age of the Smart Machine: The Future of Work and Power*, Heinemann, London, particularly Chapter 6: 'What Was Managerial Authority?'

5 Pascale, R. and Athos, A. (1981) *The Art of Japanese Management*, Simon & Schuster, New York. See in particular Chapter 4: Interdependence. The author offers additional insight on the lifetime bonds and reciprocity within Japanese companies. See also Imai, M. (1986) *Kaizen: The Key to Japan's Competitive Success*, Random House, New York.

6 Pascale, R. (1990) *Managing on the Edge: How Successful Companies Use Conflict to Stay Ahead*, Penguin Books, New York, p. 27. The quote was made by Konosuke Matsushita during an interview in 1982.

7 For more on the rise of know-how worker in general, see Dixon, J.R. Nanni, A. Vollmann, T. (1990) *The New Performance Challenge: Measuring Operations for World Class Competition*, Dow Jones Irwin, Homewood, IL; Rudie, K. Dalmia, H. and Dalmia, G. (1991) Knowledge Workers: The Last Bastion of Competitive Advantage, *Planning Review*, Nov./Dec. (special edition: The Knowledge Worker Emerges); Masuda, Y. (1990) *Managing in the Information Society: Releasing Synergy Japanese Style*, Basil Blackwell, London; Sveiby, K.E. and Lloyd, T. (1987) *Managing Know-how: Add Value . . . By Adding Creativity*, Bloomsbury Press, London; Toffler, A. (1990) *Power Shift: Knowledge, Wealth and Violence at the Edge of the 21st century*, Bantam Books, New York; Zuboff, S. (1988) *In the Age of the Smart Machine: The Future of Work and Power*, Heinemann, London.

8 Albert, M. (1991) *Capitalisme contre Capitalisme*, Seuil, Paris, in particular pp.160-168 for more on these different approaches to workers and management. Schrage, M. (1990) *Shared Minds: The New Technologies of Collaboration*, Random House, New York, p. 59, also notes the cultural and historical predisposition of countries such as Japan and Germany toward collaborative and collegial type organizations.

9 Ackoff, R. (1991) The Future of Operational Research is Past. In *Critical Systems Thinking* (ed. R. Flood and M. Jackson) John Wiley & Sons, New York. See in particular pp.54–56 where the author elaborates on the philosophical foundations for 'hard' and 'soft' systems thinking.

10 Nonaka, I. (1991) The Knowledge Creating Company, *Harvard Business Review*, Nov./Dec. The 'hard' side of management has been attributed by several commentators to the heritage of Taylor, Mayo, Max Weber and perpetuated by such contemporary organizational experts as Albert Chandler, Chester Bernard and Herbert Simon. See: Simon, H. (1945) *Administrative Behaviour*, The Free Press, New York; Taylor, F. (1929) *The Principles of Scientific Management*, Harper, New York; Weber, M.

(1947) *The Theory of Social and Economic Organization* (translated by A.M. Henderson and T. Parsons) Oxford University Press, New York.

11 Among those who have discussed the frequent need for less reliance on purely rational approaches to management today: Hampden-Turner, C. (1990) *Corporate Culture: From Vicious to Virtuous Circles*, The Economist Books, London; Hampden-Turner, C. (1990) *Charting the Corporate Mind: From Dilemma to Strategy*, Basil Blackwell, London; Lessem, R. (1990) *Developmental Management: Principles of Holistic Business*, Basil Blackwell, London; Pascale, notes 4 and 6 above; Stacey, R.D. (1991) *The Chaos Frontier: Creative Strategic Control for Business*, Butterworth-Heinemann, London, in particular pp.210-214; Weick, K. (1979) *The Social Psychology of Organizing*, 2nd edn, Addison-Wesley, Reading, MA. See also, Peace, W.H. (1991) The Hard Work of Being a Soft Manager, *Harvard Business Review*, Nov./Dec., for a more hands-on, operational approach.

12 Yutang, L. (1942) *The Wisdom of China and Asia*, Random House, New York. See in particular pp. 567–575. The author offers a deeper look at these two sides to knowing in Eastern thought – which the Confucians call the 'knowledge of externals' (facts, hard data) and the 'knowledge of essentials' (soft, understanding of human behaviour and needs).

13 Writers from a variety of domains have encouraged leaders and top executives to look to intuition as a source of problem-solving and decision-making. See Bastick, T. (1982) *Intuition: How We Think and Act*, John Wiley & Sons, New York; Bechtler, T. (ed.) (1986) *Management und Intuition*, Verlag Moderne Industrie, Zurich; Dreyfus, H.L. and Dreyfus, S.E. (1986) *Mind over Machine: The Power of Human Intuition and Expertise in the Era of the Computer*, The Free Press, New York; Hickman, C.R. (1990) *Mind of a Manager: Soul of Leader*, John Wiley & Sons, New York; Kilman, R.H. (1991) *Managing Beyond the Quick Fix*, Jossey Bass, San Francisco; Kanter, R.M. (1991) A Walk on the Soft Side, *Harvard Business Review*, Nov./Dec.; Parikh, J. (1991) *Managing Yourself – Management by Detached Involvement*, Basil Blackwell, London; Rowan, R. (1986) *The Intuitive Manager*, Little Brown, Boston.

14 From different fields, observers have remarked on the need for right/left brain skills. See Clark, K. and Fujimoto, T. (1991) *Product Development Performance: Strategy, Organization, and Management in the World Auto Industry*, Harvard University Press, Boston. See in particular pp. 332–335, where the need for 'soft' people skills and right brain/left brain dexterity is called for; Crawford, R. (1991) *In the Era of Human Capital: The Emergence of Talent, Intelligence, and Knowledge as the Worldwide Economic Force and What it Means to Managers and Investors*, New York, Harper Collins, p. 81 examines the need for 'whole-brain' thinking as a result of the emergence of the knowledge society; De Bono, E. (1992) *The Handbook for the Positive Revolution*, Penguin Books, London;

Hampden-Turner, C. (1981) *Maps of the Mind: Charts and Concepts of the Mind and Its Labyrinths*, Collier Books, London.

15 For insights on the rise of the 'organization man', see Whyte, W.H., Jr., (1956) *The Organization Man*, Doubleday, New York; Galbraith, J.K. (1958) *The Affluent Society*, Hamish Hamilton, London. Also Maccoby, M. (1976) *The Gamesman: The New Corporate Leaders*, Simon & Schuster, New York, especially beginning on p. 90.

16 Handy, C. (1991) *The Age of Unreason*, Business Books, London, pp. 112–113. Many scholars have examined the new kinds of workers who can no longer be hired, managed and retained as in previous generations. See: Delannoi, G. (1990) *Les annees folles*, Seuil, Paris; Derr, C.B. (1986) *Managing the New Careerists: The Diverse Career success Orientations of Today's Workers*, Jossey Bass, San Francisco; Kinsmann, F. (1990) *Millennium: Towards Tomorrow's Society*, Whallen, London; Toffler, A. (1981) *The Third Wave*; and Toffler, A. (1991) *Power Shift*, Bantam, New York.

17 Leinberger, P. and Tucker, B. (1991) *The New Individualists: The Generation after 'The Organization Man'*, Harper Collins, New York, p. 398.

18 Levitt, T. (1991) *Thinking About Management*, The Free Press, New York, pp. 18–19. The consequences for organizations as result of the rise of the new worker has been discussed by other writers as well. See Choate, P. and Linger, J.K. (1987) *The High-Flex Society: Shaping America's Economic Future*, Knopf, New York; Hirschorn, L. and Gilmore, T. (1992) The New Boundaries of the Boundaryless Company, *Harvard Business Review*, May/June; Kanter, R.M. (1989) *When Giants Learn to Dance: Mastering the Challenges of Strategy, Management, and Careers in the 1990s*, Simon & Schuster, New York, Part Three: Jobs, Money and People: Consequences of the Post Entrepreneurial Revolution. See also Reich, R. (1987) *Tales of a New America*, Times Books, New York.

19 Lloyd, B. (1992) Riding the Whirlwind: Managing Turbulence, *Long Range Planning*, Apr., p. 115. This quotation is from an interview with Peter Benton.

20 The family is used to denote the company rather than the tribe although the tribe is strictly speaking larger than the family. According to some anthropologists, tribes are defensive groups, formed to stake out and protect territories. See for instance Schmookler, A. (1988) *Out of Weakness: Healing the Wounds that Lead Us to War*, Anchor, New York. The image of the organization as family is probably more appropriate since it is all encompassing and the term is used quite often in corporations, especially in Japan. See Van Wolferen, K. (1989) *The Enigma of Japanese Power*, Macmillan, London, pp. 163–167.

21 Hampden-Turner, C. (1990) *Corporate Culture: From Vicious to Virtuous Circles*, Economist Publications, London, pp. 16–17. Others have also

written about the need for developing and promoting organisational learning throughout the company. See Garratt, B. (1990) *Creating a Learning Organisation: A Guide to Leadership, Learning and Development*, Director Books, London; Hayes, R., Wheelwright, S. and Clark, K. (1988) *Dynamic Manufacturing: Creating the Learning Organization*, The Free Press, New York, pp. 228–230; Peters, T.J. and Waterman, R.H., Jr. (1982) *In Search of Excellence: Lessons from America's Best Run Companies*, Harper & Row, New York; Senge, P. (1990) *The Fifth Discipline: The Art and Practice of the Learning Organization*, Doubleday, New York.

22 Argyris, C. and Schon, D. (1979) *Organizational Learning: A Theory in Action Perspective*, Addison-Wesley, Reading, MA, were among the first to examine the difference between single loop and double loop learning. Others have discussed it from a managerial viewpoint: Hunt, J. (1991) *Leadership: A New Synthesis*, Sage, London, pp. 62–65; Morgan, G. (1986) *Images of Organization*, Sage Publications, London, pp. 85–97.

23 Experimentation and consequently 'learning to fail' is key to learning theory. See Argyris, C. Putnam, R. and Smith, D.M. (1985) *Action Science*, Jossey Bass, San Francisco, in particular Chapter 9: Engaging the Learning Process; Devanna, M.A. and Tichy, N. (1990) Creating the Competitive Organization of the 21st Century: The Boundaryless Corporation, *Human Resource Management*, winter, talk about the organizational need to embrace errors; Pedler, M. Burgoyne, J. and Boydell, T. (1991) *The Learning Company: A Strategy for Sustainable Development*, McGraw Hill, London, pp. 23 and 72, encourage experimentation even at the risk of failure, as does Senge, note 21 above, p. 154.

24 Knowing more than one can tell or explain was first studied and called 'tacit' knowing by the philosopher Michael Polyani. See Polyani, M. (1958) *Personal Knowledge*, University of Chicago Press, Chicago; and Polyani, M. (1967) *The Tacit Dimension*, Doubleday, New York; Collins, H.M. (1985) *Changing Order: Replication and Induction in Scientific Practice*, Sage, London, discusses the role of tacit knowledge amongst scientists; Orr, J. (1990) Sharing Knowledge, Celebrating Identity: Community Memory in a Service Culture. In *Collective Remembering* (ed. D. Middleton and D. Edwards) Sage, London, studies its role amongst service technicians.

25 Durkheim, E. (1984) *The Division of Labour in Society* (translated by W.D. Halls) Macmillan Press, London; and Durkheim, E. (1982) *The Rules of Sociological Method*, Macmillan, London. These two studies, first published in 1893, elucidate upon the author's idea of the collective consciousness. Levi-Strauss, C. (1967) *Structural Anthropology*, (translated by C. Jacobson), Doubleday, New York, a contemporary anthropologist, has also studied this concept. For a more philosophical view, see

Popper, K. and Eccles, J.C. (1981) *The Self and Its Brain*, Springer International, Berlin. For managerial understanding and application of these concepts, see Gustavsson, B. (1992) *The Transcendent Organization: A Treatise on Consciousness in Organizations – Theoretical Discussion, Conceptual Development, and Empirical Studies*, University of Stockholm, Department of Business Administration; Heirs, B. and Pehrson, G. (1977) *The Mind of the Organization: On the Relevance of the Decision-Thinking Processes of the Human Mind to the Decision-Thinking Processes of Organizations*, Harper & Row, New York.

26 See Douglas, M. (1986) *How Institutions Think*, Syracuse University Press, Syracuse; and Middleton, D. and Edwards, D. (1990) *Collective Remembering*, Sage Publications, London.

27 Kotter, J. and Heskett, J. (1992) *Corporate Culture and Performance*, The Free Press, New York. See in particular p. 4.

28 Badaracco, J. L., Jr. (1991) *The Knowledge Link: How Firms Compete through Strategic Alliances*, Harvard Business School Press, Cambridge, MA, p. 87. See in particular Chapter 4: 'Embedded Knowledge', where the author discusses the concept of group learning. See also Cole, R.E. (1989) *Strategies for Learning: Small Group Activities in American, Japanese and Swedish Industry*, University of California Press; and Senge, note 21 above, Chapter 12: Team Learning.

29 Diversity as an ever-more sought out trait in groups is discussed by Pascale, in note 4 above. The author discusses how internal conflict, if well managed, is essential for keeping a company's momentum. Pedler, Burgoyne and Boydell, note 23 above, Chapter 35: Working with Diversity, reappraise the benefits of group diversity.

30 Numerous writers have performed research which substantiates the importance of emotions in teaming. See Fisher, R., Brown, S. and the Harvard Negotiation Project, (1989) *Getting Together*, Business Books, London. See also Gabarro, J.J. (1990) The Development of Working Relationships. In *Intellectual Teamwork: Social and Technological Foundations of Cooperative Work* (eds. J. Galagher, R. Kraut, C. Egido) Lawrence Erlbaum, Hillsdale.

31 Reich, R.B. (1987) Entrepreneurship Reconsidered: The Team as Hero, *Harvard Business Review*, May/June.

32 For more on these Japanese practices, see Pascale, R. and Athos, A. (1981) *The Art of Japanese Management*, Penguin Books, New York.

33 Many have observed the diffusion in leadership roles over the past few years. See: Kotter, J. (1990) *A Force for Change: How Leadership Differs from Management*, The Free Press, New York. Also Hirschorn, L. (1990) Leaders and Followers in a Post-Industrial Age, *The Journal of Applied Behavioral Science* (Special Issue on Character and Leadership), Vol.26, No.4. For a services perspective on new kinds of leadership skills, see Grunroos, C. (1990) *Service Marketing and Management*, Lexington

Books, Lexington, p. 250. For the notion of the leader as 'social architect', see Bennis, W. and Nanus, B. (1985) *Leaders: The Strategies for Taking Charge*, Harper & Row, New York, pp. 110–151.

34 For a discussion of cybernetic leadership, see Hampden-Turner, C. (1990) *Charting the Corporate Mind*, Basil Blackwell, London, pp. 15–23; and Hunt, note 22 above.

35 Miller, D. (1990) *The Icarus Paradox: How Exceptional Companies Bring about Their Own Downfall*, Harper Business, New York, pp. 182–183.

Chapter 7

1 Pirsig, R. (1974) *Zen and The Art of Motorcycle Maintenance*, Vintage, London. See in particular pp. 230–257 for a discussion of these aspects of quality. For more on what some call the transcendent, or subjective, approach to quality, see Garvin, D. (1984) What Does Product Quality Really Mean? *Sloan Management Review*, autumn; and Lessem, R. (1991) *Total Quality Learning: Building a Learning Organisation*, Basil Blackwell, London.

2 Berry, L., Parasuraman, A. and Zeithaml, V. (1985) Quality Counts in Services Too, *Business Horizons*, May/June. This was one of the landmark works which brought the very specific issues of service quality to the forefront. Other early works also paved the way for a new approach to service quality. See Sasser, W.E. and Leonard, F.S. (1983) The Incline of Quality, *Harvard Business Review*, Sept./Oct.; Berry, L. (1980) Services Marketing is Different, *Business*; Wyckoff, D.D. (1984) New Tools for Achieving Service Quality. *Cornell Hotel and Restaurant Administration Quarterly*, Nov.; Levitt, T. (1984) Production-Line Approach to Service, *Harvard Business Review*, Sept./Oct.

3 A number of commentators have observed what can sometimes be a tradeoff between industrial efficiency and service quality. See Albrecht, K. (1990) *Service Within: Solving the Middle Management Leadership Crisis*, Business One, Irwin, Homewood, IL. See in particular pp. 21–53; Chase, R. and Hayes, R. (1991) Beefing Up Operations in Service Firms, *Sloan Management Review*, autumn; Schlesinger, L. and Heskett, J. (1991) The Service Driven Service Company, *Harvard Business Review*, Sept./Oct.; Schneider, B. (1986) Notes on Climate and Culture. In *Creativity in Services Marketing: What's New, What Works, What's Developing* (eds M. Venkatesan, D. Schmalensee and C. Marshall) American Marketing Association, New York. For a view of the present service quality situation in the US, see *International Business Week*, Special Edition: 'The Quality Imperative', Dec. 1991. See also the *International Journal of Service Industry Management*, Special Edition: 'Service Quality', Vol. 3, 1991.

4 Garvin, D. (1983) Quality on the Line, *Harvard Business Review*, Sept./

Oct. The author compares Western and Japanese quality results in his analysis of why the latter has had the edge. Ishikawa, K. (1985) *What Is Total Quality Control? The Japanese Way* (translated by D. Lu), Prentice-Hall, Englewood Cliffs, NJ. As one of the fathers of the Japanese quality management approach, the author sees the philosophical and religious features in Eastern thought as key determinants for the success of quality moves in Japanese companies. See also Lessem, note 1 above, who discusses some of the reasons for this 'marriage' between Eastern and Western perspectives and how they resulted in the Japanese school of quality.

5 For a presentation of Deming's theories, see Deming, W.E. (1982) *Quality, Productivity and Competitive Position*, MIT Press, Cambridge, MA. Much has been written about Deming and his methods. See Gabor, A. (1990) *The Man Who Discovered Quality: How W. Edwards Deming Brought the Quality Revolution – The Stories of Ford, Xerox and GM*, Random House, New York, in particular p.134. For the views of other prominent practitioners in the area, refer to: Juran, J. (1989) *Juran on Leadership for Quality*, The Free Press, New York. For a comparison of these approaches, see March, A. and Garvin, D. (1986) A Note on Quality: The Views of Deming, Juran and Crosby, *Harvard Business School*, Note 9–687–011. For a summary of the major developments in the quality appraisals, see Schonberger, R. (1990) *Building a Chain of Customers: Linking Business Functions to Create the World Class Company*, The Free Press, New York, pp. 69–88.

6 The role of customer expectations and perceptions has been addressed by numerous writers. See Berry, L., Parasuraman, A. and Zeithaml, V. (1985) A Conceptual Model of Service Quality and Its Implications for Future Research. *Journal of Marketing*; Berry, L., Parasuraman, A. and Zeithaml, V. (1990) Five Imperatives for Service Quality, *Sloan Management Review*, summer; Berry, L., Parasuraman, A. and Zeithaml, V. (1990) *An Empirical Examination of Relationships in an Extended Service Quality Model*, Marketing Science Institute Working Paper, Dec.; Berry, L., Parasuraman, A. and Zeithaml, V. (1991) *The Nature and Determinants of Customer Expectations of Service*, Marketing Science Institute, May; Brown, S. and Swartz, T. (1989) A Gap Analysis of Professional Service Quality, *Journal of Marketing*, Apr.; Brown, S. and Swartz, T. (1991) An Evolution of Research on Professional Service Quality. In *Service Quality: Multidisciplinary and Multinational Perspectives* (eds S. Brown et al.) Lexington Books, Lexington.

7 Schlesinger, L. and Heskett, J. (1991) Reversing the Cycle of Failure in Services, *Sloan Management Review*, spring; Schlesinger, L. and Heskett, J. (1991) Enfranchisement of Service Workers, *California Management Review*, summer. Schlesinger, L. and Heskett, J. (1991) The Service-Driven Service Company, *Harvard Business Review*, Sept./Oct. Others

who have written about the need to meet employee expectations: Bowen, D. and Lawler, E. (1992) The Empowerment of Service Workers: What, Why, How and When, *Sloan Management Review*, spring; Hoffman, K.D. and Ingram, T. (1992) Service Provider Job Satisfaction and Customer-Oriented Performance, *The Journal of Services Marketing*, Vol. 6, No. 2. Among the Europeans who make this correlation, see Bloch, P. and Hababou, R. (1992) *Dinosaures et Cameleons: Neuf Paradoxes Pour Reussir dans un Monde Imprevisble*, J C Lattes, Paris, in particular pp. 89–93; Meyer, E. (1992). Comment Mesurer la Qualite de Service? *L'Entreprise*, Mar.; Normann, R. (1991) *Service Management: Strategy and Leadership in Service Business*, John Wiley & Sons, New York, pp. 148–152.

8 See Russell, B. (1959) *The Wisdom of the West*, Rathbone Books, London, p. 20.

9 Berry, L. and Parasuraman, A. (1991) *Marketing Services: Competing through Quality*, The Free Press, New York, p. 164. See also Albrecht, K. (1992) *The Only Thing That Matters: Bringing the Power of the Customer into the Center of Your Business*, Harper & Row, New York. See in particular Chapter 8: 'Empowering People with Knowledge: Winning the Hearts, Minds and Hands'.

10 Several writers have examined the hologram and its implications on business. See Davis, S. (1987) *Future Perfect*, Addison Wesley, Reading, MA, pp. 140–145; Dreyfus, H.L. and Dreyfus, S.E. (1986) *Mind over Machine: The Power of Human Intuition and Expertise in the Era of the Computer*, The Free Press, New York; Lessem, note 1 above, pp. 256–258; Zohar, D. (1991) *The Quantum Self*, Harper Collins, London, p. 55.

11 Morgan, G. (1986) *Images of Organization*, Sage, London, pp. 79–80. See also Bohm, D. (1980) *Wholeness and the Implicate Order*, Routledge & Kegan Paul, London.

12 For a discussion of Crick and Watson's DNA cell theory, see Hardison, O. B. (1989) *Disappearing through the Skylight: Culture and Technology in the 20th Century*, Penguin Books, New York. See in particular pp. 34–57; Thomas, L. (1975) *The Lives of a Cell: Notes of a Biology Watcher*, Bantam Books, New York. Gould, S.J. (1985) *The Flamingo's Smile: Reflections in Natural History*, Viking, New York. See also Chapter 2 of this book (*From Tin Soldiers to Russian Dolls*).

13 Mandelbrot, B. (1983) *The Fractal Geometry of Nature*, W.H. Freeman, New York. For more background on this subject, see Hardison, note 12 above, pp. 57–71; Stacey, R. (1991) *The Chaos Frontier: Creative Strategic Control for Business*, Butterworth-Heinemann, London, p.380. (See also Chapter 2 of this book (*From Tin Soldiers to Russian Dolls*).

14 Lessem, R. (1991) *Total Quality Learning: Building a Learning Organisation*, Basil Blackwell, London, pp. 256–258.

15 Gummesson, E. (1991) Organizing for Marketing and the Marketing Organization. In *Marketing for the Service Industries* (eds C. Congram and M. Friedman) American Management Association, AMACOM, New York, p.122. For further examination by Gummesson of the holistic nature of service quality, see Gummesson, E. (1991) Service Quality: A Holistic View. In *Service Quality: Multidisciplinary and Multinational Perspectives* (eds S. Brown et al.) Lexington Books, Lexington, pp. 3–23.

16 The softer side to service quality management is increasingly being espoused. See Bitran, G. and Hoech, J. (1990) The Humanization of Service: Respect at the Moment of Truth, *Sloan Management Review*, winter; Grunroos, C. (1990) *Service Management and Marketing*, Lexington Books, Lexington; Schmalensee, D. (1991) Soft Measurement: A Vital Ingredient in Quality Improvement, *Prism*, First Quarter.

17 Imai, M. (1986) *Kaizen: The Key to Japan's Competitive Success*, Random House, New York, p.9. The *kaizen* approach, while perhaps most integral to quality measures and procedures, embraces all the operations within a business in the pursuit of 'continuous improvement'. For additional reading on *kaizen*, see also Ishikawa, note 4 above.

18 For an examination of the concept and process of benchmarking: Camp, R. (1989) *Benchmarking: The Search for Industry Best Practices that Lead to Superior Performance*, Quality Press, Milwaukee; Hayes, R., Wheelwright, S. and Clark, K. (1988) *Dynamic Manufacturing: Creating the Learning Organisation*, The Free Press, New York, pp. 148–160; Schonberger, R. (1990) *Building a Chain of Customers: Linking Business Functions to Create the World Class Company*, The Free Press, New York; Walleck, S. O'Halloran, J.D. and Leader, C. (1991) Benchmarking World-Class Performance, *The McKinsey Quarterly*, No.1.

19 More on Xerox's use of benchmarking is in: Osterhoff, R., Locander, W. and Bounds, G. (1991) Competitive Benchmarking at Xerox. In *Competing Globally through Customer Value: The Management of Strategic Suprasystems* (eds M. Stahl and G. Bounds) Quorum Books, New York, pp. 788–798. See also Hayes, Wheelwright and Clark, note 18 above, pp. 157–158.

20 Writers who have studied complaints in this light, see Bitner, M.J., Booms, B. and Tetreault, M.S. (1990) The Service Encounter: Diagnosing Favorable and Unfavorable Incidents, *Journal of Marketing*, Jan.; Bell, C. and Zemke, R. (1987) Service Breakdown: The Road to Recovery, *Management Review*, Oct.; Clark, G.L., Kaminski, P. and Rink, D. (1992) Consumer Complaints: Advice on How Companies Should Respond Based on an Empirical Study, *The Journal of Services Marketing*, Vol. 6, No. 1; Day, G. (1990) *Market Driven Strategies: Processes for Creating Value*, The Free Press, New York, p. 366; Hart, C.L., Heskett, J. and Sasser, W.E. (1990) The Profitable Art of Service Recovery, *Harvard Business Review*, July/Aug.; Reicheld, F. and Sasser, W.E. (1990) Zero

Defections Comes to Services, *Harvard Business Review*, Sept./Oct.

21 In the United States, the Washington-based Technical Assistance Research Progress Institute (TARP) collects and analyzes data on an ongoing basis about the commercial consequences of consumer complaints, especially when unanswered. See the TARP annual reports on 'Consumer Complaint Handling in America'. For an analysis of the research results and its implications on business, see Bell, C. and Zemke, R. (1992) *Managing Knock Your Socks Off Service*, American Management Association (AMACOM), New York. See in particular Chapter 7: A Complaining Customer Is Your Best Friend; Business International, London, (1990) *Maximizing Customer Satisfaction*, BI, London; Plymire, J. (1991) Complaints as Opportunities, *Business Horizons*, Mar./Apr.

Chapter 8

1 Plato spoke about time in, among other works, *The Statesman*. For more on the notion of time through history, see Hope, M. (1991) *Time, the Ultimate Energy: An Exploration of the Scientific, Psychological and Metaphysical Aspects of Time*, Element Books, Shaftesbury. Flood, R. and Lockwood, M. (eds.) (1990) *The Nature of Time*, Basil Blackwell, London, is an anthology of articles on the mathematical, scientific and cosmological interpretations of time.

2 Prigogine, I. and Stengers, I. (1984) *Order Out of Chaos: Man's New Dialogue with Nature*, Bantam, New York, p. 8. (The brackets in this quote have been added for clarification.) There are others who question the long upheld theory of the irreversibility of time. See Penrose, R. (1989) *The Emperor's New Mind: Concerning Computers, Minds and the Laws of Physics*, Vintage Books, London. See in particular Chapter 7: 'Cosmology and the Arrow of Time'; Stewart, I. (1989) *Does God Play Dice: The New Mathematics of Physics*, Penguin, London.

3 Among those who have discussed the growing contribution of services to overall corporate revenue: Quinn, J.B., Doorley, T. and Paquette, P.C. (1988) Exploiting the Manufacturing-Services Interface, *Sloan Management Review*, summer; Shycon, H. (1991) Measuring the Payoff from Improved Customer Service, *Prism*, First Quarter; Simon, H. (1992) Service Policies of German Manufacturers: Critical Factors in International Competition. Working Paper 03–92, *Universitat Mainz, Lehrstuhl fur Betriebswirtschaftslehre und Marketing*.

4 Reichheld, F. and Sasser, W.E. (1990) Zero Defections: Quality Comes to Services, *Harvard Business Review*, Sept./Oct., p.106. Others have also commented on the correlations between losing customers, keeping customers and profitability over the long term: See Band, W. (1991)

Creating Value for Customers: Designing and Implementing a Total Corporate Strategy, John Wiley & Sons, New York; Bloch, P. and Hababou, R. (1992) *Dinosaures et Cameleons: Neuf Paradoxes pour Reussir dans un Monde Imprevisible*, Lattes, Paris; Schlesinger, L. and Heskett, J. (1991) The Service Driven Service Company, *Harvard Business Review*, Sept./Oct.

5 The benefits of long-term customer retention have been discussed by Reichheld and Sasser, note 4 above. See also Business International (1990) *Maximizing Customer Satisfaction*, BI, London, pp. 10–12; Berry, L. and Parasuraman, A. (1991) *Marketing Services: Competing through Quality*, The Free Press, New York, pp. 135–137; DeSouza, G. (1992) Designing a Customer Retention Plan, *The Journal of Business Strategy*, Mar./Apr.; Grunroos, C. (1990) *Service Management and Marketing*, Lexington Books, Lexington, p.149; Holberton, S. (1990) Customer Retention is the Key to Profitability, *Financial Times* (London), 16 July.

6 For a discussion of capacity, see Bateson, J.E.G. (1989) *Managing Services Marketing*, Dryden Press, Chicago, pp. 138–150; Eiglier, P. and Langeard, E. (1987) *Servuction: Le Marketing des Services*, McGraw-Hill, Paris; Grunroos, C. (1990) *Service Management and Marketing*, Lexington Books, Lexington; Heskett, J., Sasser, W.E. and Hart, C. *Service Breakthroughs: Changing the Rules of the Game*, The Free Press, New York; Lovelock, C. (1988) *Managing Services: Marketing, Operations and Human Resources*, Prentice Hall, Englewood Cliffs, NJ. See in particular the chapter: 'Strategies for Managing Capacity-Constrained Service Organizations.'

7 Some commentators have discussed the trend towards having permanent-temporary work: Toffler, A. (1990) *Powershift: Knowledge, Wealth and Violence at the Edge of the 21st Century*, Bantam, New York. See also Handy, C. (1991) *The Age of Unreason*, Business Books, London, who, on pp. 74–85, makes the point that members of the emerging 'flexible labor force' are characterized by a portfolio of skills which allows them to opt for part-time or temporary work, not as matter of necessity, but as a matter of choice.

8 Certain writers have encouraged firms to develop and tap multiskill capabilities to improve productivity and capacity. Refer to: Boyett, J. and Conn, H. (1991) *Workplace 2000: The Revolution Reshaping American Business*, Penguin Books, New York; Kanter, R.M. (1989) The Contingent Job and the Post-Entrepreneurial Career, *Management Review*, Apr.; Crawford, R. (1991) *In the Era of Human Capital: The Emergence of Talent, Intelligence and Knowledge as the Worldwide Economic Force and What It Means to Managers and Investors*, Harper Business, New York; Handy, note 7 above.

9 Womack, J., Jones, J. and Roos, D. (1990) *The Machine That Changed the World*, Rawson Associates, New York. See in particular pp. 61 and 150,

where they explain how Toyota shares personnel capacity with its suppliers.

10 Sheldrake, R. (1991) *The Rebirth of Nature: The Greening of Science and God*, Rider Publishers, London, pp. 68–69, examines the emergence of the concept of energy, especially in the late nineteenth and early twentieth centuries. For a discussion of some of the limitations of machine generated energy, see Foster, R. (1986) *Innovation: The Attacker's Advantage*, Summit Press, New York, pp. 76–81, and Ord-Hume, A. (1980) *Perpetual Motion*, St. Martin's Press, New York. Normann, R. (1991) *Service Management: Strategy and Leadership in Service Business*, 2nd edn, John Wiley and Sons, New York, pp. 123–124, discusses the need to develop principles of 'human energy management' and 'human capacity management' as integral to service enterprise success.

11 The fact that machines are 'closed' systems, whereas human beings are essentially 'open' systems, is one of the reasons given for the superiority of human energy: in closed systems energy dissipates into entropy, in open systems energy is constantly transformed and renewed. For more on this subject, see Prigogine and Stengers, note 2 above; Lynch, D. and Kordis, P. (1988) *Strategy of the Dolphin: Winning Elegantly by Coping Powerfully in a World of Turbulent Change*, Hutchinson Business Books, London, pp. 83–90.

12 For additional information on the speed of thought, see Hope, note 1 above, pp. 166–169, where the author synthesizes the ideas of some of the physicists and neurophysicists in the field. See also Morgan, G. (1986) *Images of Organization*, Sage, London, in particular chapter 4: 'Towards Self-Organization: Organizations as Brains'.

13 Prigogine and Stengers, note 2 above, p.xxiv.

14 For background literature on the field of ergonomics, see Oborne, D.J. (ed.) (1986) *Contemporary Ergonomics*, Taylor and Francis, London; Oborne, D.J. (1987) Ergonomics and Information Technology. In *Information Technology and People* (eds F. Beckler and D.J. Oborne) MIT Press, Cambridge, MA. For more specific points about ergonomics and mental workload, see Singleton, W.T. (1989) *The Mind at Work: Psychological Ergonomics*, Cambridge University Press, Cambridge, pp. 171–176.

15 Reich, R. (1992) *The Work of Nations: Preparing Ourselves for 21st Century Capitalism*, Random House, New York, pp. 103–105. Others have also noted this trend. See Crawford, note 8 above, pp. 24–29.

16 Crawford, note 8 above, pp. 25 and 156, concludes that 70 per cent of a typical firm's – be it a manufacturer or a service company – resource base and spending is attributable to its know-how workers: a figure far greater than spending on physical or financial capital, even though it remains uncapitalized and thus does not appear on balance sheets. Consult also Ibbotson, R. and Brinson, G. (1987) *Investment Markets*, McGraw Hill,

New York; Kuznets, S. (1966) *Modern Economic Growth*, Yale University Press, New Haven. Schultz, T. (1961) Investment in Human Capital, *American Economic Review*, was one of the first to have used the term 'human capital' in the economic literature.

17 Drucker, P. (1992) *Managing for The Future*, Butterworth-Heinemann, London. See in particular pp. 244–247 on The Emerging Theory of Manufacturing. Drucker is not alone in pointing out the present inadequacies and deficiencies of traditional cost accounting methods. For a more detailed analysis of these shortfalls, see Johnson, H.T. and Kaplan, R.S. (1990) *Relevance Lost: The Rise and Fall of Management Accounting*, Harvard Business School Press, Cambridge, MA, p. 202.

18 Roach, S. (1991) Services under Siege: The Restructuring Imperative, *Harvard Business Review*, Sept./Oct., p. 91. A new school is developing which advances an activity based accounting approach for companies overall. It is considered a potential alternative to cost accounting since it looks at the firm as comprised of processes and activities – not cost centres – and attempts to distinguish those activities which add value from those which don't. Refer to: Brimson, J. (1991) *Activity Accounting: An Activity-Based Costing Approach*, John Wiley & Sons, New York, in particular pp. 7–11. A more general, performance based approach to measurement is also being put forward as more comprehensive and meaningful than cost accounting. See: Kaplan, R.S. and Norton, D. (1992) The Balanced Scorecard: Measures That Drive Performance, *Harvard Business Review*, Jan./Feb.

19 Hall, R. (1991) The Contribution of Intangible Resources to Business Success, *Journal of General Management*, Vol. 16, No. 4; Hall, R. (1992) The Strategic Analysis of Intangible Resources, *Strategic Management Journal*, Vol. 13; the legal, fiscal and accounting issues involved in capitalizing such people-dependent, intangible resources as know-how and talent have also been addressed by the editors of the Economist Intelligence Unit in collaboration with Arthur Andersen. EIU (1992) *The Valuation of Intangible Assets: Special Report P254*, The Economist Publications, London; Smith, G.V. and Parr, R. (1989) *Valuation of Intellectual Property and Intangible Assets*, New York, John Wiley & Sons.

20 For a discussion of the growing inadequacy of goodwill as a reflection of the worth of human and intellectual capital, see Edvinsson, L. and Richardson, J. (1989) Services and Thoughtware: New Dimensions in Service Business Development. In *Strategic Trends in Services: An Inquiry into the Global Service Economy* (eds A. Bressand and K. Nicolaidis) Harper & Row, New York, pp. 46–47; Reich, note 15 above, p. 105; Smith and Parr, note 19 above, see in particular on pp. 76–88; Tearney, M. (1973) Accounting for Goodwill: A Realistic Approach, *The Journal of Accountancy*, July.

21 The time and money necessary for the ongoing education and training of know-how workers has been studied by: Sveiby, K.E. and Lloyd, T. (1987) *Managing Know-how: Add Value by Valuing Creativity*, Bloomsbury Press, London, especially on pp. 75–79.

22 Edvinsson, and Richardson, note 20 above, pp. 46–47, emphasize the importance of application value. See also Grant, R.M. (1991) The Resource-Based Theory of Competitive Advantage, *The California Management Review*, spring.

23 Some who have commented more generally on the service particularities which make pricing decisions in services even more complex than it is for manufacturers: Bateson, J. (1989) *Managing Services Marketing*, The Dryden Press, Chicago, Chapter 6: 'Service Pricing Policy'; Normann, R. (1991) *Service Management: Strategy and Leadership in Service Business*, 2nd edn, John Wiley & Sons, New York, Chapter 11: 'The Art and Science of Pricing'; Shaw, J. (1990) *The Service Focus: Developing Winning Game Plans for Service Companies*, Dow Jones Irwin, Chicago, pp. 10–17; Vandermerwe, S., Matthews, W.and Rada, J. (1989) European Manufacturers Shape Up for Services, *The Journal of Business Strategy'*, Nov./Dec.

24 For a discussion of the pros and cons of bundling, see Guiltinan, J. (1987) The Price Bundling of Services: A Normative Framework, *The Journal of Marketing*, Apr.; Normann, note 23 above, p.129; Simon, H. (1992) Service Policies of German Manufacturers: Critical Factors in International Competition. Working Paper 03–92, *Lehrstuhl fur Betriebswirtschaftslehre und Marketing, Universitat Mainz*; Lovelock, C. (1991) *Services Marketing*, 2nd edn, Prentice Hall, Englewood Cliffs, NJ, p. 243.

25 General discussions of pricing techniques in services: Cannon, H. and Morgan, F. (1990) A Strategic Pricing Framework, *Journal of Services Marketing*, spring; Corey, R. (1980) *A Note on Pricing*, Harvard Business School, Cambridge, MA, makes the point that pricing is an 'art', a 'game' played amongst competitors; Dearden, J. (1978) Cost Accounting Comes to Service Industries, *Harvard Business Review*, Sept./Oct.; Simon, H. (1992) Pricing Opportunities – And How to Exploit Them, *Sloan Management Review*, Winter, explains how pricing has long been based less on precision, and more on rules of thumb and intuition. For an examination of the issues specific to pricing for knowledge intensive technologies, see Bidault, F. (1989) *Technology Pricing: From Principles to Strategy*, Macmillan, London; Davidow, W. (1986) *Marketing High Technology*, The Free Press, New York. See in particular pp. 106–117.

26 The relationship between market share and profitability was first analysed in the 1970s by Sidney Scheffler and the Profit Impact of Market Strategy (PIMS) Group. Their research, based on information supplied by corporate members worldwide into a data pool base, is an ongoing project. For more

information on their projects, see Gale, B. and Buzzell, R. (1987) *The PIMS (Profit Impact of Market Strategy) Principles: Linking Strategy to Performance*, The Free Press, New York.

27 Stalk, G., Evans, P. and Shulman, L. (1992) Competing on Capabilities: The New Rules of Corporate Strategy, *Harvard Business Review*, Mar./Apr., p. 62.

28 Chussil, M. (1991) Does Market Share Really Matter? *Planning Review*, Sept./Oct. The author uses statistical analysis in addressing the difficulty of determining which – high market share or high ROI – causes the other. Wilson, A. (1992) *New Directions in Marketing: Business-to-Business Strategies for the 1990s*, NTC Business Books, Chicago, p.209, also questions what he calls the 'myth' of market share as a criterion for market success or high profitability.

29 See Grunroos, note 5 above, p.149.

30 Quinn, J.B., Doorley, T. and Paquette, P. (1990) Technology in Services: Rethinking Strategic Focus, *Sloan Management Review*, winter, p. 84; Quinn, J.B., Doorley, T. and Paquette, P. (1990) Beyond Products: Services Based Strategy, *Harvard Business Review*, Mar./Apr., is a similar view.

Chapter 9

1 Hofstadter, D.R. (1979) *Godel, Escher, Bach – An Eternal Golden Braid: A Metaphorical Fugue on Minds and Machines in the Spirit of Lewis Carroll*, Penguin, New York, examines some of the unique counterpoint characteristics of Bach's music. See also Buchet, E. (1986) *J.S. Bach*, Editions Buchet/Chastel, Paris; Gould, G. (1983) *Le Dernier Puritain*, Fayard, Paris, in particular the chapter entitled: 'JS Bach: le Clavier Bien Tempere at la Fugue.'

2 Braudel, F. (1982) *The Structures of Everyday Life and the Wheels of Commerce: Civilization and Capitalism 15th-18th Century*, Harper & Row, New York. The author in several of his works has traced the evolution of technology and its role in human civilization. For socio-economic examinations of technological development and its impact on work, see Piore, M. and Sabel, C. (1984) *The Second Industrial Divide: Prospects for Prosperity*, Basic Books, New York; Zuboff, S. (1988) *In the Age of the Smart Machine: The Future of Work and Power*, Heinemann, London.

3 Beninger, J. (1986) *The Control Revolution: Technological and Economic Origins of the Information Society*, Harvard University Press, Cambridge, MA; see also Beninger, J. (1990) The Evolution of Control. In *Computers in the Human Context: Information Technology, Productivity, and People* (ed. T. Forester) Basil Blackwell, London.

4 Several commentators have written about the ascendant role of information technology in services. See Bressand, A. and Nicolaidis, K. (1989) *Strategic Trends in Services: An Inquiry into the Global Service Economy*, Harper & Row, New York; Child, J. and Loveridge, R. (1990) *Information Technology in European Services: Towards a Microelectronic Future*, Blackwell, Oxford; Clutterbuck, D. (ed.) (1989) *Information 2000: Insights into the Coming Decades in Information Technology*, Pitman, London; Crawford, R. (1991) *In the Era of Human Capital: The Emergence of Talent, Intelligence and Knowledge as the Worldwide Economic Force and What It Means to Managers and Investors*, Harper Business, New York; Heskett, J., Sasser, E. and Hart, C. (1990) *Service Breakthroughs: Changing the Rules of the Game*, The Free Press, New York, especially Chapter 10: Managing Information Technologies and Chapter 13: Conceiving Future Breakthroughs; Quinn, J.B., Doorley, T. and Paquette, P. (1990) Technology in Services: Rethinking Strategic Focus, *Sloan Management Review*, winter; Quinn, J.B. and Paquette, P. (1990) Technology in Services: Creating Organizational Revolutions, *Sloan Management Review*, winter; Simon, H. (1991) Kundennahe als Wettbewerbsstrategie und Fuhrungsherausforderung. Working Paper 01–91, *Universitat Mainz, Lehrstuhl fur Betriebswirtschaftslehre und Marketing*.
5 Zuboff, note 2 above, pp. 22–23. See also Masuda, Y. (1990) *Managing in the Information Society: Releasing Synergy Japanese Style*, Basil Blackwell, London.
6 Barabba, V. and Zaltman, G. (1991) *Hearing the Voice of the Market: Competitive Advantage Through Creative Use of Market Information*, Harvard Business School Press, Cambridge, MA, p.114. Their points on the difference between data and information refer specifically to marketing research.
7 For more on intelligence amplification, or augmentation, see Rheingold, H. (1991) *Virtual Reality*, Secker & Warburg, London, p.37.
8 Several authors have discussed these unique features of information as a resource. See Badaracco, J. (1991) *The Knowledge Link: How Firms Compete through Strategic Alliances*, Harvard Business School Press, Boston; Crawford, R. (1991) *In the Era of Human Capital: The Emergence of Talent, Intelligence and Knowledge as the Worldwide Economic Force and What it Means to Managers and Investors*, Harper Business, New York; Cleveland, H. (1985) *The Knowledge Executive: Leadership in an Information Society*, E.P. Dutton, New York, pp. 19–114; Davis, S. and Davidson, B. (1991) *2020 Vision: Transform Your Business Today to Succeed in Tomorrow's Economy*, Simon & Schuster, New York; Toffler, A. (1990) *Powershift: Knowledge, Wealth and Violence at the Edge of the 21st Century*, Bantam Books, New York.
9 Primozic, K., Primozic, E. and Leben, J. (1991) *Strategic Choices:*

Supremacy, Survival or Sayonara, McGraw Hill, New York, in particular Chapter 2: 'Understanding the Waves of Innovation'. Others have also looked at problems of internally focused IT. See Hopper, M. (1990) Rattling SABRE: New Ways to Compete on Information, *Harvard Business Review*, May/June; Keen, P. (1991) *Shaping the Future: Business Design through Information Technology*, Harvard Business School Press, Cambridge, MA; Porter, M. (1985) *Competitive Advantage: Creating and Sustaining Superior Performance*, The Free Press, New York; Porter, M. and Millar, V. (1985) How Information Technology Gives You Competitive Advantage, *Harvard Business Review*, July/Aug.

10 According to one commentator who examined the rapidly decreasing costs – which have been dropping by a factor of 1,000 every decade – in the IT and computing industries, if the auto industry had experienced the same cost curve, by 1995 a Rolls Royce would be worth $1, and a gallon of gas good for 3 million miles. See Crawford, R. (1991) *In the Era of Human Capital: The Emergence of Talent, Intelligence and Knowledge as the Worldwide Economic Force and What it Means for Managers and Investors*, Harper Business, New York, pp. 37–38.

11 Wurman, R.S. (1991) *Information Anxiety*, Pan Books, London. The author analyses some of the causes and consequences of the plethora of data. See also Klapp, O. (1986) *Overload and Boredom: Essays on the Quality of Life in the Information Society*, The Greenwood Press, New York; Naisbitt, J. (1982) Megatrends, Warner Books, New York.

12 Several authors have written about the service sector's comparatively disappointing returns from their IT investments. See Hackett, G. (1990) Investment in Technology – The Service Sector Sinkhole? *Sloan Management Review*, winter; Heskett, J. and Schlesinger, L. (1991) The Service Driven Service Company, *Harvard Business Review*, Sept./Oct.; Normann, R. (1991) *Service Management: Strategy and Leadership in the Service Business*, John Wiley & Sons, New York, pp. 104–105; Roach, S. (1991) Services Under Siege – The Restructuring Imperative, *Harvard Business Review*, Sept./Oct.

13 Heskett, J., Sasser, W.E. and Hart, C. (1990) *Service Breakthroughs: Changing the Rules of the Game*, The Free Press, New York, pp. 184–187. The authors discuss the initial difficulties in getting employees and customers to embrace new technologies in service settings. For a more general analysis on the problems of instilling new ideas, including IT, in tradition bound organizations, see Kantrow, A. (1987) *The Constraints of Corporate Tradition: Doing the Correct Thing, Not Just What the Past Dictates*, Harper & Row, New York. On the effects of the introduction of technology at Federal Express, see Nehls, C. (1988) Custodial Package Tracking at Federal Express. In *Managing Innovation: Cases from the Services Industries* (eds B. Guile and J. B. Quinn) National Academy of Engineering Series on Technology and Social Priorities, National

Academy Press, Washington, DC.

14 Gilder, G. (1992) *Life after Television*, W.W. Norton, New York, p. 65, discusses this data overload.

15 For additional insight on the differences between data, information, intelligence and wisdom, Cleveland, note 8 above, pp. 22–23; Ekins, P. (1992) *Wealth Beyond Measure: An Atlas of New Economics*, Gaia Books, London, pp. 114–117; Henderson, H. (1986) The Age of Light: Beyond the Information Age, *The Futurist*, July/Aug.; Leinberger, P. and Tucker, B. (1991) *The New Individualists: The Generation after the Organization Man*, Harper Collins, New York, p. 346. See also Barabba and Zaltmann, note 6 above, in particular pp.37-49, and pp.279-288, where the authors elucidate upon the nuances between 'intelligence' and 'wisdom'. Also: Cooley, M. (1987) *Architect or Bee?* 2nd edn, Hogarth Press, London; Turing, A. (1950) Computing Machinery and Intelligence, *Mind*, Vol.LIX, No.236. The author is one of the first to pose the dilemma about 'thinking machines'. Two authors who have examined Turing's ideas: Anderson, A. (1964) *Minds and Machines*, Prentice-Hall, Englewood Cliffs, NJ; and Bolter, J.D. (1986) *Turing's Man: Western Culture in the Computer Age*, Pelican, London. Watson, L. (1991) *The Nature of Things: The Secret Life of Inanimate Objects*, Sceptre, London, p. 223, comments on the ability of machines to think like human beings.

16 Penzias, A. (1989) *Ideas and Information: Managing in a High-Tech World*, Norton, New York, p. 146.

17 For more on these 'expert systems', see Gordon, T. (1987) Better Mousetrapping, Better Ideas. In *An Agenda for the 21st Century* (ed. R. Kidder) The MIT Press, Cambridge, MA, p. 127; Sisodia, R. (1991) Expert Systems for Services – Prospects and Payoffs. *The Journal of Services Marketing*, Summer; Turban, E. (1990) *Decision Support and Expert Systems: Management Support Systems*, 2nd edn, Macmillan, New York; Wolfgram, D., Dear, T. and Galbraith, C. (1989) *Expert Systems for the Technical Professional*, John Wiley & Sons, New York.

18 Boyett, J. and Conn, H. (1991) *Workplace 2000: The Revolution Reshaping American Business*, Dutton, New York, pp. 26–27. The authors describe American Express' use of information technology and especially its moves into intelligent software and 'neural networking'.

19 Olaisen, J. and Revang, O. (1991) The Significance of Information Technology for Service Quality: From Market Segmentation to Individual Service, *International Journal of Service Industries Management*, No.3. Others have also commented on the personalization of the service offering as a result of technology: McGowan, W. (1991) *Revolution in Real Time: Managing Information Technology in the 1990s*, Harvard Business School Press, Cambridge, MA, in particular the Preface; Negroponte, N. (1991) Products and Services for Computer Networks, *Scientific American*, Sept., who emphasizes that intelligently designed networks will understand and

respond to the needs of individuals; Sasser, W.E. and Fulmer, W. (1990) Personalized Service Delivery Systems. In *Service Management Effectiveness* (ed. D. Bowen, R. Chase, and T. Cummings), Jossey Bass, San Francisco.

20 For the role of IT in creating cross-functionalization, see Scott Morton, M. (ed.) (1991) *The Corporation of the 1990s: Information Technology and Organizational Transformation*, Oxford University Press, New York. See also Macdonald, K.H. (1991) Business Strategy Development, Alignment, and Redesign. In *The Corporation of the 1990s: Information Technology and Organizational Transformation* (ed. M. Scott Morton) Oxford University Press, New York; McKersie, R. and Walton, R. (1991) Organizational Change. In *The Corporation of the 1990s: Information Technology and Organizational Transformation* (ed. M. Scott Morton) Oxford University Press, New York; Rotemberg, J. and Saloner, G. (1991) *Interfirm Competition and Collaboration. In The Corporation of the 1990s: Information Technology and Organizational Transformation* (ed. M. Scott Morton) Oxford University Press, New York. See also Boyett, J. and Conn, H. (1991) *Workplace 2000: The Revolution Reshaping American Business*, Dutton, New York. See in particular Chapter 3: 'Future Information Sharing'; Drucker, P. (1988) The Coming of the New Organization, *Harvard Business Review*, Jan./Feb.

21 Gilder, G. (1992) *Life after Television*, W.W. Norton, New York, analyzes the technology-induced move from informational hierarchies, where information was sequestered in mainframes, to 'heterarchies' where each individual has access to, and can transmit, information.

22 Schrage, M. (1990) *Shared Minds: The New Technologies of Collaboration*, Random House, New York, p. 142.

23 Jaikumar, J. (1991) The Boundaries of Business: The Impact of Technology, *Harvard Business Review*, Sept./Oct., urges that technology be used to improve communication within organizations. See also Rockart, J. and Short, J. (1991) The Networked Organization and the Management of Interdependence. In *The Corporation of the 1990s: Information Technology and Organizational Transformation* (ed. M. Scott Morton) Oxford University Press, New York.

24 Leinberger and Tucker, note 15 above, pp. 343–345. See also Davis, S. and Davidson, B. (1990) Management and Organization Principles for the Information Economy, *Human Resource Management*, winter. Johnston, R. and Lawrence, P. (1991) Beyond Vertical Integration – The Rise of the Value Adding Partnership. In *Revolution in Real Time: Managing Information Technology in the 1990s*, Harvard Business Review, Cambridge, MA, pp. 17–31, have examined how IT has contributed to the creation of value adding processes within firms.

25 For more on DuPont's overall corporate information system and how it is being linked to customers, see Mead, T. (1990) The IS Innovator at

DuPont, *Datamation*, 15 Apr.

26 Ideas on the impact of technology on services spanning time, space and distance can be found in: Carre, D. (ed.) (1990) *Info-Revolution: Usage des Technologies de l'Information*, Autrement, Paris; *Forum 91 – Policy Symposium: Towards a Global Networked Society*, Geneva, 7–10 Oct. 1991, International Telecommunication Union 6th World Telecommunication Forum Publication; *Scientific American: Communications, Computers and Networks*, Sept. 1991 Special Issue.

27 More on these new technologies, especially the impact of digitalization, in Gilder, note 21 above; Davis and Davidson, note 8 above.

28 Greater explanation of virtual reality can be found in Rheingold, note 7 above.

29 Schrage, note 22 above, is one who discusses the need for technologies which enhance what people do naturally, rather than enforce new behavior. See in particular pp. 149–150. For similar viewpoints, see the collection *Computers in the Human Context*, (T. Forester, ed.), London, Basil Blackwell, 1990.

30 Kosnik, T.(1990) Perennial Renaissance: The Marketing Challenge in High Tech Settings. In *Managing Complexity in High Technology Organizations* (ed. M.A. von Glinow and S.Mohrman) Oxford University Press, New York. See in particular pp. 143–145. The author presses for a balance between the needs to focus on new technologies and on maintaining long-term customer relationships. Also Kosnik, T. and Moriarty, R. (1989) High-Tech Marketing: Concepts, Continuity and Change, *Sloan Management Review*, summer.

31 Levitt, T. (1991) *Thinking about Management*, The Free Press, New York. See in particular p. 134 on 'The Marketing Mode.'

Chapter 10

1 The ever more rapid obsolescence of technology has been a constant of the modern era. For discussion on the subject, see Giarini, O. (1981) *Dialogue sur la Richesse et le Bien-etre*, Economica, Paris; Giarini, O. and Loubergie, H. (1979) *La Civilisation technicienne a la Derive: Les Rendements Decroissants de la Technologies*, Dunod, Paris; Giarini, O. and Stahel, W. (1989) *The Limits to Certainty*, Kluwer Academic Publishers, Dordrecht; Gimpel, J. (1992) *La Fin de l'Avenir: Le Declin Technologique et la Crise de l' Occident*, Seuil, Paris. Fukuyama, F. (1992) *The End of History and the Last Man*, Hamish Hamilton, London, p.92, states that in the most advanced technologies, product life cycles are now measured in months.

2 Crawford, R. (1991) *In the Era of Human Capital:The Emergence of Talent, Intelligence, and Knowledge as the Worldwide Economic Force*

and What It Means to Managers and Investors, Harper Business, New York, Chapter 3: 'Technology: Knowledge's Product'. Also: Boyett, J. and Conn, H. (1991) *Workplace 2000: The Revolution Reshaping American Business*, Dutton, New York; Sveiby, K.E. and Lloyd, T. (1987) *Managing Know-how: Add Value by Valuing Creativity*, Bloomsbury Press, London.

3 Discussion of the new individualism is included in Leinberger, P. and Tucker, B. (1991) *The New Individualists: The Generation after the Organization Man*, Harper Collins, New York. For more on the differences between the self-centred 'I' and the more associative 'I-we', see Etzioni, A. (1987) Seeking the Center. In *An Agenda for the 21st Century* (ed. R. Kidder) MIT Press, Cambridge, MA. Cazes, B. (1992) True Likeness or Distorted Image? Probing the Explanatory Power of Value Changes, *Futures*, May. The author also examines the already apparent emergence of a new kind of person, whose concerns and interests are markedly different from those which reigned in the latter half of the twentieth century.

4 Gundelach, P. (1992) Recent Value Changes in Western Europe, *Futures*, May, p. 317.

5 King, A., Schneider, B. and The Club of Rome, (1991) *Questions de Survie: La Revolution Mondiale a Commence*, Calmann Levy, Paris, Chapter 10: 'Motivations et Valeurs'; Reich, R. (1992) *The Work of Nations: Preparing Ourselves for 21st Century Capitalism*, Vintage Books, New York, Chapter 23: The New Community and Chapter 25: 'Who is Us?; Masuda, Y. (1991) *Managing in the Information Society*, Basil Blackwell, London, handles this theme throughout his book.

6 Sheldrake, R. (1990) *The Rebirth of Nature: The Greening of God and Science, Rider*, London, Chapter 2: The Conquest of Nature and the Scientific Priesthood. For similar analyses, see Pauchant, T. and Fortier, I. (1990) Anthropocentric Ethics in Organizations: How Different Strategic Management Schools View the Environment. In *The Corporation, Ethics and the Environment* (ed. W. M. Hoffman, R. Frederick and E. Petry) Quorum Books, New York.

7 Umehara, T. (1992) Ancient Japan Shows Postmodernism the Way, *New Perspectives Quarterly*, spring, p. 11.

8 Cairncross, F. (1991) *Costing the Earth*, Economist Publications, London. See also Elkington, J. and Knight, P. (1991) *The Green Business Guide: How to Take Up and Profit from the Environmental Challenge*, Victor Gollancz, London; Vandermerwe, S. and Oliff, M. (1990) Customers Drive Corporations Green, *Long Range Planning*, Dec.

9 Wahlstrom, B. (1991) *Management 2002*, Les Editions de l'Organisation, Paris, p. 24. (Note that the quotation is a translation.)

10 Kung, H. (1991) *Global Responsibility*, SCM Press, London. See in particular pp. 29–35.For a similar point about corporate responsibility to

stakeholders overall, see Demb, A. and Neubauer, F.F. (1992) *The Corporate Board: Confronting the Paradoxes*, Oxford University Press, London. See in particular Chapter 8: 'Imperatives for the Twenty-first Century', where the authors examine the challenges for corporate governance in the years ahead. See also Jonas, H. (1984) *The Imperative of Responsibility*, University of Chicago Press, Chicago.

11 Fukuyama, F. (1992) *The End of History and the Last Man*, Hamish Hamilton, London, on pp.81–88, discusses the emergent and necessary role of alternative technologies. See also Ekins, P. (1992) *Wealth beyond Measure: An Atlas of New Economics*, Gaia Books, London.

12 For more on sustainability, see World Commission on Environment and Development (1987) *Our Common Future (The Brundtland Report)*, Oxford University Press, London. The concept was first examined in this groundbreaking report. Davis, J. (1991) *Greening Business: Managing for Sustainable Development*, Basil Blackwell, London; Schmidheiny, S. (1992) *Changing Course: A Global Business Perspective on Development and the Environment*, MIT Press, Cambridge, MA; Smith, E. (1992) Growth vs. Environment: The Push for Sustainable Development, *International Business Week*, 11 May (Cover Story).

13 For a compilation of the recent thinking on accounting for environmental assets, see Owen, D. (1992) *Green Reporting: Accountancy and the Challenge of the Nineties*, Chapman & Hall, London. See also *The Economist*, (1992) The Price of Green, 9 May; Jacobs, M. (1991) *The Green Economy*, Pluto Press, London; Norgaard, R. (1991) *Sustainability and the Economics of Assuring Assets for Future Generations*, World Bank Publication, Washington.

14 Vandermerwe, S. and Oliff, M. (1991) Corporate Challenges for an Age of Reconsumption, *Columbia Journal of World Business*, autumn. The authors examine some of the new and adapted services which will be necessary for what they call 'reconsumption' – a system of using materials, components and goods longer and over again – to become feasible.

15 Breton, T. (1991) *La Dimension Invisible: Le Defi du Temps et de l'Information*, Editions Odile Jacob, Paris.

16 Negroponte, N. (1991) Products and Services for Computer Networks, *Scientific American*, Sept. Attali, J. (1981) *Les Trois Mondes*, Fayard, Paris; Attali, J. (1991) *Lignes d'Horizon*, Fayard, Paris, was one of the first to discuss the emergence and almost limitless potential of 'nomadic' products and services.

17 Breton, note 15 above, p. 212.

18 Grenier, R. and Metes, G. (1992) *Enterprise Networking: Working Together Apart*, Digital Press. See in particular pp. 165–167. For more on 'virtual organizations' and similar type organizational transformations, see Ettighoffer, D. (1992) *L'Entreprise Virtuelle: Ou Les Nouveaux Modes de*

Travail, Editions Odile Jacob, Paris; Mills, D.Q. (1991) *Rebirth of the Corporation*, John Wiley & Sons, New York; Scott Morton, M.S. (1991) *The Corporation of 1990s: Information Technology and Organizational Transformation*, Oxford University Press, New York; Von Glinow, M.A. and Mohrman, S.A. (eds.) (1990) *Managing Complexity in High Technology Organizations*, Oxford University Press, New York.

19 Know-why is a topic addressed by numerous authors. See Badaracco, J. (1991) *The Knowledge Link: How Firms Compete through Strategic Alliances*, Harvard Business School Press, Boston, pp.84-85; Barton, D.L. (1990) Implementing New Production Technologies: Exercises in Corporate Learning. In *Managing Complexity in High Technology Organizations* (eds M.A. Von Glinow and S.A. Mohrman) Oxford University Press, New York. Hayes, R. Wheelwright, S. and Clark, K. (1988) *Dynamic Manufacturing: Creating the Learning Organization*, The Free Press, New York, pp. 231; Reich, note 5 above, pp. 230–232.

Index